S. S. Hamill

The Science of Elocution

With Exercises and Selections Systematically Arranged for Acquiring the Art of

Reading and Speaking

S. S. Hamill

The Science of Elocution
With Exercises and Selections Systematically Arranged for Acquiring the Art of Reading and Speaking

ISBN/EAN: 9783337278366

Printed in Europe, USA, Canada, Australia, Japan

Cover: Foto ©Thomas Meinert / pixelio.de

More available books at **www.hansebooks.com**

THE

SCIENCE OF ELOCUTION:

WITH

EXERCISES AND SELECTIONS

SYSTEMATICALLY ARRANGED FOR ACQUIRING

The Art of Reading and Speaking.

By S. S. HAMILL, A.M.,

PROFESSOR OF ENGLISH, HISTORY, AND ELOCUTION IN THE STATE UNIVERSITY OF MISSOURI, COLUMBIA, MO.

NEW YORK:

NELSON & PHILLIPS

CINCINNATI: HITCHCOCK & WALDEN.

1879

PREFACE.

In the belief that Elocution should be studied as a science as well as practiced as an art, the following pages are presented to the public.

The design of the work is to unfold the principles of Elocution, to show their application to the different forms of thought and emotion, to classify selections under their appropriate styles, and, in connection therewith, to furnish sufficient exercises for the cultivation of the articulation, the tones of the voice, and the graces of manner.

That Elocution is a science, that there are certain established principles observed by all good speakers and violated by all bad ones, none will deny who have carefully investigated the subject. To understand and to practically illustrate these principles should be the prominent object of the student of Elocution.

Without this all cultivation of the voice and manner will be of little avail. Instances are numerous of students who have carefully and diligently practiced the exercises for the cultivation of the voice and manner, so abundant in the various works on Elocution, and have derived therefrom all the advantages they propose, and yet good readers and speakers are very rare.

PREFACE.

A radical defect exists somewhere, or, contrary to all experience and testimony, the ability to read and speak well is not an acquirement. An experience of nearly twenty years as a teacher in this department has convinced the author that the study of Elocution usually ceases where it really should begin, namely with the adaptation of the tones of the voice and the expression of countenance to the sentiment uttered.

To correct in some degree this defect, and to awaken a deeper interest in the subject of Elocution, is the hope of the author in the present publication.

When Elocution shall be studied in our colleges and universities as a science, its principles known and practiced, then, and not till then, will good speaking be the rule, and not, as now, the rare exception.

S. S. H.

ILLINOIS WESLEYAN UNIVERSITY,
BLOOMINGTON, *Jan.* 1, 1872.

CONTENTS.

	PAGE
ELOCUTION	19
TABULAR VIEW OF THE SCIENCE OF ELOCUTION	20

PART I.
EXPRESSION.

CHAPTER I.
ARTICULATION.

	PAGE
CHART OF ELEMENTARY SOUNDS	22
POSITION OF BODY	23
SUGGESTIONS	23
EXERCISES IN LONG VOCALS	24
" SHORT VOCALS	27
" DIPHTHONGS	30
" SUB-VOCALS	31
" ASPIRATES	37
" DIFFICULT COMBINATIONS	41

CHAPTER II.
RESPIRATION.

EXERCISES IN BREATHING	48
" EFFUSIVE VOCAL BREATHING	49
" EXPULSIVE VOCAL BREATHING	49
" EXPLOSIVE VOCAL BREATHING	49

CHAPTER III.
VOICE.

ATTRIBUTES OF VOICE	50
FORM OF VOICE	51
EFFUSIVE FORM	51
EXERCISES IN EFFUSIVE FORM	52
APPLICATION OF EFFUSIVE FORM	52

CONTENTS.

	PAGE
ILLUSTRATIONS OF EFFUSIVE FORM	53
ADVANTAGES OF EFFUSIVE FORM	53
EXPULSIVE FORM	54
EXERCISES IN EXPULSIVE FORM	54
APPLICATION OF THE EXPULSIVE	54
ILLUSTRATIONS OF EXPULSIVE FORM	55
ADVANTAGES OF EXPULSIVE FORM	57
EXPLOSIVE FORM	57
EXERCISES IN EXPLOSIVE FORM	58
APPLICATION OF EXPLOSIVE FORM	58
EXAMPLES OF EXPLOSIVE FORM	59
ADVANTAGES OF EXPLOSIVE FORM	59
QUALITY OF VOICE	60
PURE TONE	61
EXERCISES IN PURE TONE, EFFUSIVE FORM	62
APPLICATION OF PURE TONE, EFFUSIVE FORM	62
EXAMPLES OF PURE TONE, EFFUSIVE FORM	62
EXERCISES IN PURE TONE, EXPULSIVE FORM	63
APPLICATION OF PURE TONE, EXPULSIVE FORM	64
EXAMPLES OF PURE TONE, EXPULSIVE FORM	64
EXERCISES IN PURE TONE, EXPLOSIVE FORM	65
APPLICATION OF PURE TONE, EXPLOSIVE FORM	65
ADVANTAGES OF PURE TONE	66
OROTUND	66
EXERCISES IN OROTUND, EFFUSIVE FORM	67
APPLICATION OF OROTUND, EFFUSIVE FORM	68
EXAMPLES OF OROTUND, EFFUSIVE FORM	68
EXERCISES IN OROTUND, EXPULSIVE FORM	69
APPLICATION OF OROTUND, EXPULSIVE FORM	69
EXAMPLES OF OROTUND, EXPULSIVE FORM	69
EXERCISES IN OROTUND, EXPLOSIVE FORM	71
APPLICATION OF OROTUND, EXPLOSIVE FORM	72
EXAMPLES OF OROTUND, EXPLOSIVE FORM	72
ADVANTAGES OF OROTUND	73
ASPIRATE	74
EXERCISES IN ASPIRATE, EFFUSIVE FORM	74
APPLICATION OF ASPIRATE, EFFUSIVE FORM	75
EXAMPLES OF ASPIRATE, EFFUSIVE FORM	75
EXERCISES IN ASPIRATE, EXPULSIVE FORM	76
APPLICATION OF ASPIRATE, EXPULSIVE FORM	76
EXAMPLES OF ASPIRATE, EXPULSIVE FORM	77
EXERCISES IN ASPIRATE, EXPLOSIVE FORM	78
APPLICATION OF ASPIRATE, EXPLOSIVE FORM	78
EXAMPLES OF ASPIRATE, EXPLOSIVE FORM	78
ADVANTAGES OF ASPIRATE	78
PECTORAL	79
EXERCISES IN PECTORAL, EFFUSIVE FORM	79
APPLICATION OF PECTORAL, EFFUSIVE FORM	79
EXAMPLES OF PECTORAL, EFFUSIVE FORM	79
EXERCISES IN PECTORAL, EXPULSIVE FORM	81

CONTENTS.

	PAGE
Application of Pectoral, Expulsive Form	81
Examples of Pectoral, Expulsive Form	81
Exercises in Pectoral, Explosive Form	83
Application of Pectoral, Explosive Form	83
Examples of Pectoral, Explosive Form	83
Advantages of Pectoral	84
Guttural	84
Exercises in Guttural, Effusive Form	84
Application of Guttural, Effusive Form	85
Examples of Guttural, Effusive Form	85
Exercises in Guttural, Expulsive Form	85
Application of Guttural, Expulsive Form	85
Examples of Guttural, Expulsive Form	86
Application of Guttural, Explosive Form	86
Examples of Guttural, Explosive Form	86
Advantages of Guttural	86
Oral	87
Application of Oral	87
Examples of Oral	87
Advantages of Oral	88
Nasal	88
Force	89
Divisions of Force	90
Exercises in Force	90
Subdued Force—Application of	91
Examples of Subdued Force	91
Moderate Force—Application of	93
Examples of Moderate Force	92
Energetic Force—Application of	95
Examples of Energetic Force	95
Impassioned Force—Application of	97
Examples of Impassioned Force	97
Advantages of Force	99
Stress	99
Radical Stress	100
Exercises in Radical Stress	100
Application of Radical Stress	100
Examples of Radical Stress	101
Advantages of Radical Stress	102
Median Stress	103
Exercises in Median Stress	103
Application of Median Stress	103
Examples in Median Stress	104
Advantages of Median Stress	106
Final Stress	106
Exercise in Final Stress	106
Application of Final Stress	106
Examples in Final Stress	107
Advantages of Final Stress	108
Compound Stress	109

CONTENTS.

	PAGE
Exercises in Compound Stress	109
Application of Compound Stress	109
Examples in Compound Stress	110
Advantages of Compound Stress	110
Thorough Stress	110
Exercises in Thorough Stress	111
Application of Thorough Stress	111
Examples of Thorough Stress	111
Advantages of Thorough Stress	112
Intermittent Stress	113
Exercises in Intermittent Stress	113
Application of Intermittent Stress	113
Examples in Intermittent Stress	114
Advantages of Intermittent Stress	114
Pitch	115
Divisions of Pitch	116
Exercises in Pitch	117
Middle Pitch—Application of	118
Examples of Middle Pitch	118
Low Pitch—Application of	120
Examples of Low Pitch	120
High Pitch—Application of	121
Examples of High Pitch	121
Very Low Pitch—Application of	123
Examples of Very Low Pitch	123
Very High Pitch—Application of	125
Examples of Very High Pitch	125
Advantages of Pitch	126
Movement	127
Divisions of Movement	127
Exercises in Movement	127
Moderate Movement—Application of	128
Examples of Moderate Movement	128
Slow Movement—Application of	130
Examples of Slow Movement	130
Very Slow Movement—Application of	131
Examples of Very Slow Movement	132
Rapid Movement—Application of	132
Examples in Rapid Movement	132
Very Rapid Movement—Application of	134
Examples in Very Rapid Movement	135
Advantages of Movement	136
Accidents of Voice	138
Quantity	138
Long Quantity	139
Exercises in Long Quantity	139
Application of Long Quantity	139
Examples of Long Quantity	139
Short Quantity	141
Exercises in Short Quantity	141

	PAGE
APPLICATION OF SHORT QUANTITY	141
EXAMPLES OF SHORT QUANTITY	141
ADVANTAGES OF QUANTITY	142
INFLECTIONS	144
RISING INFLECTION	144
EXERCISES IN RISING INFLECTION	144
APPLICATION OF RISING INFLECTION OF SECOND	145
EXAMPLES OF RISING INFLECTION OF SECOND	145
APPLICATION OF RISING INFLECTIONS OF THIRD AND FIFTH	145
EXAMPLES OF RISING INFLECTIONS OF THIRD AND FIFTH	145
APPLICATION OF RISING INFLECTION OF OCTAVE	147
EXAMPLES OF RISING INFLECTION OF OCTAVE	147
FALLING INFLECTION	147
EXERCISES IN FALLING INFLECTION	148
APPLICATION OF FALLING INFLECTION	148
EXAMPLES OF FALLING INFLECTIONS OF SECOND AND THIRD	148
EXAMPLES OF FALLING INFLECTIONS OF THIRD AND FIFTH	149
EXAMPLES OF FALLING INFLECTIONS OF THIRD, FIFTH AND OCTAVE	149
ADVANTAGES OF INFLECTION	151
CIRCUMFLEX	151
APPLICATION OF CIRCUMFLEX	152
EXAMPLES OF CIRCUMFLEX	152
ADVANTAGES OF CIRCUMFLEX	152
CADENCE	152
EXAMPLES IN CADENCE	153
ADVANTAGES OF CADENCE	153
PAUSES	154
APPLICATION OF PAUSES	154
EXAMPLES OF PAUSES	154
EMPHASIS—KINDS OF	157
EMPHASIS OF FORCE	158
EXAMPLES OF EMPHASIS OF FORCE	159
EMPHASIS OF STRESS	159
EXAMPLES OF EMPHASIS OF RADICAL STRESS	159
EXAMPLES OF EMPHASIS OF MEDIAN STRESS	159
EXAMPLES OF EMPHASIS OF FINAL STRESS	160
EXAMPLES OF EMPHASIS OF COMPOUND STRESS	160
EXAMPLES OF EMPHASIS OF THOROUGH STRESS	160
EMPHASIS OF QUALITY	161
EXAMPLE OF EMPHASIS OF ASPIRATE QUALITY	161
EXAMPLE OF EMPHASIS OF PECTORAL QUALITY	161
EXAMPLE OF EMPHASIS OF GUTTURAL QUALITY	161
EMPHASIS OF PITCH	162
EXAMPLES OF VERY HIGH PITCH	162
EXAMPLES OF VERY LOW PITCH	162
EMPHASIS OF MOVEMENT	165
EXAMPLES OF EMPHASIS OF SLOW MOVEMENT	165
EXAMPLES OF EMPHASIS OF RAPID MOVEMENT	165
ADVANTAGES OF MOVEMENT	165
CLIMAX	167

CONTENTS.

	PAGE
EXAMPLES OF CLIMAX....	167
GROUPING—ADVANTAGES OF	170
ILLUSTRATIONS OF GROUPING	170

CHAPTER IV.
ACTION.

POSITIONS OF FEET	177
CHANGES IN POSITION OF FEET	180
POSITION OF BODY	180
POSITION OF ARMS IN REPOSE	180
POSITION OF ARMS IN GESTURE	181
THE HAND	182
POSITIONS OF HAND	182
ACCOMPANIMENTS OF GESTURE	183
QUALITIES OF GESTURE	185
ADAPTATION OF GESTURE	187
SIGNIFICANT GESTURES	188
THE EYE AND COUNTENANCE	189
THE PASSIONS	191
PICTURE OF THE PASSIONS	193

PART II.
DEDUCTIONS.

CHAPTER I.
STYLES.

DIAGRAM OF STYLES	210
EXPLANATION	211

CHAPTER II.
PATHETIC STYLE.

DEATH-BED.—*Thomas Hood*	212
THE PAUPER'S DEATH-BED.—*Mrs. Southey*	212
MY MOTHER'S BIBLE.—*G. P. Morris*	213
THE OLD ARM-CHAIR.—*Eliza Cook*	214
THE BURIAL OF ARNOLD.—*N. P. Willis*	215
THE LAST FOOTFALL	217
ANABEL LEE.—*Edgar A. Poe*	218
THE BRIDGE OF SIGHS.—*Thomas Hood*	219
THE GRAVE OF THE BELOVED.—*Washington Irving*	221

CHAPTER III.

SERIOUS STYLE.

	PAGE
NEARER HOME.—*Phebe Cary*	224
THE HEAVENLY CANAAN.—*Watts*	225
IN THE OTHER WORLD.—*Mrs. H. Beecher Stowe*	225
IF WE KNEW	227
FORTY YEARS AGO	228
THE MOUNTAINS OF LIFE.—*J. G. Clark*	230
THE ISLE OF LONG AGO.—*B. F. Taylor*	231
GOD THE TRUE SOURCE OF CONSOLATION.—*Moore*	232
GRATITUDE.—*Addison*	232
OVER THE RIVER.—*Miss Priest*	233

CHAPTER IV.

TRANQUIL STYLE.

RAIN ON THE ROOF.—*Coates Kinney*	235
NIGHT.—*Shelley*	236
THE LIGHT-HOUSE.—*Moore*	236
MUSINGS.—*Amelia*	237
THE RAINBOW.—*Amelia*	239

CHAPTER V.

GRAVE STYLE.

INSPIRATION OF THE BIBLE.—*Winthrop*	241
GOODNESS OF GOD	242
ACCESS TO GOD.—*James Hamilton*	242
INFIDELITY TESTED	243
RELIGION THE ONLY BASIS OF SOCIETY.—*W. E. Channing*	244
PROMISES OF RELIGION TO THE YOUNG.—*Alison*	245

CHAPTER VI.

DIDACTIC STYLE.

CHEERFULNESS	247
BE COMPREHENSIVE	248
HAMLET'S ADVICE.—*Shakspeare*	249
INDUSTRY AND ELOQUENCE.—*Wirt*	249
NO EXCELLENCE WITHOUT LABOR.—*Wirt*	251
ADVICE TO YOUNG LAWYERS.—*Judge Story*	252
MODULATION.—*Lloyd*	253
DON'T RUN IN DEBT.—*Eliza Cook*	254
QUERIES	254

CHAPTER VII.

LIVELY STYLE.

	PAGE
PERSONALITIES AND USES OF A LAUGH	257
PADDLE YOUR OWN CANOE.—*Mrs. Sarah T. Bolton*..........	258
I'M WITH YOU ONCE AGAIN.—*G. P. Morris*..................	260
A PSALM OF LIFE.—*Longfellow*............................	260

CHAPTER VIII.

GAY STYLE.

SPRING.—*Bryant*..	262
YOUNG LOCHINVAR.—*Scott*................................	262
LET US TRY TO BE HAPPY	264
COQUETTE PUNISHED	264
RHYME OF THE RAIL.—*Saxe*..............................	266

CHAPTER IX.

JOYOUS STYLE.

GUNEOPATHY.—*Saxe*.....................................	269
MERCUTIO'S HUMOROUS DESCRIPTION OF QUEEN MAB.—*Shakspeare*	270

CHAPTER X.

SUBLIME STYLE.

IN MEMORIAM—A. LINCOLN.—*Mrs. Buybee*..................	272
BREAK! BREAK! BREAK!—*Tennyson*........................	273
GOD.—*Derzhavin*	274
GOD'S FIRST TEMPLES.—*Bryant*..........................	277
THE CLOSING YEAR.—*Prentice*...........................	280
MORNING HYMN TO MONT BLANC.—*Coleridge*................	282

CHAPTER XI.

ORATORICAL STYLE.

REPLY TO MR. WICKHAM IN BURR'S TRIAL, 1807.—*Wirt*......	285
ARISTOCRACY.—*Robert R. Livingston*.....................	286
GENERAL GOVERNMENT AND THE STATES.—*Alexander Hamilton*..	287
PATRIOTIC SELF-SACRIFICE.—*Cay*.........................	288
AMBITION OF A STATESMAN.—*Clay*.........................	289
NATIONAL CHARACTER.—*Maxey*.............................	290
RESPONSIBILITIES OF OUR REPUBLIC.—*Joseph Story*.........	291
DUTY OF LITERARY MEN TO THEIR COUNTRY.—*Grimke*.........	291
AMERICAN LABORERS.—*Naylor*.............................	293
NAPOLEON BONAPARTE.—*Phillips*..........................	294

	PAGE
UNJUST NATIONAL ACQUISITION.—*Thomas Corwin*	296
OUR SYSTEM OF PUBLIC INSTRUCTION SHOULD DISTINCTLY INCULCATE A LOVE OF COUNTRY.—*Newton Bateman*	297
APPEAL IN BEHALF OF IRELAND.—*S. S. Prentiss*	299
GLORIOUS NEW ENGLAND.—*S. S. Prentiss*	301
SPEECH BEFORE THE VIRGINIA CONVENTION OF DELEGATES, MARCH, 1775.—*Patrick Henry*	302
SUPPOSED SPEECH OF JAMES OTIS.—*Mrs. L. M. Child*	304
RIENZI'S ADDRESS TO THE ROMANS.—*Miss Mitford*	306

CHAPTER XII.
ORATORICAL SUBLIME.

DEATH OF JOHN QUINCY ADAMS.—*L. E. Holmes*	308
DEATH OF ALEXANDER HAMILTON.—*Dr. Nott*	309

CHAPTER XIII.
IMPASSIONED POETIC STYLE.

HATE OF THE BOWL	311
THE AMERICAN FLAG.—*J. R. Drake*	312
THE RESCUE OF CHICAGO.—*H. M. Look*	314
SHERIDAN'S RIDE.—*T. Buchanan Read*	316

CHAPTER XIV.
SHOUTING STYLE.

FROM CHARGE OF LIGHT BRIGADE.—*Tennyson*	318
FROM MARMION AND DOUGLAS.—*Scott*	319
FROM MARCO BOZZARIS.—*Halleck*	319
FROM BLACK REGIMENT.—*Boker*	319
TELL'S ADDRESS TO THE ALPS.—*J. S. Knowles*	321

CHAPTER XV.
VEHEMENT STYLE.

CATALINE'S DEFIANCE.—*Croly*	322
THE SEMINOLE'S DEFIANCE.—*G. W. Patten*	323
SPARTACUS TO THE GLADIATORS AT CAPUA.—*E. Kellogg*	324

CHAPTER XVI.
DRAMATIC STYLE.

FROM ON BOARD THE CUMBERLAND, MARCH 7, 1862.—*George H. Boker*	327
ABOU BEN-ADHEM.—*Leigh Hunt*	328

CONTENTS.

	PAGE
LEAP FOR LIFE.—*G. P. Morris*	329
LORD ULLIN'S DAUGHTER.—*Campbell*	330
JOHN BURNS OF GETTYSBURG.—*F. Bret Harte*	331
POOR LITTLE JIM	334
GAMBLER'S WIFE.—*Coates*	335
THE BEAUTIFUL SNOW.—*James W. Watson*	336
MAUD MULLER.—*J. G. Whittier*	338
JOHN MAYNARD, THE HERO PILOT.—*Gough*	342
BLACK REGIMENT.—*Boker*	343
ON THE SHORES OF TENNESSEE	345
THE VAGABONDS.—*Trowbridge*	347
ON BOARD THE CUMBERLAND.—*Boker*	350
THE BELLS.—*Edgar A. Poe*	354
THE RISING, 1776.—*T. Buchanan Read*	357
THE POLISH BOY.—*Mrs. Ann S. Stephens*	360
COUNT CANDESPINA'S STANDARD.—*Boker*	364
THE BARON'S LAST BANQUET.—*A. G. Green*	367
BERNARDO DEL CARPO.—*Mrs. Hemans*	369
THE RAVEN.—*Edgar A. Poe*	375
SCENE FROM HAMLET	371

HUMOROUS STYLE.

THE NANTUCKET SKIPPER.—*J. T. Fields*	378
A CATEGORICAL COURTSHIP	379
MR. ORATOR PUFF.—*Thomas Moore*	380
SMACK IN SCHOOL.—*W. P. Palmer*	381
PYRAMUS AND THISBE.—*Saxe*	382
A VERY IMPORTANT PROCEEDING—FROM PICKWICK PAPERS.—*Dickens*	384

THE

SCIENCE OF ELOCUTION.

ELOCUTION.

ELOCUTION is the Science and Art of expressing thought and feeling by utterance and action.

As a science, it unfolds the principles of reading and speaking; as an art, it embodies in delivery every accomplishment, both of voice and action, necessary to appropriate expression.

The requisites of a good elocution are,

First, Distinct articulation;

Second, Full and free respiration;

Third, Perfect control of a clear, full, round, musical tone of voice;

Fourth, Graceful and expressive action;

Fifth, Cultivated taste and judgment.

TABULAR VIEW OF THE SCIENCE OF ELOCUTION.

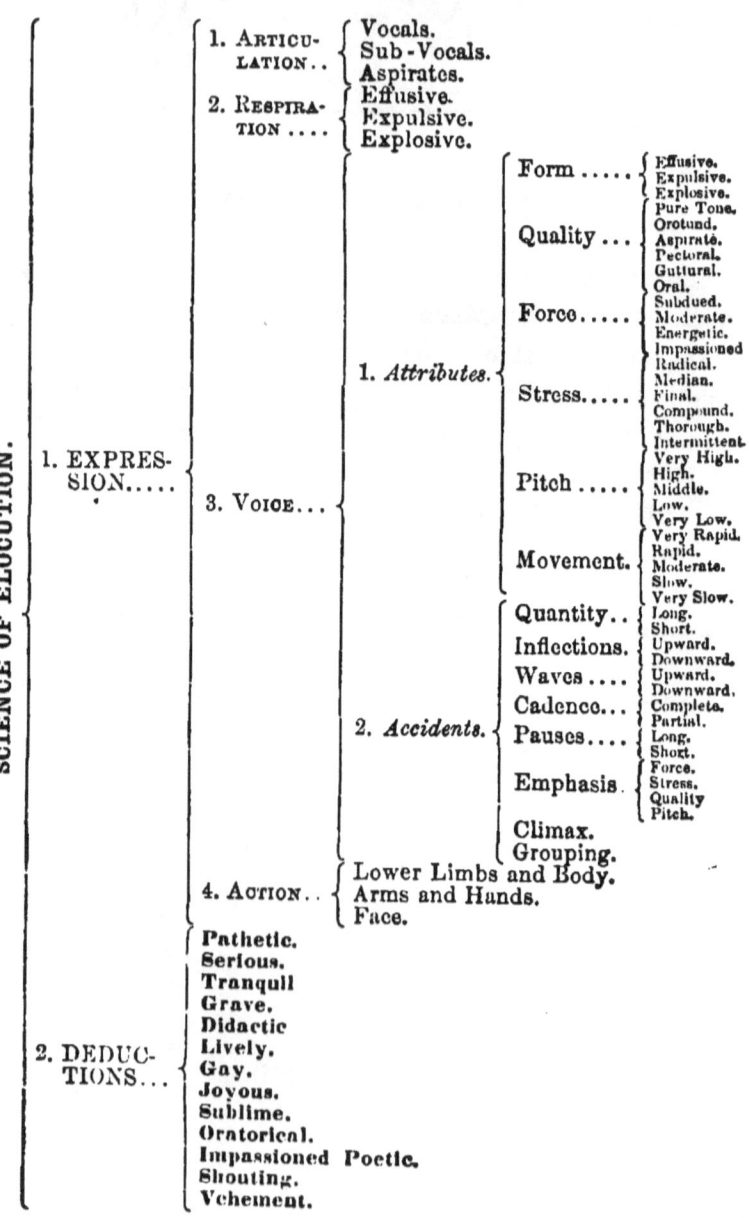

PART 1

EXPRESSION.

THE term expression includes all that part of Elocution which relates to articulation, respiration, vocalization, and action.

CHAPTER I.

ARTICULATION.

ARTICULATION is the utterance of the elementary sounds of a language by the appropriate movements of the organs of speech.

A ready and distinct articulation is an indispensable requisite to good reading.

Owing to bad habits acquired in early youth, and to defective systems of instruction, but few persons possess this invaluable accomplishment.

Frequent and careful practice on the elementary sounds will in almost every case correct defects, and impart a ready and distinct articulation.

SECTION I.

ELEMENTARY SOUNDS.

An elementary sound is a sound produced by a single impulse of the organs of speech.

Phonologists pretty generally agree that there are forty-four elementary sounds in the English language.

These sounds are represented by letters and characters. The sounds are divided into vocals, sub-vocals, and aspirates; the letters into vowels and consonants.

CHART OF THE ELEMENTARY SOUNDS.

LONG VOCALS.

1. e, as in me, eve.
2. ē, " serge, verge.
3. ā, " aim, ale.
4. â, " air, care.
5. ä, " arm, farm.
6. ô, " or, for.
7. ō, " oak, no.
8. ǫ, " ooze, do.

SHORT VOCALS.

9. ĭ, as in ill, it.
10. ĕ, " ell, let.
11. ŏ, " odd, not.
12. ŭ, " up, sup.
13. ă, " add, sad.
14. ȧ, " ask, task.
15. ụ, " full, pull.

DIPHTHONGS.

16. ī, as in ice, lie.
17. oi, " oil, boil.
18. ū, as in mute, tube.
19. ou, " out, sound.

SUB-VOCALS.—*Correlatives.*

20. b, as in boy, ebb.
21. d, " did, rod.
22. g, " go, rag.
23. ġ, " gem, judge.
24. v, " veer, valve.
25. th, " this, breathe.
26. z, " zone, zeal.
27. zh, " azure, seizure.

SUB-VOCALS.—*Liquids.*

28. l, as in lo, will.
29. r, " row, roar.
30. m, " moon, home.
31. n, " no, moon.
32. ng, " sing, ring.

ELEMENTARY SOUNDS. 23

Sub-Vocals.—*Coalescents.*

33. w, as in we, wit.
34. y, " yet, you.

Aspirates.—*Explodents.*

35. p, as in pin, pipe.
36. t, " till, spot.
37. k, " kick, neck.
38. ch, " church, which.

Aspirates.—*Continuants.*

39. f, as in fife, stiff.
40. th, " think, breath.
41. s, " see, pass.
42. sh, " shine, wish.
43. h, " he, hat.
44. wh, " whence, what.

SECTION II.

EXERCISES IN ARTICULATION.

The following exercises are designed for the cultivation of a distinct and accurate articulation. Syllabication, accent, and pronunciation, though all important in reading and speaking, do not properly belong to a work on Elocution. They can only be thoroughly learned from the unabridged dictionaries.

Position of the Body.

The pupil should be careful, when practicing the following exercises, to maintain an erect position of the body, keep the head up, the chest expanded, and the shoulders well back.

Suggestions.

These exercises are not designed merely for those whose articulation is defective. Persons who speak with even more than ordinary accuracy will be greatly benefited by frequent practice on the elementary sounds.

That the highest advantage may be derived from this practice let there be no feeble work.

Repeat each exercise with energy, clearness, and precision.

Before uttering any word or sentence repeat a number of times the element for the cultivation of which the exercise is specially designed.

In pronouncing the long vocals, which admit of indefinite prolongation, be careful not to drawl them.

Exercises on the elementary sounds are now so generally practiced in the primary schools and at colleges, and the positions and actions of the organs in the production of these sounds so accurately taught, that a detailed discussion of them here is deemed unnecessary.

Exercises on the Long Vocals.

I. ē, as in me.

he,	the,	be,	eve,
meed,	heed,	need,	seed,
breathe,	these,	please,	least.

1. I believe it every word.
2. I mean what I say.
3. Seems, madam! nay, it is.
4. Tell them we need no change.
5. Be not overcome by evil.
6. Heat me these irons hot.
7. I must be brief.
8. We must believe to be saved.

II. ẽ, as in earth.

| earth, | ermine, | verge, |
| prefer, | mirth, | serge. |

ARTICULATION.

1. The unsullied sanctity of your ermine.
2. I prefer not to do it.
3. He is on the verge of ruin.
4. Crown him with myrtle.
5. I am in earnest.

III. ā, as in aim.

aim,	ale,	pay,	may,
age,	pale,	lame,	slay,
pray,	day,	clay,	vain.

1. If we fail we can do no worse.
2. He is a saint.
3. He may pray, but it will be all in vain.
4. They say that we will fail.
5. May we pay our way?
6. He is afraid of me.
7. Nay, after that, consume away in rust.
8. Away! away! let me not see thy face.

IV. â, as in air.

| their, | lair, | dare, | hair, |
| chair, | prepare, | prayer, | despair. |

1. The air is very cool.
2. Dare to do right.
3. Swear by my sword.
4. Air, earth, and sea, resound his praise.
5. Come, boy, prepare yourself.
6. Where shall the lover rest?
7. There through the summer day.
8. Scarce are boughs waving.

V ä, as in arm.

arm,	harm,	charm,	farm,
qualm,	calm,	balm,	alarm,
palm,	psalm,	ma'am,	father.

1. To arms! to arms! they cry.
2. The night was calm and beautiful.
3. Hast thou a charm to stay the morning star?
4. I will not harm thee, boy.
5. The psalm was warrior David's song.
6. The balmy breath of incense-breathing morn.
7. A qualm of conscience brings me back again.
8. Father, thy hand hath reared this venerable column.

VI. ô, as in or.

or,	for,	nor,	fall,
north,	war,	all,	tall,
law,	corn,	small,	pall.

1. My voice is still for war.
2. The law must be obeyed.
3. The cause stands not on eloquence, but stands on laws.
4. All that I am, all that I hope in this life, I am now ready to stake on it.
5. The north is wild with alarms.
6. I come not here to talk.
7. His tall form taller seemed.
8. The pall was settled.

VII. ō, as in no.

no,	go,	lo,	woe,
home,	old,	bold,	glorious,
sold,	enrolled,	fold,	gold.

1. Paid my price in paltry gold.
2. No, no, gentlemen, gold cannot purchase it.
3. They have enrolled us.
4. Thou glorious mirror.
5. Fold her hands lightly.
6. Home, thy joys are passing lovely.

ARTICULATION.

7. Woe, unto thee, Chorazin!
8. The bold, brave boy of Glingal.

VIII. o͞o, as in ooze.

who,	ooze,	fool,	stool,
moon,	room,	boon,	soon,
loom,	doom,	noon,	choose.

1. Thy doom is fixed.
2. The fool hath said, No God.
3. There is no longer any room for hope.
4. The moon's pale light.
5. Soon we shall join the kindred dead.
6. The blood oozed from his ghastly wound.
7. Who dare assert it?
8. You denied me this.

EXERCISES ON SHORT VOCALS.

IX. ĭ, as in ill.

ill,	it,	will,	fill,
in,	rip,	inch,	ink,
rid,	pith,	risk,	till.

1. I will never submit.
2. Rid me of these vagabonds.
3. It is I; be not afraid.
4. Inch by inch we will dispute the ground.
5. I'll risk my life upon it.
6. Ill-mannered wretch.
7. If I can catch him once upon the hip.
8. Three millions of people armed in the holy cause of liberty.

X. ĕ, as in ell.

ell,	let,	end,	deck,
neck,	wreck,	pet,	send,
men,	pest,	jet,	death.

1. The end of all things is at hand.
2. Let come what may.
3. The people are in debt.
4. Men, men, for shame, thus to yield.
5. I would never lay down my arms, never, never.
6. This in a moment brings me to my end.
7. But this informs me I shall never die.
8. Up to the spar deck!

XI. ŏ, as in odd.

odd,	not,	on,	stop,
cot,	rob,	rock,	rod,
got,	nod,	sod,	rot.

1. And the rock shall rear its head.
2. Stop! for thy tread is on an empire's dust.
3. Odd! 'tis very odd indeed.
4. Let the carrion rot.
5. Unconsciously he executes the will of God.
6. His lot is a hard one.
7. This rock shall fly from its firm base as soon as I
8. On, on, you noble English.

XII. ŭ, as in up.

up,	sup,	cup,	skull,
but,	us,	hut,	hub,
hug,	bud,	run,	gun.

1. Up, comrades, up!
2. Give me rum! O give me rum!
3. The cup is full of poison.
4. They sup full well.
5. Your apprehension must be dull.
6. That skull had a tongue in it once.
7. Don't give up the ship.
8. They tell us that we are weak.

ARTICULATION.

XIII. ă, as in add.

add,	sad,	had,	mat,
bad,	back,	cat,	rat,
battle,	scaffold,	satisfy,	that.

1. His countenance was sad.
2. The battle, sir, is not to the strong alone.
3. What will satisfy you?
4. Back to thy punishment, false fugitive.
5. Add to your virtue, faith.
6. The scaffold has no terrors for me.
7. Let me die like a man.
8. That will be justice.

XIV. á, as in ask.

ask,	task,	flask,	mask,
fast,	hasp,	grant,	branch
grass,	pass,	mass,	clasp.

1. Pass the shadow but a hair.
2. Ask and you shall receive.
3. The grass grows green above her grave.
4. The task is done.
5. Fast hurrying through the outer door.
6. Grant me but an hour of life.
7. And clasping to his heart his boy, he fainted on the deck.
8. Fast bind, fast find.

XV. ụ, as in full.

| full, | pull, | put, | puss, |
| push, | bullet, | bullion, | fuller. |

1. Full many a gem of richest ray serene.
2. Pull, pull for your lives.
3. The bullet passed near his face.
4. The fuller fulls his cloth.

EXERCISES ON DIPHTHONGS.

XVI. ĭ, as in ice.

ice,	lie,	try,	fie,
mile,	fight,	kite,	ripe,
spike,	bide,	vise,	isle

1. A mile or two at most.
2. Let him bide his time.
3. My name, my fame, must be unsullied.
4. And give thee in thy teeth the lie.
5. His form is held as in a vise.
6. The vile wretch.
7. The isles of Greece, the isles of Greece.
8. I'll fight till from my bones my flesh be hacked

XVII. oi, or oy, as in oil.

oil,	boil,	foil,	soil,
voice,	toil,	boy,	joy,
boisterous,	noise,	rejoice,	turmoil.

1. My voice is still for war.
2. What noise is that I hear?
3. Rejoice, ye men of Angiers.
4. The boisterous waves lashed the shore.
5. Let not the sacred soil be polluted.
6. The toil-worn traveler enters.
7. Joy, joy! shout aloud for joy!
8. The spoil shall be the victor's reward.

XVIII. ū, as in mute.

tube,	duke,	beauty,	amuse,
subdue,	fury,	usage,	use,
value,	statue,	renew,	few.

1. Few shall part where many meet.
2. The demand determines the value.
3. The curfew tolls.

4. He knew that it was wrong.
5. The general reviewed his army.
6. He was mute with astonishment.
7. The statute forbids it.
8. Renew it o'er and o'er.

XIX. ou, as in out.

out,	sound,	hour,	thou,
plow,	now,	thousand,	round,
pound,	bound,	mount,	fount.

1. Out, out, brief candle!
2. Put out the light, and then put out the light.
3. Now, by the gods above us, sires!
4. A thousand at thy side shall fall.
5. A day, an hour, of virtuous liberty is worth a whole eternity of bondage.
6. Bound thy desires by thy means.
7. Thou hast destroyed us.
8. Sound, sound the alarm!

Exercises on Sub-Vocals.—*Correlatives.*

XX. b, as in boy.

bad,	boon,	bind,	bend,
brown,	beck,	beat,	beg,
orb,	tube,	curb,	rub,
dub,	nib,	mob,	rob.

1. Bind beauteous boughs upon his brow.
2. Bend not before the beauteous vision.
3. Be brave, be bold, for good.
4. Brave boys of Bengal.
5. Basely they bound him to the beach.
6. The bards of the Bible.
7. Benjamin Brown bought the book.
8. He is a bold, brave, bad boy.

XXI. d, as in did.

doom,	duty,	dead,	delve,
day,	defy,	deep,	deed,
add,	mad,	sad,	lad,
head,	hard,	bard,	defend

1. Dare to do right.
2. Down on thy knees, thy doom is sealed.
3. Deep calleth unto deep.
4. Do you dare defy my authority?
5. Down the long dark line.
6. Despair not of success in the darkest day.
7. Did you say David is dead?
8. Despise not the day of small things.

XXII. g, as in go.

give,	gone,	gad,	grind,
grant,	gasp,	glad,	guilt,
hag,	rag,	lag,	log,
tug,	sag,	fag,	dog.

1. Gold gave thee all thy grace.
2. Grasp the goal and gain the prize.
3. Grant ye, O grant ye this boon to me!
4. Gather graces from the groves.
5. Go, give thy gains away.
6. Gather not greedily the gold.
7. God grant thee grace.
8. Glory gathers on his brow.

XXIII. g, as in judge.

gem,	join,	cage,	jade,
jam,	jag,	jeer,	jar,
jump,	June,	jolt,	jovial.

1. Join, all ye people, in his praise.
2. Gems of richest ray serene.

3. Justice should join with mercy.
4. Justly judge the cause.
5. Journeymen do not always deal justly.
6. Juno, the sister and wife of Jupiter.
7. Jocund John jokes jocosely.
8. Join the everlasting jubilee.

XXIV. v, as in veer.

vale,	void,	value	vile,
vary,	vase,	vent,	valve,
have,	live,	brave,	save,
love,	above,	give,	behave

1. Value virtue highly.
2. Vile villains vent their vengeance.
3. Valiant deeds deserve praise.
4. Vengeance belongeth to the Lord.
5. Verily, verily, I say unto you.
6. Vagabonds wander idly around.
7. Vain, vain are all thy efforts.
8. Various views are entertained.

XXV. th, as in this.

this,	their,	them,	then,
thence,	there,	than,	that,
breathe,	beneath,	wreathe,	weather.

1. This is the place, the center of the grove.
2. Thou breathest, silent the submissive waves.
3. Beneath those rugged elms, that yew tree's shade
4. Breathes there a man with soul so dead.
5. Wreathe flowers for the valiant dead.
6. That thou shouldst die.
7. The vessel weathered the storm.
8. There is now no longer any room for hope.

XXVI. z, as in zone.

  zone, zeal, zest, zebra,
  zero, zinc, zigzag, zenith,
  has, was, cause, rouse.

1. The zeal of thy house hath eaten me up.
2. He has reached the zenith of his glory.
3. Zeno was zealous in his work.
4. He has zeal without knowledge.
5. The cause will raise up men.
6. Rouse, ye Romans, rouse!
7. The zephyr breathes calmly.
8. Zion, the joy of all the earth.

XXVII. zh, as in azure.

  azure, pleasure, seizure, measure,
  erasure, treasure, composure, disclosure.

1. The measure of man is mind.
2. Your pleasure shall be the law.
3. The treasures of the universe are his.
4. The seizure was made according to law.
5. Not like those steps on heaven's azure.

  Exercises on Sub-Vocals.—*Liquids.*

XXVIII. l, as in lo.

  loud, long, leave, last,
  land, lend, least, loose,
  fall, all, call, wall.

1. Lo, the poor Indian!
2. Leaves have their time to fall.
3. Leave me, leave me to die alone.
4. Land, land ahead.
5. Little lads like looking about.
6. Learned lads like long lessons.
7. Last, last, lordliest of lords.
8. Lord Leland long loved the landlady of Leicester

ARTICULATION.

XXIX. r, as in row

roar,	roam,	roast,	reel,
round,	rise,	river,	reap,
flour,	fear,	near,	sear.

1. Rough and rugged rocks rear their heads high in air.
2. Round the rude ring the ragged rascal ran.
3. Robert rebuked Richard, who ran roaring.
4. Rich, ripe, round fruit hung round the room.
5. Real riches rise from within.
6. Return, O holy Dove, return!
7. Roderick Random ran a ridiculous race.
8. Rivers to the ocean run.

XXX. m, as in mow.

moon,	morn,	move,	mop,
man,	mind,	malt,	mine,
arm,	farm,	harm,	warm.

1. Many men are misled by fame.
2. More than mortal man may not be.
3. Much learning hath made thee mad.
4. Milestones mark the march of time.
5. More misery may yet be mine.
6. Mournfully they march to the martial music.
7. Men may rise by their own merit.
8. May thy memory be embalmed in the hearts of men.

XXXI. n, as in no.

noon,	now,	near,	name,
new,	nice,	never,	nest,
fan,	man,	ran,	won.

1. Name not the gods, thou boy of tears.
2. No nation need despair.

3. Not now, Neighbor Norton.

4. Near by the spring upon a tree you know I cut your name.

5. No man knows the future.

6. Now none so poor to do him reverence.

7. I would never lay down my arms, never, never, never!

8. Napoleon's noble nature knew no niggardly notions.

XXXII. ng, as in sing.

wing,	ring,	long,	song,
bring,	thing,	doing,	ringing,
arming,	learning,	rising,	warring.

1. Bring flowers, sweet flowers.
2. Long may it wave.
3. Standing on the confines of another world.
4. Living, we will maintain it.
5. Dying we will assert it.
6. It is my living sentiment.
7. By the blessing of God it will be my dying sentiment.
8. Nothing but death can separate us.

EXERCISES ON SUB-VOCALS.—*Coalescents.*

XXXIII. w, as in wit.

was,	wise,	word,	wind,
war,	wan,	wild,	well,
weed,	weld,	wear,	week.

1. Wild was the night.
2. Weep not for me.
3. When wisdom shall return.
4. Well have they done their part.
5. Wise men will rule well.
6. Wisdom is above rubies.

7. Was ever woman in this humor wooed?
8. Was ever woman in this humor won?

XXXIV. y, as in yet.

you,	yes,	yard,	yea,
yawn,	year,	yacht,	yawl,
yell,	yellow,	yelk,	yelp,
yield,	young,	youth,	your.

1. Yield to mercy while 'tis offered to you.
2. Yet I say unto you that Solomon in all his glory was not arrayed like one of these.
3. Yield, madman, yield, thy horse is down.
4. Young men ahoy!
5. Youth is the seed-time of life.
6. Yonder comes the powerful king of day.
7. Yesterday shall be as to-day.
8. Year after year our blessings continue.

Exercises on Aspirates.—*Explodents*.

XXXV. p, as in pin.

pipe,	place,	page,	post,
port,	play,	poor,	pope,
pony,	pop,	point,	ply,
poem,	press,	prove,	proud.

1. Prove all things.
2. Poverty and pride are poor companions.
3. Perish my name!
4. Perhaps her love, perhaps her kingdom, charmed him.
5. Pickwick Papers, part first.
6. Pour this pestilence into her eyes.
7. Pictures of palaces please the eye.
8. Pious people praise the Lord.

XXXVI. t, as in tip.

top,	till,	toy,	time,
tap,	tag,	tat,	tart,
test,	tent,	tight,	trout,
tartar,	tassel,	tangle,	tartan.

1. Touch not, taste not, handle not.
2. Time and tide wait for no man.
3. Turn their uprooted trunks toward the skies.
4. Tremble and totter, ye adamantine mountains.
5. Teaching the rustic moralist to die.
6. Teach the truant child to pray.
7. Two guests sat at the feast.
8. Tar, tallow, tumeric, turpentine, and tin.

XXXVII. k, as in kick.

kin,	keel,	keep,	ken,
key,	kind,	king,	kiss,
kite,	kirk,	cart,	cape,
kink,	kith,	call,	cost.

1. Keep thy own counsels.
2. Come in consumption's ghastly form.
3. Kites rise against the wind.
4. Clean, placid Leman.
5. Kill a king.
6. Crown the victor.
7. Kindness kills the cause of hate.
8. Come one, come all.

XXXVIII. ch, as in church.

choose,	chaste,	chat,	check,
cheese,	cheer,	cheat,	cheap,
chide,	cherish,	choice,	child,
chief,	chess,	cherub,	chick.

1. Children choose trifling toys.
2. Chaucer's poetry charmed the chief.

3. Charge, Chester! charge!
4. Change cannot change thee.
5. Cheery, changeless, chieftainless.
6. Chaplets of chainless charity are for thee.
7. Chalice of childlike cheerfulness is thine.
8. Charity suffereth, and is kind.

Exercises on Aspirates.—*Continuants.*

XXXIX. f, as in fame.

fast,	fate,	far,	fane,
fatal,	fearful,	favor,	feed,
felon,	fellow,	fenny,	fetter,
friend,	filcher,	finger,	finical.

1. Fast bind, fast find.
2. Fasting he went to sleep, and fasting waked.
3. Fast by the throne obsequious Fame resides.
4. Father, from above bend down thine ear.
5. Fortune favors the brave.
6. False face must hide what the false heart doth know.
7. Firm in his faith he falters not.
8. First in war, first in peace, and first in the hearts of his countrymen.

XL. th, as in think.

thick,	thin,	through,	thanks,
thought,	thrust,	thong,	thousand,
breath,	hath,	birth,	death.

1. Three thousand thistles were thrust through his thumb.
2. Thanks to the thoughtful giver.
3. Thick and thicker fell the hail.
4. Through the thronged crowd he thrust his way.
5. Thrust the thorn into the flesh.

6. Three thousand soldiers thoughtlessly threw themselves away.

7. Think thoughtfully three times.

XLI. s, as in sound.

 sing, sour, sight, south,
 sigh, soon, stop, safe,
 song, suns, systems, strand.

1. Sans teeth, sans eyes, sans taste, sans every thing
2. Star after star from heaven's high arch shall rush.
3. Send us the spirit of the Son.
4. See the stars from heaven falling.
5. Soldiers, sailors, seamen, all were lost.
6. Suns sink on suns, and systems systems crush.
7. See sinners in the Gospel glass.
8. Softly, slowly see the sun arise.

XLII. sh, as in shame.

 shun, show, shear, shove,
 shout, sham, shroud, shelf,
 shine, ship, shore, shrine.

1. Shakspeare, Shelley and Sheridan.
2. She sang the song of the shirt.
3. Ships, sailorless, lay rotting on the sea.
4. Shout, shout aloud for joy!
5. Shrines shall guard the sacred dust.
6. So shalt thou rest secure.
7. Shroud my shame, night's gathering darkness
8. She then shall dress a sweeter sod.

XLIII. h, as in hope.

 hold, hand, hard, harp,
 head, help, half, hart,
 harsh, herds, hero, hermit

1. How heavy the hunter's tread.
2. His horsemen hard behind us ride.
3. Heroes have hearts for noble deeds.
4. How sweet to my heart are the scenes of my childhood.
5. Hail, holy light.
6. How high the heavens appear!
7. He heaved a huge stone up the hill.
8. Hark! hark! for bread my children cry.

XLIV. wh, as in what.

when,	whip,	where,	whet,
wheel,	wheat,	whine,	white,
whips,	whence,	what,	whirl.

1. Whence and what art thou?
2. What whim led Whitney to invent the cotton gin?
3. Whither, O whither shall I fly!
4. What white-winged sail is that?
5. Why will kings forget that they are men!
6. Whither when they came they fell at words.
7. Whither away so fast?
8. Whisper softly in the assembly.

Initial Combinations.

1. Br. brick, bread, bran, brought, brush, breeze, broom.
2. Bl. bloom, blur, blaze, blight, blood, blow, blue.
3. Dr. drill, dread, dram, dross, drum, dream, droll.
4. Dw. dwell, dwarf, dwindle.
5. Fl. fling, fled, flat, flood, flee, flare, flaw.
6. Fr. froze, fruit, frame, fry, from, frieze.
7. Gl. glib, glon, glad, gloss, glut, glean, glare.

8. Gr.   grasp, graze, grind, growl, grow, groom.
9. Kl.   click, clef, clam, clot, cluck, clean, claw.
10. Kr. crane, crime, crown, crow, crude, cram.
11. Kw. quick, quench, quack, queer, quart, quirk.
12. Ku. cue, cube, cute, cure, curate.
13. Pr. prim, priest, prong, prayer, praise, prime, proud.
14. Pl. plat, plot, plush, please, play, ply, plow.
15. Sp. spin, spend, span, spar, spur, spear, spare, spawn.
16. Spr. spring, spread, sprat, sprung, spree, sprawl. spray.
17. Spl. split, splash, spleen, splice, splint.
18. Sph. sphere, sphinx, spheric, spherule.
19. St. stick, stem, stand, star, stood, stun, steel.
20. Str. straw, stray, strive, strow, strong, strength.
21. Sn. snip, snag, snarl, snub, sneeze, snores, snail.
22. Sm. smut, smear, small, smile, smote, smooth, smell.
23. Sl. slip, slept, slang, sloth, slung, sleep, slur, slay.
24. Sk. skip, scan, scot, scar, scaled, score, scale, sky.
25. Skl. Sclave, sclerotic.
26. Skr. scrip, scrap, scrub, scream, scrawl, scribe, screw.
27. Skw. squib, square, squash, squat, squeak, squall.
28. Shr. shrimp, shrug, shrill, shrive, shroud, shrew.
29. Tr. trill, tread, trash, trot, trust, tree, train, try.
30. Tw. twinge, twang, tweed, twain, twine, tweak.
31. Thr. thrill, thread, throb, thrush, three, thrice.

Terminal Combinations.

COMBINATIONS.	EXAMPLES.
bd, bdst.	Pro-*b'd'st,* blab-*b'd'st,* robb*'d'st,* or-*b'd.*
bl, blst, bld, bldst, blz.	trou-*ble,* trou-*bl'st,* trou-*bl'd,* trou-*bl'dst,* trou-*bles.*
bz.	ni-*bs,* na-*bs,* pro-*bes,* tri-*bes,* sta-*bs,* cur-*bs.*
bst.	fib-*b'st,* stub-*b'st,* rob-*b'st,* sob-*b'st,* ro-*b'st.*
dl, dlst, dld, dldst, dlz.	han-*dle,* han-*dl'st,* han-*dl'd,* han-*dl'dst,* han-*dles.*
dn, dnz, dnst, dnd, dndst.	har-*den,* har-*dens,* har-*d'n'st,* har-*d'n'd,* har-*d'n'dst.*
dz.	fa-*des,* hi-*des,* dee-*ds,* loa-*ds,* broo-*ds,* hee-*ds.*
dst.	mi-*dst,* bred-*d'st,* di-*dst,* coul-*d'st,* ha-*d'st,* loa-*d'st.*
dth, dths.	wi-*dth,* brea-*dth,* brea-*dths,* wi-*dths.*
gd, gdst.	beg-*g'd,* brag-*g'd,* brag-*g'dst,* beg-*g'd'st.*
gl, glst, gld, gldst, glz.	man-*gle,* man-*gl'st,* man*gl'd,* man-*gl'dst,* man-*gles.*
gz.	di-*gs,* dre-*gs,* wa-*gs,* lo-*gs,* bu-*gs,* eg-*gs,* ho-*gs.*
gst.	lag-*g'st,* wag-*g'st,* dog-*g'st,* dug-*g'st.*
jd.	brid-*g'd,* hed-*g'd,* dred-*g'd,* jud-*g'd.*
fl, flst, fld, fldst, flz.	tri-*fle,* tri-*fl'st,* tri-*fl'd,* tri-*fl'dst,* tri-*fles.*
ft, fts, ftst.	swi-*ft,* wa-*ft,* wa-*fts,* wa-*ft'st,* quaf-*ft'st.*

44 SCIENCE OF ELOCUTION.

COMBINATIONS.	EXAMPLES
fs, fst.	snu-*fs*, lau-*ghs*, lau-*gh'st*, stuf-*f'st*.
fth, fths.	fi-*fth*, fi-*fths*.
sl, slst, sld, sldst, slz.	ne-*stle*, ne-*stl'st*, ne-*stl'd*, ne-*stl'dst* ne-*stles*.
sk, skt, sks, skst.	ma-*sk*, ma-*sk'd*, ma-*sks*, ma-*sk'st*.
sp, spt, sps.	ra-*sp*, ra-*sp'd*, ra-*sps*, cla-*sps*.
st, sts.	fi-*st*, bu-*st*, bu-*sts*, co-*sts*.
cht.	hit-*ch'd*, fet-*ch'd*, sket-*ch'd*, hat-*ch'd*.
lb, lbd, lbz.	bu-*lb*, bu-*lb'd*, bu-*lbs*.
ld, ldz, ldst.	fil-*led*, ho-*ld*, ho-*lds*, ho-*ld'st*, fil-*ld'st*.
lj, ljd.	bi-*lge*, bu-*lge*, bu-*lg'd*, bi-*lg'd*.
lm, lmd, lmz.	whe-*lm*, whe-*lm'd*, whe-*lms*.
ln.	swol-*len*, fal-*len*, sto-*len*, wool-*len*, sul-*len*.
lv, lvd, lvz.	de-*lve*, she-*lve*, she-*lv'd*, she-*lves* de-*lv'd*, de-*lves*.
lz.	fil-*ls*, tel-*ls*, bal-*ls*, hul-*ls*, tol-*ls*, cal-*ls*.
lk, lks, lkt, lkts.	e-*lk*, si-*lk*, si-*lks*, mu-*lct*, mu-*lcts*.
lp, lpt, lps, lpst.	pu-*lp*, he-*lp*, he-*lp'd*, he-*lps*, he-*lp'st*.
lt, lts, ltst.	hi-*lt*, ha-*lt*, ha-*lts*, ha-*lt'st*, sha'*lt*, sha-*lt'st*.
lf, lfs.	de-*lf*, gu-*lf*, gu-*lfs*, se-*lf*.
ls, lst.	fa-*lse*, fal-*l'st*, dwel-*l'st*, cal-*l'st*.
lth, lths.	ti-*lth*, hea-*lth*, hea-*lths*, wea-*lth*.
lch, lcht.	fi-*lch*, fi-*lch'd*.
md, mdst.	dim-*m'd*, ento-*mb'd*, ento-*mb'dst*, hem-*m'd*.
mz.	la-*mbs*, to-*mbs*, he-*ms*, su-*ms*, ha-*ms*.

COMBINATIONS.	EXAMPLES.
mp, mps, mpt, mpts.	i-*mp*, i-*mps*, atte-*mpt*, atte-*mpts*.
mf, mfs.	ly-*mph*, ny-*mph*, ny-*mphs*.
mst.	dim-*m'st*, ento-*mb'st*, hem-*m'st* roa-*m'st*.
nd, ndz, ndst.	fi-*nd*, se-*nd*, se-*nds*, se-*nd'st*, fi-*nd'st*.
nj, njd.	si-*nge*, ra-*nge*, ra-*ng'd*, si-*ng'd*.
nz.	pe-*ns*, fi-*ns*, fa-*ns*, tu-*ns*, quee-*ns*.
ngd, ngdst, ngz, ngth, ngths.	ha-*ng'd*, ha-*ng'dst*, ha-*ngs*, stre-*ngth*, stre-*ngths*.
nk, nkt, nks, nkst.	wi-*nk*, wi-*nk'd*, wi-*nks*, wi-*nk'st*, dri-*nk'st*.
nt, nts, ntst.	wa-*nt*, wa-*nts*, wa-*nt'st*, be-*nt'st*.
ns, nst.	pe-*nce*, wi-*nce*, wi-*nc'd*, da-*nce*, da-*nc'st*.
nch, ncht.	que-*nch*, fli-*nch*, fli-*nch'd*, que-*nch'd*.
rb, rbst, rbd, rbdst, rbz.	ba-*rb*, ba-*rb'st*, ba-*rb'd*, ba-*rb'dst*, ba-*rbs*.
rd, rdst, rdz.	fur-*r'd*, hea-*rd*, hea-*rd'st*, ba-*rds*, ca-*rds*.
rg, rgz.	bu-*rgh*, bu-*rghs*.
rj, rjd.	me-*rge*, u-*rge*, u-*rg'd*, me-*rg'd*.
rl, rlst, rld, rldst, rlz.	hu-*rl*, hu-*rl'st*, hu-*rl'd*, hu-*rl'dst*, hu-*rls*.
rm, rmst, rmd, rmdst, rmz, rmth.	wa-*rm*, wa-*rm'st*, wa-*rm'd*, wa-*rm'dst*, wa-*rms*, wa-*rmth*.
rn, rnst, rnd, rndst, rnt, rnz.	bu-*rn*, bu-*rn'st*, bu-*rn'd*, bu-*rn'dst*, bu-*rnt*, bu-*rns*.
rv, rvst, rvd, rvdst, rvz.	cu-*rve*, cu-*rv'st*, cu-*rv'd*, cu-*rv'dst*, cu-*rves*.
rz.	fi-*rs*, sta-*rs*, wa-*rs*, bea-*rs*, o-*res*, fi-*res*.

COMBINATIONS.	EXAMPLES.
rk, rks, rkst, rkt, rktst.	ha-*rk*, ha-*rks*, ha-*rk'st*, ha-*rk'd*, ha-*rk'dst*.
rp, rps, rpst, rpt, rptst.	ha-*rp*, ha-*rps*, ha-*rp'st*, ha-*rp'd*, ha-*rp'dst*.
rt, rts, rtst.	spi-*rt*, hu-*rt*, hu-*rts*, hu-*rt'st*, spi *rts*, spi-*rt'st*.
rf, rft, rfs.	sca-*rf*, tu-*rf*, tu-*rf'd*, tu-*rfs*, sca-*rfs*.
rs, rst, rsts, rstst.	cu-*rse*, hea-*rse*, bu-*rst*, bu-*rsts*, cu-*rs'd*, cu-*rs'dst*.
rth, rths.	wor-*th*, hea-*rth*, hea-*rths*, mi-*rth*, bi-*rths*.
rsh.	ma-*rsh*, ha-*rsh*.
rch, rcht.	sea-*rch*, sea-*rch'd*, lu-*rch*, lu-*rch'd*.
vd, vdst.	li-*v'd*, li-*v'dst*, mo-*v'd*, mo-*v'dst*.
vl, vlst, vld, vldst, vlz.	dri-*v'l*, dri-*v'l'st*, dri-*v'l'd*, dri-*v'l'dst*, dri-*v'ls*.
vn, vnz, vnth.	hea-*v'n*, hea-*v'ns*, cle-*v'nth*, dri-*v'n*.
vz.	el-*ves*, del-*ves*, li-*ves*, mo-*ves*, lea-*ves*, do-*ves*.
vst.	mo-*v'st*, li-*v'st*, del-*v'st*, ra-*v'st*.
zd.	plea-*sed*, ama-*z'd*, rai-*sed*, clo-*sed*.
zl, zlst, zld, zldst, zlz.	muz-*zle*, muz-*zl'st*, muz-*zl'd*, muz-*zl'dst*, muz-*zles*.
zm, zmz.	cha-*sm*, spa-*sm*, spa-*sms*, cha-*sms*.
zn, znst, znd, zndst, znz.	pri-*son*, impri-*son'st*, impri-*son'd*, impri-*son'dst*, pri-*sons*.
thd, thz, thst.	wrea-*th'd*, wrea-*ths*, wrea-*th'st*.
kl, klst, kld, kldst, klz.	truc-*kle*, truc-*kl'st*, truc-*kl'd*, truc-*kl'dst*, truc-*kles*.
kn, knst, knd, kndst, knz.	blac-*ken*, blac-*ken'st*, blac-*ken'd*, blac-*ken'dst*, blac-*kens*.
kt, kts.	pic-*k'd*, a-*ct*, a-*cts*, roc-*k'd*, kic-*k'd*.
ks.	mo-*cks*, ra-*cks*, pi-*cks*, de-*cks*.

ARTICULATION.

COMBINATIONS.	EXAMPLES.
pl, plst, pld, pldst, plz.	*pl*-uck, rip-*ple*, rip-*pl'st*, rip-*pl'd*, rip-*pl'dst*, rip-*ples*.
pt, pts.	clip-*ped*, cry-*pt*, cry-*pts*, strap-*ped*
ps, pst.	ro-*pes*, cli-*ps*, clip-*p'st*, rip-*ped'st*.
pth, pths.	de-*pth*, de-*pths*.
tl, tlst, tld, tldst, tlz.	set-*tle*, set-*tl'st*, set-*tl'd*, set-*tl'dst*, set-*tles*.
ts, tst.	mee-*ts*, pe-*ts*, pe-*t'st*, ro-*ts*, rot-*t'st*.

CHAPTER II.

RESPIRATION.

The ability to speak well is in a great degree dependent on appropriate respiration. Without a sufficient supply of breath the vocal organs cannot perform their functions properly.

Ignorance of the right method of using the lungs and the larynx in reading and speaking has produced more cases of pulmonary consumption than all other causes combined.

Exercises for acquiring control of these organs should, then, first claim the attention of the student of Elocution.

SECTION I.

POSITION.

Preparatory to every vocal exercise the pupil should place the body in a perfectly erect and easy position, the chest fully projected, the shoulders thrown backward and downward, the head erect, the body supported on the left foot, the right foot placed a little in advance of the left, and forming with it an angle of forty-five degrees, the hands hanging naturally by the side.

SECTION II.

I. EXERCISE IN BREATHING.

Inhale very slowly until the lungs are inflated to their utmost capacity, then, after retaining the breath for a moment, as slowly exhale.

Repeat this exercise at least a dozen times. In the act of inhalation carefully avoid a harsh, aspirate sound, as no habit is more injurious to the vocal organs.

II. Exercise in Effusive Vocal Breathing.

Inflate the lungs as before, then exhale in a prolonged sound of the letter *h*.

In the exhalation give out only sufficient breath to keep the sound audible. Continue each exercise as long as you can sustain the breath, and repeat at least a dozen times.

This exercise is called Effusive Breathing, because the breath is gently sent forth from the organs.

III. Exercise in Expulsive Vocal Breathing.

Inhale the breath rapidly but quietly, and emit it suddenly and forcibly in the sound of the letter *h*. In this exercise the breath is expelled from the organs forcibly, and it is known as expulsive breathing.

Repeat a number of times.

IV. Exercise in Explosive Vocal Breathing.

Draw in the breath very quickly, and send it forth abruptly and violently from the organs in the sound of the letter *h*.

This exercise is called explosive breathing because the breath is violently and abruptly emitted from the organs.

Repeat at least a dozen times.

CHAPTER III.

VOICE.

Voice is sound produced by the passage of the air through the larynx and cavities of the mouth and nose.

It is not the purpose of the present work to give a detailed description of the mechanical movements of the organs, and the action of the air upon them in the production of vocal sound, nor is such a knowledge necessary to excellence in vocal expression. The student who desires to investigate this subject will find it fully discussed in works upon physiology.

An analysis of the attributes and accidents of voice, and their effect on expression, is more properly the work of the student of elocution, and to this his attention is invited.

SECTION I.

ATTRIBUTES OF VOICE.

Having acquired by the preceding exercises control of the organs of articulation and respiration, attention is now directed to those attributes of voice which give expression to thought and feeling irrespective of articulate utterance.

An analysis of the human voice exhibits six essential elements, namely: Form, Quality, Force, Stress, Pitch, and Movement. These are called attributes, because in the utterance of every sentence each of these elements is found.

ATTRIBUTES OF VOICE.

We may read or speak without employing Quantity, long or short, Inflection, rising or falling, Waves, upward or downward, Cadence, Pauses, Emphasis, Climax, or Grouping; but it is impossible to utter a sentence without exhibiting Form, either effusive, expulsive, or explosive, Quality, pure or impure, Force, in some degree, Stress, of some kind, Pitch—some place upon the musical scale—and Movement of some rate.

And it is by the various combinations of these attributes that we give appropriate expression to the different forms of thought and emotion.

A knowledge, then, of their effect on utterance, and the ability to give at pleasure any desired combination, is indispensable to excellence in reading and speaking. To this end it will be necessary to consider each attribute separately, determine its characteristic effect on expression, and present exercises by which control of it may be acquired.

SECTION II.
FORM OF VOICE.

Form of voice is the manner in which the sound is sent forth from the vocal organs.

This must be Effusive, Expulsive, or Explosive, as every sound, whether produced by the vocal organs or by any other means, must be in one of these forms.

SECTION III.
EFFUSIVE FORM.

Effusive is that form of voice in which the sound issues from the organs in a tranquil manner, without abruptness either in the beginning or ending.

The breath is not sent forth by any forcible effort, but is gently effused into the surrounding air.

To acquire control of this form of voice practice the following exercises as directed:

Inhale a large volume of air before uttering each sound. In the formation of the sound give out only sufficient breath to produce the required tone.

Repeat each of the elements, continuing the sound as long as you can sustain the breath.

Effusive Form—First Exercise.

1. ē, as heard in eve, mete.
2. ĕ, " ermine, earth.
3. ā, " ale, may.
4. â, " air, care.
5. ä, " arm, farm.
6. ô, " order, form.
7. ō, " old, note.
8. ōō, " ooze, moon.

Repeat each of the following words several times in a moderately prolonged tone, being careful to avoid all abruptness both in the beginning and close of the utterance.

Effusive Form—Second Exercise.

All,	arm,	our,	use,
hall,	harm,	oil,	duty,
fall,	farm,	vow,	beauty,
awful,	calm,	howl,	amuse,
pall,	afar,	balm,	refuse.

The **effusive** is the appropriate form of voice for the expression of *pathos, solemnity, sublimity, grandeur, reverence, adoration, devotion, awe,* and *amazement,* of a quiet and tranquil character.

The following selections should be practiced with special reference to the effusive form.

EXAMPLES: I. PATHOS.

[From "The Death Bed."—*Hood.*]

We watched her breathing through the night,
  Her breathing soft and low,
As in her breast the wave of life
  Kept heaving to and fro.

II. SOLEMNITY.

[From "Gratitude."]

When all thy mercies, O my God,
  My rising soul surveys,
Transported with the view, I'm lost
  In wonder, love, and praise.

III. REVERENCE AND ADORATION.

[From "The Morning Hymn in Paradise."—*Milton.*]

These are thy glorious works, Parent of Good,
Almighty! Thine this universal frame,
Thus wondrous fair. Thyself how wondrous then!
Unspeakable! who sitt'st above these heavens,
To us invisible, or dimly seen
Midst these thy lowest works.

IV. AWE AND AMAZEMENT.

[From "Macbeth."—*Shakspeare.*]

  Now o'er the one half world
Nature seems dead, and wicked dreams abuse
The curtained sleep; now witchcraft celebrates
Pale Hecate's offerings; and withered murder,
Alarmed by his sentinel, the wolf,
Whose howl's his watch, thus, with his stealthy pace,
Toward his design moves like a ghost.

The **effusive** gives a softness and smoothness to the tone, which, in the expression of pathos, solemnity, devotion, and reverence, produces one of the most pleasing effects in delivery, calling out at once all the purer and nobler feelings, and fitting the mind for the contemplation of the higher and holier scenes, while the absence of this property of utterance renders the reading of the most sublime passages in prayer and praise harsh and unpleasant.

In the utterance of the milder forms of **awe and horror** the effusive gives intensity to the expression.

SECTION IV.

EXPULSIVE FORM.

The **expulsive** is that form of voice in which the sound is emitted from the organs in an abrupt and forcible manner.

The breath, by a vigorous inward and upward action of the abdominal muscles, is sent forth from the lungs to the vocal organs, where it is converted into an expulsive sound.

To acquire control of this form of voice, great care should be taken while practicing the exercises to maintain a vigorous play of the abdominal, dorsal and intercostal muscles, to keep the head erect and the shoulders well back.

Repeat the following exercises in a clear, full, expulsive form of voice.

Expulsive Form—First Exercise.

1. ĕ, as heard in end, ell.
2. ă, " add, have.
3. à, " ask, dance.
4. ŏ, " odd, not.
5. ĭ, " ill, fin.
6. ŭ, " up, study.
7. u̞, " pull, push.

EXPULSIVE FORM—SECOND EXERCISE.

Add,	on,	air,	end,
eve,	up,	no,	fair,
orb,	awful,	law,	live,
dare,	own,	die,	few,
ice,	send,	fool,	fame,
art,	ale,	arm,	isle,
sink,	read,	heard,	swim,
brave,	down,	this,	slave.

The **expulsive** is the appropriate form of voice for the utterance of *narrative, descriptive, didactic, animated, argumentative,* and *impassioned* thought as expressed in scientific and literary lectures, doctrinal and practical sermons, senatorial, political, and judicial speeches, and formal orations.

EXAMPLES: I. NARRATION.
[From "A Soldier's Funeral."—*A. H. Quint.*]

The first funeral at which I officiated was at Harper's Ferry, while our regiment occupied that post. There had been brought into our hospital a soldier of the Fifteenth Pennsylvania—then on its way home at the expiration of its three months' service—whom that regiment left with us one afternoon as they passed through the place. That evening, as I passed at a late hour through the hospital, I noticed this new face, and, on inquiry, found the facts. He was sick with typhoid fever—very sick. Little more than a boy in years, he was to me, then, nameless, not one of ours; but he was a suffering soldier, and may God bless every one of such!

II. DIDACTIC.
[From "Industry and Eloquence."—*Wirt.*]

In the ancient republics of Greece and Rome, oratory was a necessary branch of a finished education. A much smaller proportion of the citizens were educated than among us, but of these a much larger number became orators. No man could hope for distinction or influence and yet slight this art. The commanders of their armies were orators as well as soldiers, and ruled as well by their rhetorical as by their military skill. There was no trusting with them, as with us, to a natural facility, or the acquisition of an accidental fluency by occasional practice.

III. ARGUMENTATIVE ORATORICAL.

[From "Our Duty to our Country."—*Story.*]

We stand the latest, and, if we fail, probably the last, experiment of self-government by the people. We have begun it under circumstances of the most auspicious nature. We are in the vigor of youth. Our growth has never been checked by the oppressions of tyranny; our constitutions have never been enfeebled by the vices or luxuries of the Old World. Such as we are we have been from the beginning —simple, hardy, intelligent, accustomed to self-government and to self-respect. The Atlantic rolls between us and any formidable foe. Within our territory, stretching through many degrees of latitude and longitude, we have the choice of many products and many means of independence. The government is mild, the press is free, religion is free; knowledge reaches, or may reach, every home. What fairer prospect of success could be presented? What means more adequate to accomplish the sublime end? What more is necessary than for the people to preserve what they have themselves created? Already has the age caught the spirit of our institutions. It has already ascended the Andes and snuffed the breezes of both oceans; it has infused itself into the life-blood of Europe, and warmed the sunny plains of France and the low lands of Holland; it has touched the philosophy of Germany and the North, and, moving onward to the South, has opened to Greece the lessons of her better days. Can it be that America, under such circumstances, can betray herself? Can it be that she is to be added to the catalogue of republics, the inscription upon whose ruins is, They were, but they are not? Forbid it, my countrymen! Forbid it, Heaven!

IV. IMPASSIONED.

[From "Eloquence of James Otis."—*Mrs. Childs.*]

The flame of liberty is extinguished in Greece and Rome, but the light of its glowing embers is still bright and strong on the shores of America. Actuated by its sacred influence, we will resist unto death; but we will not countenance anarchy and misrule. The wrongs that a desperate community have heaped upon their enemies shall be amply and speedily repaired. Still it may be well for some proud men to remember that a fire is lighted in these colonies which one breath of their king may kindle into such a flame that the blood of all England cannot extinguish it.

The **expulsive form** gives energy, life, and spirit to all direct and forcible speaking. Divested of this form of voice the manly and powerful eloquence of Demosthenes, Chatham, Webster, and Clay, would become ridiculous and contemptible.

No exercise is more beneficial for strengthening and developing the voice than practice on the expulsive form.

SECTION V.

EXPLOSIVE FORM.

The **explosive** is that form of voice in which the sound bursts forth instantaneously from the organs.

It resembles in suddenness the crack of a pistol or the report of a rifle.

"This form of voice proceeds from a violent and abrupt exertion of the abdominal muscles acting on the diaphragm, and thus discharging a large volume of air previously inhaled. The breath in this process is, as it were, dashed against the glottis or lips of the larynx, causing a loud and instantaneous explosion."

"In the act of 'explosion' the chink of the glottis is for a moment closed, and resistance at first offered to the escape of the breath by a firm compression of the lips of the larynx and downward pressure of the epiglottis.

"After this instant pressure and resistance, follows the explosion, caused by the appulsive act of the abdominal muscles and diaphragm, propelling the breath with powerful and irresistible volume on the glottis and epiglottis, which at length give way and suffer the breath to escape with a loud and sudden report of a purely explosive character."

Practice the following elements and words with all the force and abruptness you can command. Inflate the lungs before each effort, and then expel the breath violently as directed above.

In connection with these exercises practice the mechanical act of coughing.

Explosive Form—First Exercise.

1. ĭ, as heard in it, ill.
2. ĕ, " let, met.
3. ă, " add, lad.
4. á, " ask, task.
5. ŏ, " odd, clod.
6. u̧, " pull, full.
7. ŭ, " up, cup.

Explosive Form—Second Exercise.

In,	art,	on,	ebb,
air,	up,	all,	let,
back,	hacked,	trip,	skip,
down,	flit,	stick,	stuck,
mock,	old,	lie,	down.

The **explosive** is the appropriate form for the expression of *joy, gladness, intense passion,* as *anger, scorn, hatred, revenge,* the *sudden cry of terror* and *alarm,* **and** the *shout of courage* and *defiance.*

Examples: I. Ecstatic Joy.

Joy, joy! shout aloud for joy!

II. Anger and Defiance.

[From "The Parting of Marmion and Douglas."—*Scott.*]

And if thou said'st I am not peer
To any lord in Scotland here,
Lowland or highland, far or near,
Lord Angus, thou hast lied.

III. Scorn.

[From "Seminole's Defiance."—*Patten.*]

I loathe you with my bosom;
I scorn you with mine eye;
I'll taunt you with my latest breath,
And fight you till I die.

IV. Courage.

[From "Warren's Address."—*Pierpont.*]

Stand! the ground's your own, my braves:
Will ye give it up to slaves?
Will ye look for greener graves?
Hope ye mercy still?
What's the mercy despots feel?
Hear it in that battle-peal!
Read it on yon bristling steel!
Ask it, ye who will.

No exercise is so effectual for imparting energy to the tone or strengthening weak organs as practice on the explosive form of voice. Combined with the expulsive, in argumentative discourse, it gives life and energy to the utterance.

Murdoch and Russell in their excellent work, "Vocal Culture," say: "This form of the human voice (the explosive) is one of the most impressive in its effects. By a law of our constitution it acts with an instantaneous shock on the sympathetic nerve, and rouses the sensibility of the whole frame; it summons to instant action all the senses, and in the thrill which it sends from nerve to brain we feel its awakening and inciting power over the mind."

With the rapidity of lightning it penetrates every faculty and sets it instinctively on the alert.

It seems designed by nature as the note of alarm to the citadel of the soul.

SECTION VI.

QUALITY OF VOICE.

Quality of voice is the purity or impurity of the tone. The different qualities are, Pure Tone, Orotund, Aspirate, Pectoral, Guttural, Oral and Nasal.

Of these the first two are the appropriate qualities for the expression of unimpassioned forms of thought and the higher and nobler feelings and emotions.

The Aspirate, Pectoral and Guttural are the natural language of the malignant feelings and passions. Even the lower animals express their feelings of hate, anger, rage in the aspirate, pectoral and guttural qualities, as heard in the hissing of the serpent, the low pectoral growl of the wolf, and the deep guttural roar of the tiger.

In continuous, unimpassioned discourse these impure qualities are often employed to give emphasis to certain words and phrases.

The Nasal and Oral are used chiefly in personation, mimicry and burlesque.

Each of these qualities admit of the three forms already presented, and will be discussed in their relations to the Effusive, Expulsive and Explosive.

SECTION VII.

PURE TONE.

Pure tone is that quality of voice in which all the breath is converted into a clear, round, smooth, musical sound, with the resonance in the back part of the roof of the mouth. It is free from all aspirate, oral, nasal, or other impure qualities.

Owing to our defective system of education this quality of voice, so peculiar to childhood, is rarely possessed in more mature age.

The restraining influences of the school-room tend directly to destroy all the natural purity and sweetness of the voice.

To restore this natural quality, practice daily the following exercises with the strictest attention to the purity of the tone.

That the highest advantage may be derived from these exercises, special regard should be given to the quality.

Repeat a number of times each of the following elements in the effusive form with the utmost purity of tone. It will be noticed that the object of the exercise on page 52 was to cultivate form of voice without reference to quality or other attributes. The special object of this exercise is to cultivate purity of tone, and at the same time to retain and strengthen what was gained by the exercises under form. It should be constantly borne in mind that, in connection with each additional exercise, attention should be given to all the previous exercises, so that when the exercises in Movement of Voice are presented, (the last exercises under the attributes,) they will be not only exercises in Movement, but also in Form, Quality, Force, Stress, and Pitch.

Pure Tone, Effusive Form—First Exercise.

1. ē, as heard in me, see.
2. ā,   "   ale, pale.
3. â,   "   air, pare.
4. ä,   "   father, arm.
5. a̤,   "   all, talk.
6. ō,   "   no, old.
7. ōō,   "   moon, food.

Repeat the words as directed above, only with less prolongation

Pure Tone, Effusive Form—Second Exercise.

All,	fall,	breathe,	softly,
soldiers,	peacefully,	brother,	mother,
gently,	wondrous,	bow,	heaven,
beauteous,	brow,	sleep,	pall.

Pure tone, in the **effusive form,** is the appropriate quality of voice for the utterance of *pathetic, solemn, serious* and *tranquil thought,* not mingled with grandeur and sublimity, where the purpose is to awaken the feelings rather than to enlighten the mind.

Examples: I. Solemnity.

Pure Tone, Effusive Form.

[From "An Evening Revery."—*Phebe Cary.*]

One sweetly solemn thought
   Comes to me o'er and o'er;
I'm nearer my home to-day
   Than ever I've been before.

II. Serious Thought.
Pure Tone, Effusive Form.

There is often sadness in the tone,
  And a moisture in the eye,
And a trembling sorrow in the voice,
  When we bid a last good-bye;
But sadder far than this, I ween,
  O, sadder far than all,
Is the heart-throb with which we strain
  To catch the last footfall.—*Anon.*

III. Tranquillity.
Pure Tone, Effusive Form.

My soul to-day
Is far away,
Sailing the Vesuvian Bay;
My wingéd boat,
A bird afloat,
Swims round the purple peaks remote.—*T. B. Read.*

Repeat the following elements and words a number of times in the Expulsive Form, Pure Tone, with the closest attention to the quality of voice:

Pure Tone, Expulsive Form—First Exercise.

1. ĕ, as heard in earth, ermine.
2. ā,   "   aim, age.
3. ă,   "   add, lad.
4. ĕ,   "   ell, end.
5. ŏ,   "   odd, sod.
6. ŭ,   "   up, cup.

Pure Tone, Expulsive Form—Second Exercise.

Arm,	put,	bet,	let,
fit,	met,	up,	on,
back,	down,	live,	victory,
last,	again,	friend,	think.

Pure tone, in the **expulsive form,** is the appropriate quality of voice for the delivery of *narrative, descriptive,* and *didactic thought,* in which the purpose of the speaker is more to enlighten the mind than to awaken the feelings or rouse the passions.

EXAMPLES: I. NARRATIVE, DESCRIPTIVE.
Pure Tone, Expulsive Form.
[From "The Blind Preacher."—*Wirt.*]

It was one Sunday, as I traveled through the County of Orange, that my eye was caught by a cluster of horses tied near a ruinous old wooden house in the forest, not far from the roadside. Having frequently seen such objects before in traveling through these States, I had no difficulty in understanding that this was a place of religious worship.

Devotion alone should have stopped me to join in the duties of the congregation, but I must confess that curiosity to hear the preacher of such a wilderness was not the least of my motives. On entering I was struck with his preternatural appearance. He was a tall and very spare old man; his head, which was covered with a white linen cap, his shriveled hands, and his voice, were all shaking under the influence of palsy, and a few moments ascertained to me that he was perfectly blind.

II. DIDACTIC.
Pure Tone, Expulsive Form.
[From "The Puritans."—*Macaulay.*]

The Puritans were men whose minds had derived a peculiar character from the daily contemplation of superior beings and eternal interests. Not content with acknowledging in general terms an overruling Providence, they habitually ascribed every event to the will of the Great Being, for whose power nothing was too vast, for whose inspection nothing was too minute. To know him, to serve him, to enjoy him, was with them the great end of existence. They rejected with contempt the ceremonious homage which other sects substituted for the pure worship of the soul. Instead of catching occasional glimpses of the Deity through an obscuring vail, they aspired to gaze full on the intolerable brightness, and to commune with him face to face. Hence originated their contempt for terrestrial distinctions.

PURE TONE, EXPLOSIVE FORM.

Repeat the following elements and words in the Explosive Form, Pure Tone:

PURE TONE, EXPLOSIVE FORM—FIRST EXERCISE.

1. ĭ, as heard in ill, fill.
2. ŭ, " up, sup.
3. ĕ, " ell, end.
4. ă, " add, mad.
5. à, " ask, task.
6. ŏ, " odd, on.
7. u̯, " pull, full.

PURE TONE, EXPLOSIVE FORM—SECOND EXERCISE.

You,	the,	cup,	tip,
on,	bit,	end,	may,
me,	no,	will,	tap,
nut,	fill,	rat,	pit.

Pure tone in its **explosive form** is the quality appropriate for the expression of *ecstatic joy* and *mirth*.

EXAMPLES: I. ECSTATIC JOY.

Pure Tone, Explosive Form.

[From "The Voice of Spring."—*Mrs. Hemans.*]

I come, I come! ye have called me long;
I come o'er the mountains with light and song,
Ye may trace my step o'er the wak'ning earth,
By the winds which tell of the violet's birth,
By the primrose stars in the shadowy grass,
By the green leaves opening as I pass.

II. GAYETY.

Pure Tone, Explosive Form.

[From "Lochinvar."—*Scott.*]

O, young Lochinvar is come out of the west!
Through all the wide border his steed was the best;

And save his good broadsword he weapon had none;
He rode all unarmed, and he rode all alone.
So faithful in love, and so dauntless in war,
There never was knight like the young Lochinvar.

The advantages of Pure Tone are twofold—first, to the speaker; second, to the hearer. It is produced with less expenditure of breath than any other quality; its effect upon the vocal organs is beneficial rather than injurious; with the same effort it is heard at a greater distance than any other quality; its clear musical properties give a distinctness to articulation and an ease to utterance grateful to the ear; it produces none of the jarring effects experienced in listening to a speaker whose voice is harsh, hard, or in any way impure in quality.

SECTION VIII.

OROTUND.

The **orotund** is that quality of voice in which the breath is converted into a full, round, deep, musical tone, with the resonance in the upper part of the chest.

It is distinguished from the Pure Tone by a fullness, clearness, strength, smoothness, and sub-sonorous quality resembling the resonance of certain musical instruments.

"In the orotund, volume and purity of tone, to the greatest extent of the one and the highest perfection of the other, are blended in one vast sphere of sound."

This quality is possessed naturally by very few. Even among public speakers it is rarely heard, save in a limited degree. Actors and orators of eminence and distinction understand and appreciate the value of the orotund, and have spared no pains to obtain control of it. It is heard in all their utterance of grand, lofty and sublime thoughts.

Though rarely possessed, it is susceptible of cultivation, and may by judicious practice be acquired by almost every one.

Dr. Rush mentions it as the highest perfection of the cultivated utterance of the public speaker.

To acquire control of the orotund, practice the following exercise with the freest opening of the vocal organs.

Before repeating each element inhale a large quantity of air. Give to each sound all the volume and quantity you can command.

OROTUND, EFFUSIVE FORM—FIRST EXERCISE.

1. ä, as in father, arm.
2. å, " ask, grass.
3. ạ, " all, talk.
4. ō, " old, note.

Repeat the words as directed above, carefully observing both the Effusive Form and Orotund Quality.

OROTUND, EFFUSIVE FORM—SECOND EXERCISE.

Loud,	deep,	dread,	profound,
long,	full,	broad,	sublime,
round,	honor,	moon,	endless,
father,	holy,	roll,	majesty,
soul,	hour,	universe,	dark,
torrid,	silence,	blue,	grandeur.

The **orotund, in the effusive form,** is the quality of voice appropriate for the expression of *solemnity, sublimity, grandeur* and *reverence.*

EXAMPLES: I. GRANDEUR AND SUBLIMITY.
Orotund, Effusive Form.
[From the "Apostrophe to the Ocean."—*Byron.*]

Thou glorious mirror, where the Almighty's form
   Glasses itself in tempests; in all time—
Calm or convulsed, in breeze, or gale, or storm,
   Icing the pole, or in the torrid clime,
   Dark, heaving, boundless, endless, and sublime,
The image of Eternity—the throne
   Of the Invisible! even from out thy slime
The monsters of the deep are made: each zone
Obeys thee: thou goest forth, dread, fathomless, alone.

II. SUBLIMITY AND REVERENCE.
Orotund, Effusive Form.
[From "God."—*Derzhavin.*]

O thou Eternal One! whose presence bright
   All space doth occupy, all motion guide:
Unchanged through time's all-devastating flight;
   Thou only God! There is no God beside!
Being above all beings! Mighty One!
   Whom none can comprehend, and none explore;
Who fill'st existence with thyself alone·
   Embracing all—supporting—ruling o'er;
   Being whom we call God, and know no more!

III. REVERENCE AND SOLEMNITY.
Orotund, Effusive Form.
[From "Psalm CIV."]

Bless the Lord, O my soul! O Lord, my God, thou art very great; thou art clothed with honor and majesty: who coverest thyself with light as with a garment; who stretchest out the heavens like a curtain: who layeth the beams of his chambers in the waters; who maketh the clouds his chariot; who walketh upon the wings of the wind; who maketh his angels spirits, his ministers a flaming fire; who laid the foundations of the earth, that it should not be removed forever.

Repeat the following elements and words in the Expulsive Form with the fullest Orotund Quality. Inflate the lungs fully before each effort.

OROTUND, EXPULSIVE FORM—FIRST EXERCISE.

1. ā, as heard in ale, hale.
2. ă, " add, have.
3. â, " air, share.
4. a, " what, wander.
5. ī, " ice, fine.
6. ō, " old, bold.
7. ū, " use, tube.

OROTUND, EXPULSIVE FORM—SECOND EXERCISE.

Sink,	sword,	down,	live,
die,	mercy,	slave,	read,
this,	army,	spurn,	head,
even,	drawn,	above,	never,
dissever,	revive,	induce,	amuse,
accuse,	ambition,	present,	forever.

The **orotund**, in the **expulsive form**, is the quality appropriate for the delivery of *earnest, bold, grand* and *lofty thought* in the form of argumentative and oratorical speeches and sermons, and impassioned poetry.

EXAMPLES: I. GRAND AND LOFTY SENTIMENT.
Orotund, Expulsive Form.
[From "Supposed Speech of John Adams."—*Webster.*]

Read this declaration at the head of the army: every sword will be drawn from its scabbard, and the solemn vow uttered to maintain it, or perish on the bed of honor. Publish it from the pulpit; religion will approve it, and the love of religious liberty will cling around it, resolved to stand with it or fall with it. Send it to the public halls; proclaim it there. Let them hear it who heard the roar of the enemy's cannon; let them see it who saw their brothers and their sons fall on the field of Bunker Hill, and in the streets of Lexington and Concord, and the very walls will cry out in its support.

II. Oratorical Appeal.
Orotund, Expulsive Form.
[From "Speech in Virginia Convention."—*Patrick Henry.*]

It is in vain, sir, to extenuate the matter. Gentlemen may cry Peace! peace! but there is no peace. The war is actually begun! The next gale that sweeps from the North will bring to our ears the clash of resounding arms! Our brethren are already in the field! Why stand we here idle? What is it that gentlemen wish? What would they have? Is life so dear, or peace so sweet, as to be purchased at the price of chains and slavery? Forbid it, Almighty God! I know not what course others may take; but as for me, give me liberty, or give me death!

III. Earnest Exhortation.
Orotund, Expulsive Form.
[From "Motives of the Gospel."—*Dwight.*]

Ministers proclaim to you the glad tidings of great joy, and point out to you the path to heaven. The Sabbath faithfully returns its mild and sweet seasons of grace that earthly objects may not engross your thoughts and prevent your attention to immortality. The sanctuary unfolds its doors and invites you to enter in and be saved.

The Gospel still shines to direct your feet and to quicken your pursuit of the inestimable prize. Saints wait with fervent hope of renewing their joy over your repentance. Angels spread their wings to conduct you home. The Father holds out the golden scepter of forgiveness that you may touch and live. The Son died on the cross, ascended to heaven, and intercedes before the throne of mercy that you may be accepted. The Spirit of grace and truth descends with his benevolent influence to allure and persuade you. While all things, and God at the head of all things, are thus kindly and solemnly employed to encourage you in the pursuit of this inestimable good, will you forget that you have souls which must be saved or lost?

Will you forget that the only time of salvation is the present? that beyond the grave there is no Gospel to be preached? that there no offers of life are to be made? that no Redeemer will there expiate your sins, and no forgiving God receive your souls?

IV. IMPASSIONED POETIC.
Orotund, Expulsive Form.
[From "Launching of Ship."—*Longfellow.*]

Thou, too, sail on, O Ship of State!
Sail on, O Union, strong and great!
Humanity, with all its fears,
With all its hopes of future years,
Is hanging breathless on thy fate!
We know what Master laid thy keel,
What workmen wrought thy ribs of steel,
Who made each mast, and sail, and rope,
What anvils rang, what hammers beat,
In what a forge, and what a heat,
Were shaped the anchors of thy hope.

Fear not each sudden sound and shock;
'Tis of the wave, and not the rock;
'Tis but the flapping of the sail,
And not a rent made by the gale.
In spite of rock and tempest roar,
In spite of false lights on the shore,
Sail on, nor fear to breast the sea!
Our hearts, our hopes, are all with thee:
Our hearts, our hopes, our prayers, our tears,
Our faith triumphant o'er our fears,
Are all with thee—are all with thee.

Repeat the following elements and words in the Explosive Form, fullest Orotund Quality. Be careful to give each exercise the sudden, startling explosive.

OROTUND, EXPLOSIVE FORM—FIRST EXERCISE.

1. ă, as heard in add, fat.
2. ĕ,   "   end, met.
3. ĭ,   "   ill, fin.

4. ŏ, as heard in odd, not.
5. ŭ, " us, tub.

OROTUND, EXPLOSIVE FORM—SECOND EXERCISE.

Up,	but,	study,	have,
random,	end,	add,	odd,
done,	order,	put,	push,
lie,	admit,	not,	sit,
back,	neck,	pick,	sick,
hack,	mock,	tuck,	luck.

The **orotund,** in the **explosive form,** is the quality appropriate for the expression of *courage, warning, alarm, terror* and *abrupt exclamation.*

EXAMPLES: I. COURAGE.
Orotund, Explosive Form.
[From "Marco Bozzaris."—*Halleck.*]

Strike! till the last armed foe expires;
Strike! for your altars and your fires;
Strike! for the green graves of your sires,
 God, and your native land!

II. TERROR.
Orotund, Explosive Form.
[From "Marco Bozzaris."—*Halleck.*]
To arms! they come! the Greek! the Greek!

III. ALARM.
Orotund, Explosive Form.
[From "The Bells."—*Poe.*]

Hear the loud alarum bells—
 Brazen bells!
What a tale of terror now their turbulency tells!
 In the startled ear of night
 How they scream out their affright!

OROTUND, EXPLOSIVE FORM.

Too much horrified to speak,
They can only shriek, shriek,
Out of tune,
In a clamorous appealing to the mercy of the fire,
In a mad expostulation with the deaf and frantic fire,
Leaping higher, higher, higher,
With a desperate desire,
And a resolute endeavor,
Now—now to sit, or never,
By the side of the pale-faced moon.
O the bells, bells, bells!
What a tale their terror tells
Of despair!
How they clang, and clash, and roar!
What a horror they outpour
On the bosom of the palpitating air!
Yet the ear, it fully knows,
By the twanging
And the clanging,
How the danger ebbs and flows,
Yet the ear distinctly tells,
In the jangling
And the wrangling,
How the danger sinks and swells,
By the sinking or the swelling in the anger of the bells—
Of the bells—
Of the bells, bells, bells, bells,
Bells, bells, bells—
In the clamor and the clangor of the bells!

The **orotund** is fuller in volume and purer in quality than the common voice; it is more musical in tone; it is more efficient in the production of long quantity; it is more under command; it is freer from all impurities; it is, in short, the only quality appropriate for the solemnity of the Church service, the grandeur and energy of the oration, and the majesty and sublimity of Shakspeare and Milton.

It must not, however, be imagined that the orotund, when once acquired, is to entirely supersede the common voice. Students of Elocution and public speakers frequently render themselves ridiculous, and the study of Elocution disgusting, by parading their powers of orotund on all occasions. Such exhibitions resemble

> "Ocean into tempest tossed
> To waft a feather or to drown a fly."

Except in the expression of grand, lofty, and sublime thought, the Pure Tone should form the basis of utterance.

SECTION IX.

ASPIRATE.

The **aspirate** is that quality of voice in which the breath is sent forth from the organs without being converted into vocal sound. The whisper is the perfection of the aspirate quality.

Like the Pure Tone and Orotund, it has its effusive, expulsive and explosive forms.

To acquire control of this quality, practice in a whispered tone the elements and words and sentences in which the element *h* predominates.

ASPIRATE, EFFUSIVE FORM—FIRST EXERCISE.

1. ē, as heard in me, eve.
2. ā, " fate, gray.
3. ō, " old, note.
4. ū, " use, lute.
5. ōō, " moon, food.
6. ī, " ice, fine.

ASPIRATE, EFFUSIVE FORM—SECOND EXERCISE.

Hope,	home,	have,	house,
high,	host,	heaven,	hand,
had,	heart,	hear,	huge,
hum,	think,	thrust,	thousand.

ASPIRATE, EFFUSIVE FORM.

The **aspirate**, in the **effusive form,** is the quality appropriate for the expression of *secret thought, suppressed fear* and *profound repose.*

Combined with the orotund, the aspirate intensifies the expression of sublimity, awe, reverence and amazement.

It is in this combined form that the aspirate will be of the greatest practical advantage to the general student.

Examples: I. Stillness.
Aspirate, Effusive Form.
[From "Dying Request."—*Mrs. Hemans.*]

Leave me! Thy footstep with its lightest sound,
   The very shadow of thy waving hair,
Wakes in my soul a feeling too profound,
   Too strong, for aught that lives and dies to bear;
O bid the conflict cease!

II. Profound Repose.
Aspirate, Effusive Form.
[From "Stillness of Night."—*Byron.*]

All heaven and earth are still, though not in sleep,
   But breathless, as we grow when feeling most,
And silent, as we stand in thoughts too deep;
   All heaven and earth are still: from the high host
Of stars to the lulled lake and mountain coast,
All is concentrated in a life intense,
   Where not a beam, nor air, nor leaf, is lost,
But hath a part of being, and a sense
Of that which is of all Creator and Defense.

III. Sublimity and Reverence.
Aspirate, Orotund, Effusive Form.
[From a Russian Hymn.—*Browning.*]

Thou breathest, and the obedient storm is still;
   Thou speakest; silent the submissive wave:
Man's shattered ship the rushing waters fill,
   And the hushed billows roll across his **grave.**

Sourceless and endless God! Compared to thee,
  Life is a shadowy, momentary dream:
And time, when viewed through thy eternity,
  Less than the mote of morning's golden beam

IV. SUBLIMITY AND AWE.

Aspirate, Orotund, Effusive Form.

[From "The Closing Year."—*Prentice.*]

'Tis midnight's holy hour, and silence now
Is brooding, like a gentle spirit, o'er
The still and pulseless world. Hark! on the winds
The bell's deep tones are swelling—'tis the knell
Of the departed year.

        No funeral train
Is sweeping past; yet on the stream and wood,
With melancholy light, the moonbeams rest
Like a pale, spotless shroud; the air is stirred
As by a mourner's sigh; and on yon cloud,
That floats so still and placidly through heaven,
The spirits of the seasons seem to stand—
Young Spring, bright Summer, Autumn's solemn form,
And Winter with his aged locks, and breathe,
In mournful cadences, that come abroad
Like the far wind-harp's wild and touching wail,
A melancholy dirge o'er the dead year,
Gone from the earth forever.

ASPIRATE, EXPULSIVE FORM—EXERCISE.

Repeat the elements and words on page 74 in the expulsive form, aspirate quality.

The **aspirate,** in the **expulsive form,** is the quality appropriate for the expression of *sudden fear, alarm* and *terror.* Combined with the orotund, **it gives intensity to awe and horror.**

ASPIRATE, EXPULSIVE FORM.

EXAMPLES: I. ALARM AND FEAR.

Aspirate, Expulsive Form.

[From "The Battle of Waterloo."—*Byron.*]

While thronged the citizens with terror dumb,
Or whispered with white lips, "The foe!
   They come! they come!"

II. SUPPRESSED COMMAND, FEAR.

Aspirate, Expulsive Form.

[From "Military Command."—*Anon.*]

Soldiers, you are now within a few steps of the enemy's outposts! Our scouts report them as slumbering in parties around their watch-fires, and utterly unprepared for our approach. A swift and noiseless advance around that projecting rock, and we are upon them—we capture them without the possibility of resistance. One disorderly noise or motion may leave us at the mercy of their advanced guard. Let every man keep the strictest silence under the pain of instant death.

III. INTENSE FEAR, AWE, AND HORROR.

Aspirate, Orotund, Expulsive Form.

[From "Hamlet."—*Shakspeare.*]

Angels and ministers of grace defend us!
Be thou a spirit of health, or goblin damned,
Bring with thee airs from heaven, or blasts from hell,
Be thy intents wicked or charitable,
Thou com'st in such a questionable shape
That I will speak to thee; I'll call thee Hamlet,
King, father, royal Dane: O answer me:
Let me not burst in ignorance! but tell
Why thy canonized bones, hearsed in death,
Have burst their cerements! why the sepulcher,
Wherein we saw thee quietly in-urned,
Hath op'd his ponderous and marble jaws,
To cast thee up again! What may this mean,
That thou, dead corse, again, in complete steel,
Revisitest thus the glimpses of the moon,
Making night hideous: and we fools of nature,
So horribly to shake our disposition,
With thoughts beyond the reaches of our souls?
Say, why is this? wherefore? what should we **do?**

when combined with the Orotund, it intensifies the utterance of deep solemnity, sublimity, adoration and profound reverence.

Examples: I. Awe and Horror.
Pectoral, Effusive Form.

[From "Darkness."—*Byron*.]

I had a dream, which was not all a dream.
The bright sun was extinguished, and the stars
Did wander, darkling, in the eternal space,
Rayless and pathless, and the icy earth
Swung blind and blackening in the moonless air.
Morn came, and went—and came, and brought no day
And men forgot their passions, in the dread
Of this their desolation; and all hearts
Were chilled into a selfish prayer for light.
And they did live by watch-fires; and the thrones,
The palaces of crownéd kings, the huts,
The habitations of all things which dwell,
Were burnt for beacons: cities were consumed,
And men were gathered round their blazing homes,
To look once more into each other's face.
Happy were those who dwelt within the eye
Of the volcanoes and their mountain torch.

II. Horror and Dread.
Pectoral, Effusive Form.

[From "Macbeth."—*Shakspeare*.]

Now o'er the one half world
Nature seems dead; and wicked dreams abuse
The curtained sleep; now witchcraft celebrates
Pale Hecate's offerings; and withered murder,
Alarumed by his sentinel, the wolf,
Whose howl's his watch, thus, with his stealthy pace,
Toward his design
Moves like a ghost. Thou sure and firm-set earth!
Hear not my steps, which way they walk; for fear
The very stones prate of my whereabout,
And take the present horror from the time,
Which now suits with it.

III. Awe and Deep Solemnity.

Orotund-Pectoral, Effusive Form.

[Jacob's Exclamation after his Dream.—*Bible.*]

How dreadful is this place! This is none other than the house of God, and the gate of heaven!

IV. Awe and Profound Sublimity.

Orotund-Pectoral, Effusive Form.

[From the Psalms.]

Of old Thou hast laid the foundation of the earth; and the heavens are the work of thy hands. They shall perish, but thou shalt endure; yea, all of them shall wax old like a garment; as a vesture shalt thou change them, and they shall be changed: but thou art the same; and thy years shall have no end.

Before the mountains were brought forth, or ever thou hadst formed the earth and the world, even from everlasting to everlasting thou art God. Thou turnest man to destruction; and sayest, "Return, ye children of men."

For a thousand years in thy sight are but as yesterday when it is past, and as a watch in the night.

Thou carriest them away as with a flood; they are as a sleep: in the morning they are like grass which groweth up. In the morning it flourisheth and groweth up: in the evening it is cut down and withereth.

Pectoral, Expulsive Form—Exercise.

Repeat the elements and words on page 79 in the expulsive form, pectoral quality.

The **pectoral**, in the **expulsive form**, is the quality appropriate for the expression of *hate, malice, scorn, revenge,* etc.

Examples: I. Hatred and Malice.

Pectoral, Expulsive Form.

[From "Merchant of Venice."—*Shakspeare.*]

How like a fawning publican he looks
I hate him, for he is a Christian

But more, for that, in low simplicity,
He lends out money gratis, and brings down
The rate of usance with us here in Venice.
If I can catch him once upon the hip,
I will feed fat the ancient grudge I bear him!
He hates our sacred nation; and he rails,
Even there where merchants most do congregate,
On me, my bargains, and my well-won thrift,
Which he calls interest. Cursed be my tribe
If I forgive him!

II. Horror and Terror.

Pectoral, Expulsive Form.

[From "Richard III."—*Shakspeare.*]

O I have passed a miserable night!
So full of fearful dreams, of ugly sights,
That, as I am a Christian, faithful man,
I would not spend another such a night,
Though 'twere to buy a world of happy days;
So full of dismal terror was the time!
    My dream was lengthened after life:
O then began the tempest to my soul!
    With that, methought, a legion of foul fiends
Environed me, and howléd in mine ears
Such hideous cries, that, with the very noise,
I trembling waked, and, for a season after,
Could not believe but that I was in hell;
Such terrible impression made my dream!

III. Scorn and Abhorrence.

Pectoral, Expulsive Form.

[Masaniello, in reply to the base suggestions of Genuino.]

I would that now
I could forget the monk who stands before me;
For he is like the accursed and crafty snake!
Hence! from my sight! Thou Satan, get behind me
Go from my sight! I hate and I despise thee!

Pectoral, Explosive Form—Exercise.

Practice the elements and words on page 79 in the explosive form, with pectoral quality.

The **pectoral**, in the **explosive form**, is the quality for the expression of *anger, rage, threatening, defiance,* etc.

It is usually more or less mingled with the aspirate and orotund in the expression of these passions.

Examples: I. Anger and Threatening.
Pectoral, Explosive Form.
[From "Cataline's Defiance."—*Croly.*]

"Traitor!" I go; but I return. This—trial?
Here I devote your senate! I've had wrongs
To stir a fever in the blood of age,
Or make the infant's sinews strong as steel.
This day's the birth of sorrow! This hour's work
Will breed proscriptions! Look to your hearths, my lords
For there, henceforth, shall sit, for household gods,
Shapes hot from Tartarus! all shames and crimes!
Wan treachery, with his thirsty dagger drawn;
Suspicion, poisoning his brother's cup;
Naked rebellion, with the torch and ax,
Making his wild sport of your blazing thrones;
Till anarchy comes down on you like night,
And massacre seals Rome's eternal grave!

II. Hatred and Rage.
Pectoral, Explosive Form.
[From "Paradise Lost."—*Milton.*]

Be then his love accursed! Since love or hate,
To me alike, it deals eternal woe.
Nay, cursed be thou! since against his thy will
Chose freely what it now so justly rues
Me miserable! which way shall I fly?
Infinite wrath and infinite despair!
Which way I fly is hell, myself am hell;
And in the lowest deep, a lower deep
Still threatens to devour me, opens wide,
To which the hell I suffer seems a heaven

III. Anger and Defiance.
Pectoral, Aspirate, Orotund, Explosive Form.
[From "Seminole's Defiance."—*Patten.*]

Blaze, with your serried columns!
  I will not bend the knee!
The shackles ne'er again shall bind
  The arm which now is free.
I've mailed it with the thunder,
  When the tempest muttered low;
And where it falls, ye well may dread
  The lightning of its blow!

The **pectoral**, like the **aspirate**, is the natural language of *intense passion*. Without control of this quality of voice many of the finest passages of the Bible, Shakspeare, and Milton, cannot be impressively uttered.

Emphasis not unfrequently requires the use of the pectoral quality. Great care will be required on the part of the pupil that the too frequent use of this quality do not injure the Pure Tone and Orotund.

SECTION XI.
GUTTURAL.

The **guttural** is that quality of voice in which the sound is sent forth from the organs in a rough, harsh, discordant tone, with the resonance in the lower part of the throat. It resembles in quality the growling utterance of the lower animals. To cultivate this quality of voice practice the elements and words with a muffled, harsh, smothered tone.

GUTTURAL, EFFUSIVE FORM—FIRST EXERCISE.

1. l, as heard in lull, fill.
2. r,   "   round, rise.
3. g,   "   give, hag.

Guttural, Effusive Form—Second Exercise.

Revenge,	hinder,	mocked,	losses,
cooled,	gulped,	enemies,	bargains,
hates,	gratitude,	harshness,	arose,
despise,	lives,	dies,	million.

The **guttural**, in the **effusive form,** is the quality appropriate for the expression of *settled hate, malice, loathing* and *contempt*.

Examples: I. Settled Hate and Malice.
Guttural, Effusive Form.
[From "Merchant of Venice."—*Shakspeare.*]

I'll have my bond : I will not hear thee speak:
I'll have my bond; and therefore speak no more
I'll not be made a soft and dull-eyed fool,
To shake the head, relent, and sigh, and yield
To Christian intercessors. Follow not;
I'll have no speaking; I will have my bond.

II. Loathing and Contempt.
Guttural, Effusive Form.
[From "Merchant of Venice."—*Shakspeare.*]

Yes, to smell pork: to eat of the habitation which your prophet, the Nazarite, conjured the devil into. I will buy with you, sell with you, talk with you, walk with you, and so following; but I will not eat with you, drink with you, nor pray with you.

Guttural, Expulsive Form—Exercise.

Repeat the elements and words of last exercise in the expulsive form, guttural quality.

The **guttural** in the **expulsive form** is appropriate for the expression of *deep-seated revenge, settled rage, intense loathing,* and similar malignant passions.

Examples: I. Deep-Seated Revenge.
Guttural, Expulsive Form.
[From "Merchant of Venice."—*Shakspeare.*]

To bait fish withal: if it will feed nothing else, it will feed **my revenge.** He hath disgraced me, and hindered me of half a million: laughed at my losses, mocked at my gains, scorned my nation, thwarted my bargains, cooled my friends, heated my enemies; and what's his reason? I am a Jew. Hath not a Jew eyes? Hath not a Jew hands, organs, dimensions, senses, affections, passions? Fed with the same food, hurt with the same weapons, subject to the same diseases, healed by the same means, warmed and cooled by the same winter and summer, as a Christian is? If you prick us, do we not bleed? if you tickle us, do we not laugh? if you poison us, do we not die? and if you wrong us, shall we not revenge? If we are like you in the rest, we will resemble you in that. If a Jew wrong a Christian, what is his humility? Revenge! If a Christian wrong a Jew, what should his sufferance be by Christian example? Why, revenge! The villainy you teach me I will execute! and it shall go hard but I will better the instruction!

Guttural, Explosive Form—Exercise.

Repeat the elements and words on pages 85, 86 in the explosive form, guttural quality.

The **guttural** in the **explosive form** is the language of *intense anger, hate* and *detestation.*

Example: Intense Hate, Loathing and Anger.
Guttural, Explosive Form.
[From "Seminole's Defiance."—*Patten.*]

I loathe you with my bosom! I scorn you with mine eye!
And I'll taunt you with my latest breath, and fight you till I die!
I ne'er will ask for quarter, and I ne'er will be your slave;
But I'll swim the sea of slaughter till I sink beneath the wave!

The **guttural** is only employed in the expression of the more violent forms of the malignant passions.

In the utterance of these it is powerful in its effect

over the mind and heart. Practiced moderately, its effect on the vocal organs is beneficial; but if carried too far injurious.

SECTION XII.
ORAL.

The **oral** is that quality of voice in which the sound is sent forth from the organs in a thin, feeble tone, with the resonance in the forward part of the mouth.

It is heard in the utterance of persons in a feeble state of health, and frequently by those who are afflicted with affectation.

But little difficulty will be experienced in producing this quality of voice sufficiently perfect for practical purposes.

The great difficulty with most public speakers will be to avoid its unconscious use.

No defect is more common than the improper use of the oral tone.

One or two illustrations will be sufficient for practice.

Exercises on the elements and words will be unnecessary.

The **oral** is the quality of voice appropriate for the expression of *feebleness, exhaustion* and *fatigue*.

EXAMPLES : I. FEEBLENESS.

Oral, Effusive Form.

[From "Little Jim."—*Anon.*]

"Mother, the angels, they do smile, and beckon 'Little Jim.'
I have no pain, dear mother, now; but O, I am so dry!
Just moisten poor Jim's lips again; and, mother, don't ye cry."
With gentle, trembling haste she held the liquid to his lips;
He smiled to thank her as he took each little tiny sip—
"Tell father, when he comes from work, I said good-night to **him**·
And, mother, now I'll go to sleep." Alas! poor " Little Jim."

II.

Oral, Expulsive Form.
[From " Wounded."—*Rev. W. E. Miller.*]

   Let me lie down.
Just here in the shade of this cannon-torn tree,
Here, low on the trampled grass, where I may see
The surge of the combat, and where I may hear
The glad cry of victory, cheer upon cheer:
   Let me lie down.

   O, it was grand!
Like the tempest we charged, in the triumph to share;
The tempest—its fury and thunder were there:
On, on, o'er intrenchments, o'er living and dead,
With the foe underfoot, and our flag overhead:
   O, it was grand!

The **oral** quality of voice is indispensable in the personation of characters exhibiting *feebleness, weakness, languor,* or *sickness*.

Works on Elocution generally ignore altogether the Aspirate, Pectoral, Guttural, and Oral, regarding them as defects in quality. And for the utterance of ordinary thought they are defects, but for the expression of passion and emotion they are quite as important as Pure Tone and Orotund.

Without command of these qualities it is impossible to express appropriately many of the higher and nobler forms of feeling, or any of the baser and malignant passions.

That the student of Elocution may know when to use, as well as when to avoid, these qualities, they have been presented in detail in their appropriate relations.

The **nasal** is that quality of voice in which the sound seems to have a resonance in the nasal organs.

It is used only in *mimicry* and *burlesque,* and hence no exercises or illustrations are needed.

SECTION XIII.

FORCE.

Force is the degree of intensity with which the sound is sent forth from the vocal organs.

Volume and loudness, though not identical with force, are dependent upon it. A full volume is produced by energetic or impassioned force with Orotund quality in all forms; great loudness by impassioned force, Pure Tone, or Orotund, High Pitch, and in all forms.

No amount of force can give volume or loudness to aspirate quality in any of its forms.

Volume relates to the amount of space filled with the sound, loudness to the distance at which a sound can be heard. The low, deep tones of the organ fill a vast space, though they would not be heard at a great distance. The high, shrill notes of the fife can be heard at a great distance, yet they do not have great volume of sound.

Force may, for convenience, be divided into Subdued, Moderate, Energetic, and Impassioned.

These may again be subdivided at pleasure.

Perfect command of force, in all its divisions, is indispensable to excellence in Reading and Speaking.

To acquire this power the voice must be disciplined by cultivation. This may be done by practicing the elements, words, and sentences as directed in the following exercise. Repeat each element and word at least a dozen times, beginning with the most delicate sound that can be uttered in Pure Tone, and gradually increase the force until the utmost power of the voice is reached.

In this exercise be very careful to retain the same pitch in the repetition of each element.

SCIENCE OF ELOCUTION.

After practicing a number of times on one key change the pitch, first two or three notes higher, and then two or three notes lower.

Exercises of this kind practiced for a few minutes daily will, in a short time, greatly increase the power and vigor of the vocal organs.

The scale of dots indicates to the eye the exercise described above.

Each dot represents the same word or sound repeated with gradually increasing force. The repetition of the same word or sound is preferred to a change of elements, as thereby the ear will more readily observe the different degrees of force, and detect any change in pitch.

Force—First Exercise.

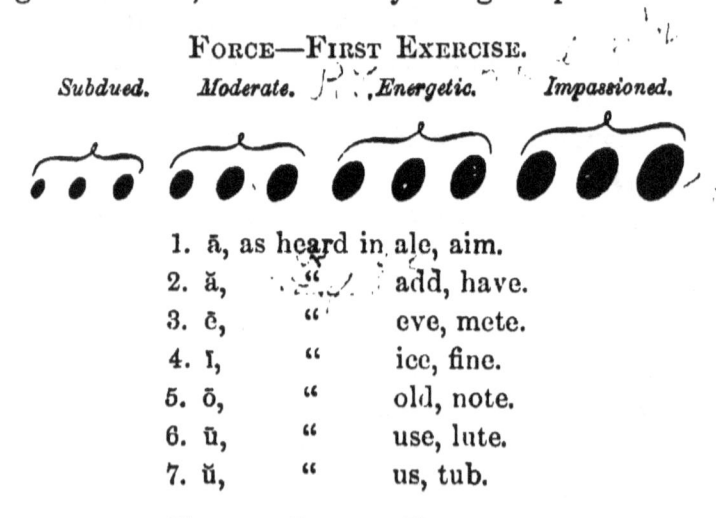

Subdued. Moderate. Energetic. Impassioned.

1. ā, as heard in ale, aim.
2. ă, " add, have.
3. ē, " eve, mete.
4. ī, " ice, fine.
5. ō, " old, note.
6. ū, " use, lute.
7. ŭ, " us, tub.

Force—Second Exercise.

Repeat in the same manner the following words. To these may be added numerous others.

Bar,	car,	mar,	ear,
fear,	hear,	ore,	lure,
orb,	arm,	mire,	art,
fare,	dart,	turn,	part.

SECTION XIV.
SUBDUED FORCE.

Subdued is that degree of force which ranges from the slightest sound that can be uttered in Pure Tone to the milder tones of ordinary conversation.

It is the degree of force, in connection with the Pure Tone, Effusive Form, appropriate for the expression of *pathetic, solemn, serious* and *tranquil thought.*

EXAMPLES: I. PATHOS.
Subdued Force, Pure Tone, Effusive Form.
[From "Burial of Arnold."—*Willis.*]

Tread lightly, comrades; ye have laid
  His dark locks on his brow;
Like life, save deeper light and shade,
  We'll not disturb them now.
Tread lightly, for 'tis beautiful,
  That blue-veined eyelids' sleep;
Hiding the eye death left so dull,
  Its slumber we will keep.

II. SOLEMNITY.
Subdued Force, Pure Tone, Effusive Form.
[From "Only Waiting."—*Anon.*]

Only waiting till the shadows
  Are a little longer grown;
Only waiting till the glimmer
  Of the day's last beam is flown;
Till the night of earth is faded
  From the heart once full of day;
Till the stars of heaven are breaking
  Through the twilight soft and gray.

Only waiting till the reapers
  Have the last sheaf gathered home,
For the summer time is faded,
  And the autumn winds have come.
Quickly, reapers, gather quickly
  The last ripe hours of my heart,
For the bloom of life is withered,
  And I hasten to depart.

III. Tranquillity.

Subdued Force, Pure Tone, Effusive Form.
[From "The Heart of the War."—*Anon.*]

Peace in the clover-scented air,
  And stars within the dome,
And underneath, in dim repose,
  A plain New England home.
Within a murmur of low tones
  And sighs from hearts oppressed,
Merging in prayer at last, that brings
  The balm of silent rest.

SECTION XV.
MODERATE FORCE.

Moderate force is the degree of intensity heard in the ordinary conversational tones. It is the appropriate force, combined with Pure Tone, Expulsive Form, for the utterance of *narrative, descriptive, didactic* and *unemotional thought;* with the Orotund, Effusive Form, for the utterance of *sublimity, reverence* and *devotion;* and with the Orotund, Expulsive Form, for the *introduction to orations, speeches* and *oratorical sermons.*

Examples: I. Narrative.

Moderate Force, Pure Tone, Expulsive Form.
[From "The Blacksmith of Ragenbach."—*Anon.*]

In the principality of Hohenlohe, now a part of the kingdom of Wirtemberg, is a village called Ragenbach, where, about twenty years ago, the following event took place: One afternoon in early autumn, in the tavern-room of Ragenbach, several men and women, assembled from the village, sat at their ease. The smith formed one of the merry company. He was a strong man, with resolute countenance and daring mien, but with such a good-natured smile on his lips that every one who saw him admired him. His arms were like bars of iron, and his fists like a forge-hammer, so that few could equal him in strength of body.

II. Descriptive.

Moderate Force, Pure Tone, Expulsive Form.

[From "The Cynic."—*Beecher.*]

The Cynic is one who never sees a good quality in a man, and never fails to see a bad one. He is the human owl, vigilant in darkness and blind to light, mousing for vermin, and never seeing noble game.

The Cynic puts all human actions into only two classes: *openly* bad and *secretly* bad. All virtue, and generosity, and disinterestedness, are merely the *appearance* of good, but selfish at the bottom. He holds that no man does a good thing except for profit. The effect of his conversation upon your feelings is to chill and sear them; to send you away sour and morose.

III. Didactic.

Moderate Force, Pure Tone, Expulsive Form.

[From "Talk to the Point."]

Talk to the point, and stop when you reach it. The faculty which some possess of making one idea cover a quire of paper is despicable. To fill a volume upon nothing is a credit to nobody, though Chesterfield wrote a very clever poem upon Nothing.

There are men who get one idea into their heads, and but one, and they make the most of it. You can see it and almost feel it in their presence. On all occasions it is produced, till it is worn as thin as charity. They remind you of a twenty-four pounder discharging at a humming-bird. You hear a tremendous noise, see a volume of smoke, but you look in vain for the effects. The bird is scattered to atoms.

IV. Animated Thought.

Moderate Force, Pure Tone, Expulsive Form.

[From "The Personality and Uses of a Laugh."—*Anon.*]

I would be willing to choose my friend by the quality of his laugh, and abide the issue. A glad, gushing outflow, a clear, ringing, mellow note of the soul, as surely indicates a genial and genuine nature, as the rainbow in the dew-drop heralds the morning sun, or the frail flower in the wilderness betrays the zephyr-tossed seed of the parterre.

A laugh is one of God's truths. It tolerates no disguises. Falsehood may train its voice to flow in softest cadences, its lips to wreathe into smiles of surpassing sweetness, its face

"to put on
That look we trust in;..."

but its laugh will betray the mockery. Who has not started and shuddered at the hollow "he-he-he!" of some velvet-voiced Mephistopheles, whose sinuous fascinations, without this note of warning— this premonitory rattle—might have bound the soul with a strong spell!

V. Sublimity, Reverence and Devotion.

Moderate Force, Orotund, Effusive Form.

[From "God's First Temples."—*Bryant.*]

Father, thy hand
Hath reared these venerable columns: thou
Did'st weave this verdant roof. Thou didst look down
Upon the naked earth, and forthwith rose
All these fair ranks of trees. They in thy sun
Budded, and shook their green leaves in thy breeze,
And shot toward heaven. The century-living crow,
Whose birth was in their tops, grew old and died
Among their branches; till at last they stood,
As now they stand, massy, and tall, and dark,
Fit shrine for humble worshiper to hold
Communion with his Maker.

VI. Introduction to an Oration.

Moderate Force, Orotund, Expulsive Form.

[From Webster's Speech in the Senate, Jan. 26, 1830, in reply to Hayne.]

Mr. President: When the mariner has been tossed for many days in thick weather, and on an unknown sea, he naturally avails himself of the first pause in the storm, the earliest glance of the sun, to take his latitude, and ascertain how far the elements have driven him from his true course. Let us imitate this prudence, and before we float farther, refer to the point from which we departed, that we may at least be able to conjecture where we now are. I ask for the reading of the resolution.

SECTION XVI.
ENERGETIC FORCE.

Energetic force is that degree of intensity heard in earnest, excited conversation. It is the force of voice, combined with Pure Tone, Expulsive and Explosive Forms, for the expression of *joy, gladness, mirth;* with the Orotund, Expulsive and Explosive Forms, for the delivery of *senatorial, political* and *judicial speeches, orations* and *sermons of an oratorical character;* with the Orotund, Effusive Form, for the utterance of *profound sublimity, grandeur,* and *adoration.*

EXAMPLES: I. JOY AND GLADNESS.

Energetic Force, Pure Tone, Expulsive and Explosive Forms.

[From "Greeting to Friends after an Absence."—*Morris.*]

I'm with you once again, my friends;
No more my footsteps roam;
Where it began my journey ends,
Amid the scenes of home.
No other clime has skies so blue,
Or streams so broad and clear;
And where are hearts so warm and true
As those that meet me here?

II. SENATORIAL SPEECH.

Energetic Force, Orotund, Expulsive and Explosive Forms.

[From "Webster's Reply to Hayne."]

Mr. President, I shall enter on no encomium upon Massachusetts—she needs none. There she is—behold her, and judge for yourselves. There is her history—the world knows it by heart. The past, at least, is secure. There is Boston, and Concord, and Lexington, and Bunker Hill—and there they will remain forever. The bones of her sons, fallen in the great struggle for independence, now lie mingled with the soil of every State from New England to Georgia—and there they will lie forever. And, sir, where American liberty raised its first voice, and where its youth was nurtured and sustained, there it still lives, in the strength of its manhood, and full of its original spirit. If discord and disunion shall wound it—if party strife and blind ambition shall hawk at and tear it—if folly and madness, if uneasiness under salutary and necessary restraints, shall succeed to separate it from that Union by which alone its existence is made sure—it will stand in the end by the side of that cradle in which its infancy was rocked; it will stretch forth its arm, with whatever vigor it may still retain, over the friends who gather round it; and it will fall at last, if fall it must, amid the proudest monuments of its own glory, and on the very spot of its origin!

III. Oration.

Energetic Force, Orotund, Expulsive and Explosive Forms.

[From "Washington."]

It matters very little what immediate spot may have been the birthplace of such a man as Washington. No people can claim, no country appropriate him. The boon of Providence to the human race—his fame is eternity, and his residence creation. Though it was the defeat of our arms, and the disgrace of our policy, I almost bless the convulsion in which he had his origin. If the heavens thundered, and the earth rocked, yet, when the storm had passed, how pure was the climate that it cleared! How bright in the brow of the firmament was the planet which it revealed to us! In the production of Washington it does really appear as if nature was endeavoring to improve upon herself, and that all the virtues of the ancient world were but so many studies preparatory to the patriot of the new.

Individual instances, no doubt, there were—splendid exemplifications of some single qualification. Cæsar was merciful, Scipio was continent, Hannibal was patient; but it was reserved for Washington to blend them all in one, and, like the lovely masterpiece of the Grecian artist, to exhibit, in one glow of associated beauty, the pride of every model, and the perfection of every master.

IV. Oratorical Sermon.

Energetic Force, Orotund, Expulsive and Explosive Forms.

[From "Living to God."—*Griffin.*]

My brethren, let us no longer live to ourselves. Let us arise and put our hands to the great work in which the nations are now moving. Wondrous things are taking place in the four quarters of the globe. The world is waking up after a long sleep, and is teeming with projects and efforts to extend the empire of truth and happiness. This is the day of which the prophets sung. Let us not sleep, while all others are rousing themselves to action. Let every soul come up to the help of the Lord. Let not one be left behind. He that has absolutely nothing to give, let him pray. Let no one be idle This is a great day, and the Lord requires every hand in the work.

SECTION XVII.

IMPASSIONED FORCE.

Impassioned force is the degree of intensity heard in the expression of *violent* and *impetuous emotion*. Combined with Pure Tone, Effusive and Expulsive Forms, Impassioned is the degree of force appropriate for *calling* and *commanding ;* with Pure Tone, Explosive Form, the expression of *ecstatic joy* and *gladness*. With the Orotund, Expulsive and Explosive Forms, it is employed in the utterance of *rousing* and *exciting appeals ;* with the Aspirate, Pectoral and Guttural, Expulsive and Explosive, in the expression of *anger, threatening, scorn, defiance, revenge,* etc.

EXAMPLES: I. CALLING.

Impassioned Force, Pure Tone, Effusive Form.

[From The Herald's Call, "King John."—*Shakspeare.*]

Rejoice, ye men of Angiers! Ring your bells:
King John, your king and England's, doth approach.
Open your gates, and give the victors way!

II. COMMANDING.

Impassioned Force, Pure Tone, Effusive Form.

[From "Charge of Light Brigade."—*Tennyson.*]

Forward, the Light Brigade,
Charge for the guns!

III. Ecstatic Joy.

Impassioned Force, Pure Tone, Expulsive and Explosive Forms

[From "The Life Boat."—*Anon.*]

Hurrah! the life-boat dashes on,
   Though darkly the reef may frown;
The rock is there, the ship is gone
   Full twenty fathoms down.
But cheered by hope, the seamen cope
   With the billows single-handed:
They are all in the boat. Hurrah! they're afloat!
And now they are safely landed
     By the life-boat! Cheer the life-boat!

IV. Rousing and Exciting Appeal.

Impassioned Force, Orotund, Expulsive and Explosive Forms.

[From "Spartacus to the Gladiators."—*Kellogg.*]

Ye stand here now like giants, as ye are! The strength of brass is in your toughened sinews; but to-morrow some Roman Adonis, breathing sweet perfume from his curly locks, shall with his lily fingers pat your red brawn, and bet his sesterces upon your blood. Hark! hear ye yon lion roaring in his den? 'Tis three days since he has tasted flesh; but to-morrow he shall break his fast upon yours, and a dainty meal for him ye will be. If ye are beasts, then stand here like fat oxen waiting for the butcher's knife. If ye are men, follow me. Strike down yon guard, gain the mountain passes, and then do bloody work, as did your sires at old Thermopylæ! Is Sparta dead? Is the old Grecian spirit frozen in your veins, that you do crouch and cower like a belabored hound beneath his master's lash? O comrades! warriors! Thracians! if we must fight, let us fight for ourselves! If we must slaughter, let us slaughter our oppressors! If we must die, let it be under the clear sky, by the bright waters, in noble, honorable battle!

V. Anger, Scorn, Defiance.

Impassioned Force, Aspirate, Pectoral and Guttural Qualities, Expulsive and Explosive Forms.

[From "The Seminole's Defiance."]

Blaze with your serried columns! I will not bend the knee;
The shackle ne'er again shall bind the arm which now is free!

I've mailed it with the thunder when the tempest muttered low,
And where it falls ye well may dread the lightning of its blow.
I've scared you in the city; I've scalped you on the plain;
Go, count your chosen where they fell beneath my leaden rain!
I scorn your proffered treaty: the pale face I defy;
Revenge is stamped upon my spear, and "blood" my battle-cry!

Perfect command of every degree of force enables the public speaker to readily adapt his tones to the sentiment he expresses, and to the circumstances by which he is surrounded.

Expressing pathos, his voice easily drops to subdued force; uttering bold and rousing thought, it as readily rises to impassioned force; in the delivery of didactic thought, it is pleasingly modulated to moderate force; speaking in a small room, the degree of force is so regulated as not to be painful to the hearers; addressing a vast assembly in the open air, the voice is perfectly audible to the most distant hearer; speaking under the influence of strong excitement, the intensity of his feelings does not hinder his utterance, nor drive him into ranting and vociferation.

Such are some of the advantages of perfect command of Force of Voice.

Exercises similar to the above not only give vigor and pliancy to the vocal organs, but are invaluable aids to health, cheerfulness, and mental activity.

SECTION XVIII.

STRESS.

Stress is the application of the force of the voice to the different parts of the word or sound.

The divisions of stress are Radical, Median, Final, Compound, Thorough, and Intermittent.

SECTION XIX.

RADICAL STRESS.

Radical stress is the application of the force of the voice to the first part of the word or sound. "The clear and forcible radical stress can take place only after an interruption of the voice."

"It would seem as if there is some momentary occlusion in the larynx, by which the breath is barred and accumulated for the purpose of a full and sudden discharge. This occlusion is most under command, and the explosion is most powerful, on syllables beginning with a tonic element, or with an abrupt one preceding a tonic, for in this last case an obstruction in the organs of articulation is combined with the function of the larynx."

To acquire control of this style of stress practice the following elements and words in the Expulsive and Explosive Forms, first with Pure Tone, then with Orotund, in the Moderate, Energetic and Impassioned degree of Force.

In this exercise be careful to expend the full force of the voice upon the first part of the word or sound.

RADICAL STRESS—FIRST EXERCISE.

1. ă, as heard in add, fat.
2. ĕ, " end, met.
3. ĭ, " ill, fin.
4. ŏ, " odd, not.
5. ŭ, " us, tub.
6. y, " nymph, lyric.
7. ā, " ale, fate.
8. ē, " eve, mete.
9. ī, " ice, fine.

Radical Stress—Second Exercise.

Add,	end,	orb,	ail,
ease,	isle,	inch,	use,
oil,	up,	on,	aid,
entire,	obey,	end,	bend,
think,	live,	defy,	blaze,
rouse,	down,	slave,	round.

The **radical stress** is heard in various degrees. In its milder form it is the stress appropriate for the delivery of *narrative, descriptive* and *didactic thought* in the style of *essays, lectures* and *sermons;* in a more energetic form it is appropriate for the utterance of *argumentative speeches* and *orations;* and in its most impassioned form for the expression of *intense feeling* and *emotion,* as *anger, scorn, defiance,* etc.

Examples: I. Narrative.
Radical Stress, Moderate Force, Pure Tone, Expulsive Form.
[From "The Heart's Charity."—*Eliza Cook.*]

A rich man walked abroad one day,
And a poor man walked the self-same way,
When a pale and starving face came by,
With a pallid lip and a hopeless eye;
And that starving face presumed to stand
And ask for bread from the rich man's hand.
But the rich man sullenly looked askance,
With a gathering frown and a doubtful glance;
"I have nothing," said he, "to give to you,
Nor any such rogue of a canting crew;"
And he fastened his pocket, and on he went,
With his soul untouched and his conscience content.

II. Didactic.
Radical Stress, Moderate Force, Pure Tone, Expulsive Form.
[From "Advice to a Young Lawyer."—*Judge Story.*]

Whene'er you speak, remember every cause
Stands not on eloquence, but stands on laws;

Pregnant in matter, in expression brief,
Let every sentence stand with bold relief;
On trifling points nor time nor talents waste,
A sad offense to learning and to taste;
Nor deal with pompous phrase, nor e'er suppose
Poetic flights belong to reasoning prose.

III. Argumentative Speech.

Radical Stress, Energetic Force, Orotund, Expulsive Form.

[From "Barbarity of National Hatreds."—*Rufus Choate.*]

Mr. President, let me say that, in my judgment, this notion of a national enmity of feeling toward Great Britain belongs to a past age of our history. My younger countrymen are unconscious of it. They disavow it. That generation in whose opinions and feelings the actions and the destiny of the next are unfolded, as the tree in the germ, do not at all comprehend your meaning, nor your fears, nor your regrets. We are born to happier feelings. We look to England as we look to France. We look to them from our new world—not unrenowned, yet a new world still—and the blood mounts to our cheeks, our eyes swim, our voices are stifled, with emulousness of so much glory; their trophies will not let us sleep; but there is no hatred at all; no hatred, no barbarian memory of wrongs, for which brave men have made the last expiation to the brave.

IV. Anger, Scorn and Defiance.

Radical Stress, Impassioned Force, Aspirate, Orotund, Guttural Quality, Explosive Form.

[From "Paradise Lost."—*Milton.*]

Whence and what art thou, execrable shape!
That dar'st, though grim and terrible, advance
Thy miscreated front athwart my way
To yonder gates? Through them I mean to pass,
That be assured, without leave asked of thee:
Retire! or taste thy folly, and learn by proof,
Hell-born, not to contend with spirits of heaven.

Radical stress is one of the most important properties of utterance. Without it reading and speaking become dull and lifeless.

The argumentative speaker who has not this property at command fails to produce conviction in the minds of his hearers.

Dr. Rush says of the Radical Stress: "It is this which draws the cutting edge of words across the ear, and startles even stupor into attention; this which lessens the fatigue of listening, and outvoices the stir and rustle of an assembly."

Murdoch and Russell say: "The utter absence of radical stress bespeaks timidity and indecision, confusion of thought, and feebleness of purpose.

"The speaker who fails in regard to the effect of this property of utterance solicits our pity rather than commands our respect. The right degree of this function indicates the manly, self-possessed speaker."

SECTION XX.
MEDIAN STRESS.

Median stress is the application of the force of the voice to the middle of the word or sound.

It is a gradual increase of force and elevation of pitch through the concrete movement to the middle of the word, and then as gradual a diminution and lowering to the close. Median stress is generally heard in connection with the effusive form.

To acquire control of this style of stress practice the following elements and words, beginning each with very subdued force and low pitch, which gradually increase and elevate to the middle, and then as gradually diminish and lower.

MEDIAN STRESS—FIRST EXERCISE.

1. ā, as heard in ale, fate.
2. ä,   "   arm, far.

3. ȧ, as heard in ask, grass.
4. a̤,   "   all, talk.
5. ō,   "   old, note.
6. ōō,   "   moon, food.

Median Stress—Second Exercise.

Gray,	tolls,	day,	softly,
old,	arm,	father,	palm,
oh,	more,	roll,	round,
beams,	prayer,	slow,	tread,
full,	fled,	pure,	snow.

Median is the appropriate stress for the utterance of *pathos, solemnity, sublimity, reverence, grandeur* and *devotion*.

It is heard in different degrees, varying with the depth and power of the emotion.

Serious, solemn and tranquil thought require only the milder forms of the Median; while reverence, grandeur, sublimity and devotion require the fullest form.

Examples: I. Tranquillity.
Median Stress, Subdued Force, Pure Tone, Effusive Form.
[From "Evening."—*Moir.*]

'Tis twilight now:
How deep is the tranquillity! The trees
Are slumbering through their multitude of boughs,
Even to the leaflet on the frailest twig!
A twilight gloom pervades the distant hills,
An azure softness mingling with the sky.

II. Solemnity
Median Stress, Subdued Force, Pure Tone, Effusive Form.
[From "Death."—*Mrs. Hemans.*]

Leaves have their time to fall,
  And flowers to wither at the north wind's breath,
And stars to set; but all,
  Thou hast all seasons for thine own, O Death!

> We know when moons shall wane,
>   When summer birds from far shall cross the sea,
>   When autumn's hue shall tinge the golden grain:
>   But who shall teach us when to look for thee?

III. SUBLIMITY AND GRANDEUR.

Median Stress, Moderate and Energetic Force, Orotund, Effusive Form.

[From "Ossian's Address to the Sun."—*Macpherson*.]

O thou that rollest above, round as the shield of my fathers! whence are thy beams, O sun! thy everlasting light! Thou comest forth in thy awful beauty: the stars hide themselves in the sky; the moon, cold and pale, sinks in the western wave. But thou thyself movest alone: who can be a companion of thy course?

The oaks of the mountain fall; the mountains themselves decay with years; the ocean sinks and grows again; the moon herself is lost in the heavens; but thou art forever the same, rejoicing in the brightness of thy course.

When the world is dark with tempests, when thunders roll, and lightnings fly, thou lookest in thy beauty from the clouds, and laughest at the storm.

But to Ossian thou lookest in vain; for he beholds thy beams no more, whether thy yellow hair floats on the eastern clouds, or thou tremblest at the gates of the west. But thou art, perhaps, like me, for a season: thy years will have an end. Thou wilt sleep in thy clouds, careless of the voice of the morning.

IV. REVERENCE AND ADORATION.

Median Stress, Moderate and Energetic Force, Orotund, Effusive Form.

[From "Morning Hymn in Paradise."—*Milton*.]

> These are thy glorious works, Parent of Good,
>   Almighty! Thine this universal frame,
>   Thus wondrous fair. Thyself how wondrous then!
>   Unspeakable! who sitt'st above these heavens,
>   To us invisible or dimly seen,
>   'Midst these thy lowest works.
>   Yet these declare thy goodness beyond thought
>   And power divine!

The **median stress** is one of the greatest beauties in reading.

It prevents the drawling and lifeless style so prevalent in the reading of the Bible and the Church service, and gives a most impressive beauty, power and grandeur to the utterance of *pathos, sublimity, reverence, devotion* and *adoration*.

Destitute of its ennobling effect, the reading of many passages in prose and poetry sinks into a monotonous and tedious utterance.

It is indispensable to the highest success in Elocution. Carried to excess it becomes a fault. The habit of mouthing, so prevalent on the stage among stock actors, has for one of its principal elements an excessive median stress. Like every element of utterance, it must be judiciously used.

SECTION XXI.

FINAL STRESS.

The **final stress** is the application of the force of the voice to the last part of the word or sound.

The force, at first but slight, is gradually increased, until it closes in an abrupt and violent sound. In its effect on the ear it is not unlike the report of a pistol when it hangs fire.

To acquire control of this style of stress practice the elements and words as directed. Repeat each of the elements, beginning with a slight sound, which gradually increase, and close with an abrupt and forcible sound.

FINAL STRESS—FIRST EXERCISE.

1. ē, as heard in me, see.
2. ā,   "   ale, pale.
3. â,   "   air, fair.
4. ä,   "   father, arm.

5. ä, as heard in ask, grass.
6. Ï,   "   ice, fine.
7. ū,   "   use, tube.

Final Stress—Second Exercise.

Slave,	wretch,	coward,	great,
villainy,	revenge,	hatred,	defiance,
birth,	sorrows,	beasts,	slaves,
extreme,	rights,	bid,	push,
determined,	proceed,	fortune,	friends,
barren,	rugged,	rock,	refuge.

The **final stress** is employed in the expression of *determined purpose, earnest resolve, stern rebuke, contempt, astonishment, horror, revenge, hate* and similar passions.

It is usually combined with the Expulsive and Explosive Forms of Voice, and, in the expression of passion, with the Aspirate, Pectoral, or Guttural Qualities.

Examples: I. Earnest Resolve.

Final Stress, Energetic Force, Orotund, Expulsive Form.

[From "Supposed Speech of John Adams."— *Webster.*]

Sir, before God, I believe the hour is come. My judgment approves this measure, and my whole heart is in it. All that I have, and all that I am, and all that I hope in this life, I am now ready here to stake upon it; and I leave off as I began, that, live or die, survive or perish, I am for the declaration. It is my living sentiment, and, by the blessing of God, it shall be my dying sentiment; independence now, and independence forever.

II. Determined Purpose.

Final Stress, Impassioned Force, Orotund Aspirate Quality, Expulsive and Explosive Forms.

[From "Speech on Writs of Assistance."—*Otis.*]

Let the consequences be what they may, I am determined to proceed. The only principles of public conduct that are worthy of a gentleman or a man are to sacrifice ease, estate, health, happiness, and even life itself, at the sacred call of his country.

III. Stern Rebuke.

Final Stress, Impassioned Force, Orotund Pectoral Quality, Expulsive and Explosive Forms.

[From "Speech against American War."—*Chatham*.]

I cannot, my lords, I will not, join in congratulation on misfortune and disgrace. This, my lords, is a perilous and tremendous moment It is not a time for adulation; the smoothness of flattery cannot save us in this rugged and awful crisis. It is now necessary to instruct the throne in the language of truth. We must, if possible, dispel the delusion and darkness which envelop it, and display, in its full danger and genuine colors, the ruin which is brought to our doors. Can ministers still presume to expect support in their infatuation? Can Parliament be so dead to its dignity and duty as to give their support to measures thus obtruded and forced upon them? Measures, my lords, which have reduced this late flourishing empire to scorn and contempt!

IV. Mockery, Contempt and Scorn.

Final Stress, Impassioned Force, Orotund Pectoral Guttural Quality, Expulsive and Explosive Forms.

[From Queen Constance to the Archduke of Austria.—*Shakspeare*.]

Thou slave! thou wretch! thou coward!
Thou little valiant, great in villainy!
Thou ever strong upon the stronger side!
Thou Fortune's champion, that dost never fight
But when her humorous ladyship is by
To teach thee safety!

V. Determined Stubborn Will.

Final Stress, Impassioned Force, Pectoral and Guttural Qualities, Expulsive and Explosive Forms.

[From Shylock's Refusal.—*Shakspeare*.]

I'll have my bond; I will not hear thee speak:
I'll have my bond; and therefore speak no more.
I'll not be made a soft and dull-eyed fool,
To shake the head, relent, and sigh, and yield

To Christian intercessors. Follow not;
I'll have no speaking! I will have my bond.

Without the full command of the Final Stress, determined purpose, earnest resolve, manly protest, degenerates into childish and angry utterance, and the expression of scorn, revenge, and contempt sink to the ridiculous tones of the shrew. In the delivery of lyric and dramatic poetry, in which high-wrought emotion is so frequently found, the Final Stress is an indispensable element of utterance.

SECTION XXII.
COMPOUND STRESS.

Compound stress is the application of the force to the first and last parts of the word, passing over the intermediate parts lightly.

Command of this style of stress can be best acquired **by** practicing words and sentences.

COMPOUND STRESS—EXERCISE.

Gone,	heaven,	married,	dead,
survive,	despise,	literary,	gospel,
sermons,	people,	earnest,	history,
canopy,	traitor,	tribune,	convicted.

The **compound** is the stress appropriate for the expression of *surprise, contempt,* and *mockery,* and sometimes of *sarcasm* and *raillery.*

EXAMPLES: I. EXTREME SURPRISE.
Compound Stress, Energetic Force, Aspirate Pure Tone, Expulsive Form.
[From "Hamlet."—*Shakspeare.*]

Ham. A bloody deed; almost as bad, good mother,
As kill a king, and marry with his brother.
Queen. As kill a king?

II. Extreme Surprise.

Compound Stress, Impassioned Force, Aspirate Pure Tone, Expulsive Form.

[From Queen Constance, when confounded with the intelligence of the union of Lewis and Blanche, and the consequent injury to her son Arthur.—*Shakspeare.*]

Gone to be married! Gone to swear a peace!
False blood to false blood joined! Gone to be friends!
Shall Lewis have Blanche, and Blanche these provinces?
It is not so; thou hast misspoke, misheard;
Be well advised, tell o'er thy tale again:
It cannot be; thou dost but say 'tis so.

III. Contempt and Mockery.

Compound Stress, Impassioned Force, Aspirate Pectoral Orotund, Explosive Form.

[From "Cataline's Defiance."—*Croly.*]

Banished from Rome! What's banished, but set free
From daily contact of the things I loathe?
"Tried and convicted traitor!"

The **compound stress** gives intensity and energy to the utterance of *surprise, contempt* and *mockery* most impressive in its effect. "The use of this form of stress belongs appropriately to feelings of peculiar force or acuteness; but on this very account it becomes an indispensable means of natural expression and true effect in many passages of reading and speaking. The difference between vivid and dull or flat utterance will often turn on the exactness with which this expressive function of voice is exerted."

SECTION XXIII.
THOROUGH STRESS.

Thorough stress is the application of the force of the voice to all parts of the word or sound equally.

To acquire control of this element of expression practice the elements and words with all the force you can command in the Orotund Expulsive.

Thorough Stress—First Exercise.

1. ō, as heard in no, go.
2. ā, " ale, pale.
3. ä, " arm, farm.
4. ī, " ice, fine

Thorough Stress—Second Exercise.

Ale,	arm,	home,	come,
lend,	send,	grave,	death,
call,	fall,	all,	lawn,
seize,	spirits,	fallen,	woe,
awake,	arise,	shout,	burn.

The **thorough stress** is appropriately employed in the expression of *rapture, joy, exultation, lofty command, indignant emotion, oratorical apostrophe,* and *virtuous indignation.*

Examples: I. Triumph and Exultation.
Thorough Stress, Impassioned Force, Orotund Quality, Expulsive Form.

[From "Sheridan's Ride."—*T. B. Read.*]

Hurrah! hurrah for Sheridan!
Hurrah! hurrah for horse and man!
And when their statues are placed on high,
Under the dome of the Union sky,
The American soldiers' Temple of Fame,
There with the glorious General's name
Be it said, in letters both bold and bright:
"Here is the steed that saved the day
By carrying Sheridan into the fight,
From Winchester—twenty miles away!"

II. Lofty Command.

Thorough Stress, Impassioned Force, Orotund, Expulsive **Form**

[From "Paradise Lost."—*Milton.*]

Princes! potentates!
Warriors, the flower of heaven! once yours, now lost,
If such astonishment as this can seize
Eternal spirits,
Awake! arise! or be forever fallen!

III. Oratorical Apostrophe.

Thorough Stress, Impassioned Force, Orotund, Expulsive Form.

O liberty! O sound once delightful to every Roman ear! O sacred privilege of Roman citizenship! once sacred, now trampled upon! But what then—is it come to this? Shall an inferior magistrate, a governor, who holds his power of the Roman people, in a Roman province, within sight of Italy, bind, scourge, torture with fire and red-hot plates of iron, and at last put to the infamous death of the cross, a Roman citizen? Shall neither the cries of innocence expiring in agony, nor the tears of pitying spectators, nor the majesty of the Roman commonwealth, nor the fear of the justice of his country, restrain the licentious and wanton cruelty of a monster, who, in confidence of his riches, strikes at the root of liberty and sets mankind at defiance?

IV. Vehement Indignation.

Thorough Stress, Impassioned Force, Orotund, Expulsive and Explosive Forms.

[From "Rebuke of Lord Suffolk."—*Chatham.*]

These abominable principles, and this more abominable avowal of them, demand the most decisive indignation. I call upon that right reverend and this most learned bench to vindicate the religion of their God, to defend and support the justice of their country. I call upon the bishops to interpose the unsullied sanctity of their lawn, upon the judges to interpose the purity of their ermine, to save us from this pollution. I call upon the honor of your lordships to reverence the dignity of your ancestors, and to maintain your own. I call upon the spirit and humanity of my country to vindicate the national character.

Thorough stress is one of the most powerful weapons of oratory. Its effect, when judiciously used, is magical.

It rouses the feelings, kindles the emotions, and stirs the very soul of an audience. If employed injudiciously and too frequently it degenerates into rant and vociferation, exciting only disgust and contempt in the mind of every cultivated hearer.

SECTION XXIV.

INTERMITTENT STRESS.

The **intermittent stress** is a tremulous emission of the voice from the organs.

To acquire control of this style of stress practice the elements and words with a short, quick, broken utterance.

Intermittent Stress—First Exercise.

1. ē, as heard in me, see.
2. ā,   "   ale, pale.
3. ă,   "   add, sad.
4. a̤,   "   talk, all.
5. ō,   "   old, bold.
6. ŏ,   "   odd, not.

Intermittent Stress—Second Exercise.

O!	die,	food,	go,
old,	man,	door,	your,
days,	down,	store,	lost,
gone,	blow,	hold,	grave.

The **intermittent stress** is the natural expression of all emotions attended with a weakened condition of the bodily organs, such as *feebleness* from *age, exhaustion, fatigue, sickness* and *grief*.

It is also appropriate in the expression of *extreme tenderness* and *ecstatic joy*.

Examples: I. Sickness.

Intermittent Stress, Subdued Force, Oral, Aspirate Quality, Effusive Form.

[From "Death of Little Jim."—*Anon.*]

Mother, the angels do so smile, and beckon little Jim.
I have no pain, dear mother, now, but O, I am so dry!
Just moisten poor Jim's lips again, and, mother, don't you cry

II. Feebleness.

Intermittent Stress, Moderate Force, Pectoral Quality, Expulsive Form.

[From "The Old Man's Request."—*Thomas Moss.*]

Pity the sorrows of a poor old man,
  Whose trembling limbs have borne him to your door,
Whose days are dwindled to the shortest span;
  O, give relief! and Heaven will bless your store!

III. Age and Exhaustion.

Intermittent Stress, Energetic Force, Pectoral and Guttural Quality, Expulsive Form.

[From "Death of Baron Rudiger."—*Green.*]

They come around me here, and say
  My days of life are o'er,
That I shall mount my noble steed
  And lead my band no more;
They come, and to my beard they dare
  To tell me now that I,
Their own liege lord and master born,
  That I—ha! ha!—must die!

The **intermittent stress** gives a vivid and touching expression to utterance, for the absence of which nothing can atone. "Without its appeal to sympathy, and its peculiar power over the heart, many of the most beautiful and touching passages of Shakspeare and Milton become dry and cold."

SECTION XXV.

PITCH.

Pitch is the place upon the musical scale on which the sound is uttered. Every sound, whether produced by the vocal organs, or by other means, is found somewhere on this musical scale. Thus we speak of the low notes of the organ, the high notes of the fife; of the low tones of the male voice, the high tones of the female voice.

Excellence in reading and speaking requires so perfect control of the different divisions of pitch that at pleasure the voice can be raised or lowered according to the feeling or emotion uttered.

The Author of our being has so attuned the sensibilities of the soul that certain notes of voice indicate certain emotions.

A low, subdued tone heard from an adjoining room suggests devotion; while a high pitch as naturally suggests a joyous conversation or angry dispute.

In singing, the divisions of pitch are absolute. Two persons singing the same tune, however widely different their natural pitch of voice, use precisely the same key. In Elocution the divisions of pitch are relative. Two persons may read the same selection on widely different keys, yet each be entirely appropriate.

In singing, the key is determined by musical instruments, in which there is comparatively little variation.

In Elocution the key appropriate for each person is determined by his own voice.

Students of Elocution make no greater mistake than in attempting to regulate their pitch of voice by that of some favorite teacher or speaker.

Many teachers of Elocution injure the majority of their pupils by impressing them with the idea that their peculiar pitch is the only true standard.

Not unfrequently do students indicate where they have been educated by their ridiculous efforts to conform a voice naturally of a high pitch to the low key of their instructor.

It cannot be too earnestly impressed upon the minds of pupils that each voice is its own index in pitch.

The divisions of Pitch in Elocution are Very High, High, Middle, Low, Very Low. These divisions should include a compass of at least two octaves, but have no definite position on the musical scale, varying according to the natural key of the different voices.

That key upon which each person naturally strikes in ordinary unimpassioned conversation will be his Middle Pitch. This will vary three or five notes. From this Middle Pitch all other divisions are to be determined.

The Low Pitch will be three, four, or five notes below the Middle. The Very Low will be two, three, or four notes below the Low; the range in the lower notes being much less than in the high notes. The High Pitch will be five, six, or eight notes above the Middle; the Very High will be five or eight notes above the High.

The above arrangement of the divisions of pitch is on the supposition that the compass of voice embraces from two and a half to three octaves. This is perhaps not far from the average, though the compass may be greatly increased by cultivation.

It may be well here to remark that a knowledge of music is not essential in the practice of the following exercises, nor indeed to the highest excellence in elocution. It is a significant fact that those who have made the highest attainments in reading and speaking have been very deficient in musical cultivation. Indeed it will be found, by a careful investigation of the subjects, that, though reading and singing are not incompatible, they are by no means mutual helpers. Singing implies the passage of the voice through the discrete movement. Reading and speaking require the passage of the voice through the concrete movement. Persons who sing a great deal, when they attempt to read unconsciously glide into these musical intervals. That which in singing constitutes one of the greatest beauties, namely, the discrete movement, in reading is the chief element of the defect known as tone, or singing-reading.

Singing may cultivate the voice, but it is exceedingly questionable if it improves the vocal delivery.

Repeat the following elements and words several times, first in a Middle Pitch, then in a Low Pitch, then in a High Pitch, then in a Very Low, and last in a Very High Pitch.

This exercise may be varied by beginning on a Very Low Pitch, and, on each repetition, raising the key two or three notes, until all the divisions have been passed over.

Pitch—First Exercise.

1. ā, as heard in ale, pale.
2. ă, " add, fat.
3. â, " air, pair.
4. ä, " far, palm.
5. á, " ask, dance.
6. a̯, " all, talk.
7. ō, " old, note.
8. ū, " use, tube.

PITCH—SECOND EXERCISE.

Old,	orb,	fate,	find,
arm,	harm,	boat,	coat,
but,	prove,	moon,	palm,
obey,	loud,	broad,	road,
deep,	dark,	ocean,	liberty,
glorious,	mirror,	tempest,	brand.

SECTION XXVI.

MIDDLE PITCH.

The **middle pitch** is the appropriate key for the delivery of *narrative, didactic* and *descriptive* thought in the form of scientific and literary lectures, introductions to speeches, orations and sermons.

EXAMPLES: I. DIDACTIC THOUGHT.

Middle Pitch, Radical Stress, Moderate Force, Pure Tone, Expulsive Form.

[From "Cheerfulness."—*Anon.*]

There is no one quality that so much attaches man to his fellow-man as cheerfulness. Talents may excite more respect, and virtue more esteem; but the respect is apt to be distant and the esteem cold. It is far otherwise with cheerfulness. It endears a man to the heart, not the intellect or the imagination. There is a kind of reciprocal diffusiveness about this quality that recommends its possessor by the very effect it produces. There is a mellow radiance in the light it sheds on all social intercourse which pervades the soul to a depth that the blaze of intellect can never reach.

II. DESCRIPTIVE THOUGHT.

Middle Pitch, Radical Stress, Moderate Force, Pure Tone, Expulsive Form.

[From "A Scene of Arab Life."—*Anon.*]

All that has been related concerning the passion for tales, which distinguishes the Arabs, is literally true. During the night which we passed on the shore of the Dead Sea we observed our Bethlehemites seated around a large fire, with their guns laid near them on the ground, while their horses, fastened to stakes, formed a kind of circle about them. These Arabs, after having taken their coffee, and conversed for some time with great earnestness, and with their usual loquacity, observed a strict silence when the sheik began his tale. We could, by the light of the fire, distinguish his significant gestures, his black beard, his white teeth, and the various plaits and positions which he gave to his tunic during the recital. His companions listened to him with the most profound attention; all of them with their bodies bent forward, and their faces over the flame, alternately sending forth shouts of admiration, and repeating with great emphasis the gestures of the historian. The heads of some few of their horses and camels were occasionally seen elevated above the group, and shadowing, as it were, the picture. When to these was added a glimpse of the scenery about the Dead Sea and the mountains of Judea, the whole effect was striking and fanciful in the highest degree.

III. NARRATION.

Middle Pitch, Radical Stress, Moderate Force, Pure Tone, Expulsive Form.

[From "Life of Raleigh."—*Anon.*]

Raleigh's cheerfulness during his last days was so great, and his fearlessness of death so marked, that the Dean of Westminster, who attended him, wondering at his deportment, reprehended the lightness of his manner. But Raleigh gave God thanks that he had never feared death, for it was but an opinion and an imagination; and as for the manner of death, he had rather die so than in a burning fever; that some might have made shows outwardly, but he felt the joy within.

IV. INTRODUCTION TO JUDICIAL SPEECH.

Middle Pitch, Radical Stress, Moderate Force, Pure Tone, Expulsive Form.

["Trial of a Murderer."—*Webster.*]

Against the prisoner at the bar, as an individual, I cannot have the slightest prejudice. I would not do him the smallest injury or injustice; but I do not affect to be indifferent to the discovery and the punishment of this deep guilt. I cheerfully share in the opprobrium, how much soever it may be, which is cast on those who feel and manifest an anxious concern that all who had a part in planning, or a hand in executing, this deed of midnight assassination, may be brought to answer for their enormous crime at the bar of public justice.

SECTION XXVII.

LOW PITCH.

Low pitch is the key appropriate for the delivery of *serious, solemn, pathetic, grave, devotional, sublime* and *grand* thought not of an earnest or impassioned character.

EXAMPLES: I. SOLEMN DIDACTIC.

Low Pitch, Radical Stress, Moderate Force, Pure Tone, Expulsive Form.

[From " Religion the Only Basis of Society."—*Channing.*]

Few men suspect, perhaps no man comprehends, the extent of the support given by religion to every virtue. No man, perhaps, is aware how much our moral and social sentiments are fed from this fountain; how powerless conscience would become without the belief of a God; how palsied would be human benevolence, were there not the sense of a higher benevolence to quicken and sustain it; how suddenly the whole social fabric would quake, and with what a fearful crash it would sink into hopeless ruin, were the ideas of a Supreme Being, of accountableness, and of a future life, to be utterly erased from every mind.

II. SOLEMN DESCRIPTIVE.

Low Pitch, Median Stress, Moderate Force, Pure Tone, Effusive Form

[From " Isle of Long Ago."]

There's a magical isle up the river of Time,
  Where the softest of airs are playing;
There's a cloudless sky, and a tropical clime,
And a song as sweet as a vesper chime,
  And the Junes with the roses are straying.

And the name of that isle is the Long Ago,
  And we bury our treasures there;
There are brows of beauty and bosoms of snow;
There are heaps of dust—but we loved them so!
  There are trinkets and tresses of hair.

There are fragments of song that nobody sings,
   And a part of an infant's prayer;
There's a lute unswept, and a harp without strings,
There are broken vows and pieces of rings,
   And the garments she used to wear.

III. SUBLIMITY.

Low Pitch, Median Stress, Moderate and Energetic Force, Orotund, Effusive Form.

[From In Memoriam: "Abraham Lincoln."—*Mrs. E. G. Bugbee.*]

There's a burden of grief on the breezes of spring,
And a song of regret from the bird on its wing;
There's a pall on the sunshine and over the flowers,
And a shadow of graves on these spirits of ours;
For a star hath gone out from the night of our sky,
On whose brightness we gazed as the war-cloud rolled by
So tranquil and steady and clear were its beams,
That they fell like a vision of peace on our dreams.

SECTION XXVIII.

HIGH PITCH.

High pitch is the key appropriate for the delivery of *animated, joyous, gay, earnest* and *impassioned* thought.

EXAMPLES: I. ANIMATED.

High Pitch, Radical Stress, Energetic Force, Pure Tone, Expulsive Form.

[From "Paddle Your Own Canoe."—*Mrs. Bolton.*]

   Voyager upon life's sea,
     To yourself be true;
   And where'er your lot may be,
     Paddle your own canoe.
   Never, though the winds **may rave,**
     Falter nor look back,
   But upon the darkest **wave**
     Leave a shining track.

Nobly dare the wildest storm,
  Stem the hardest gale;
Brave of heart and strong of arm,
  You will never fail.
When the world is cold and dark,
  Keep an end in view,
And toward the beacon mark
  Paddle your own canoe.

II. Joy.

High Pitch, Radical Stress, Energetic Force, Pure Tone, Expulsive and Explosive Forms.

[From "Voice of Spring."—*Mrs. Hemans.*]

I come! I come! ye have called me long:
I come o'er the mountains with light and song.
Ye may trace my step o'er the wakening earth,
By the winds which tell of the violet's birth,
By the primrose stars in the shadowy grass,
By the green leaves opening as I pass.

From the streams and founts I have loosed the chain;
They are sweeping on to the silvery main;
They are flashing down from the mountain brows;
They are flinging spray o'er the forest-boughs;
They are bursting fresh from their sparry caves,
And the earth resounds with the joy of waves.

III. Impassioned Oratorical.

High Pitch, Radical Stress, Impassioned Force, Orotund, Expulsive and Explosive Forms.

[From Speech in Virginia Convention.—*Patrick Henry.*]

Sir, we are not weak if we make a proper use of those means which the God of nature hath placed in our power. Three millions of people, armed in the holy cause of liberty, and in such a country as that which we possess, are invincible by any force which our enemy can send against us. Besides, sir, we shall not fight our battles alone. There is a just God who presides over the destinies of nations, and who will raise up friends to fight our battles for us. The battle, sir, is not to the strong alone; it is to the vigilant, the active, the brave. Besides, sir, we have no election. If we were base enough to desire it, it is now too late to retire from the contest There is no retreat but in submission and slavery. Our chains are forged. Their

clanking may be heard on the plains of Boston. The war is inevitable, and let it come! I repeat it, sir, let it come!
It is in vain, sir, to extenuate the matter. Gentlemen may cry Peace! peace! but there is no peace. The war is actually begun! The next gale that sweeps from the North will bring to our ears the clash of resounding arms! Our brethren are already in the field! Why stand we here idle? What is it that gentlemen wish? What would they have? Is life so dear, or peace so sweet, as to be purchased at the price of chains and slavery? Forbid it, Almighty God! I know not what course others may take; but as for me, give me liberty, or give me death!

IV. IMPASSIONED POETRY.
High Pitch, Thorough Stress, Impassioned Force, Orotund, Expulsive Form.

[From "Sheridan's Ride."—*T. B. Read.*]

Under his spurning feet, the road
Like an arrowy Alpine river flowed,
And the landscape sped away behind,
Like an ocean flying before the wind;
And the steed, like a bark fed with furnace ire,
Swept on, with his wild eye full of fire.
But lo! he is nearing his heart's desire;
He is snuffing the smoke of the roaring fray,
With Sheridan only five miles away.

SECTION XXIX.
VERY LOW PITCH.

Very low pitch is the key appropriate for the expression of *deep solemnity* when mingled with *awe, sublimity, grandeur, amazement, horror, despair, melancholy* and *gloom*.

EXAMPLES: I. SOLEMNITY AND SUBLIMITY.
Very Low Pitch, Median Stress, Energetic Force, Orotund Effusive Form.

[From "Apostrophe to the Ocean."—*Byron.*]

Roll on, thou deep and dark blue ocean, roll!
Ten thousand fleets sweep over thee in vain!
Man marks the earth with ruin—his control
Stops with the shore; upon the watery plain

The wrecks are all thy deed, nor doth remain
A shadow of man's ravage, save his own,
When for a moment, like a drop of rain,
He sinks into thy depths with bubbling groan,
Without a grave, unknelled, uncoffined, and unknown.

II. Solemnity, Sublimity and Awe.

Very Low Pitch, Median Stress, Energetic Force, Orotund, Aspirate, Effusive Form.

[From " Cato's Soliloquy."—*Addison.*]

It must be so; Plato, thou reasonest well!
Else whence this pleasing hope, this fond desire,
This longing after immortality?
Or whence this secret dread and inward horror
Of falling into nought? Why shrinks the soul
Back on herself, and startles at destruction?
'Tis the Divinity that stirs within us:
'Tis Heaven itself that points out an hereafter,
And intimates Eternity to man.
Eternity! thou pleasing, dreadful thought!
Through what variety of untried being,
Through what new scenes and changes must we pass!
The wide, th' unbounded prospect lies before me;
But shadows, clouds and darkness rest upon it.

III. Awe, Dismay and Despair.

Very Low Pitch, Median Stress, Energetic Force, Orotund, Aspirate-Pectoral, Effusive Form.

[From " The Pestilence."—*Porteus.*]

At dead of night,
In sullen silence stalks forth Pestilence:
Contagion, close behind, taints all her steps
With poisonous dew: no smiting hand is seen;
No sound is heard; but soon her secret path
Is marked with desolation: heaps on heaps
Promiscuous drop. No friend, no refuge near:
All, all is false and treacherous around,
All that they touch, or taste, or breathe, is Death.

IV. Solemnity and Awe.

Very Low Pitch, Median Stress, Energetic Force, Orotund, Aspirate, Pectoral, Effusive Form.

[From "Marco Bozzaris."—*Halleck.*]

Come to the bridal chamber, Death!
  Come to the mother when she feels
For the first time her first-born's breath;
  Come when the blessed seals
Which close the pestilence are broke,
And crowded cities wail its stroke;
Come in consumption's ghastly form,
The earthquake shock, the ocean storm;
Come when the heart beats high and warm,
  With banquet-song, and dance, and wine,
And thou art terrible: the tear,
The groan, the knell, the pall, the bier,
And all we know, or dream, or fear
  Of agony are thine.
But to the hero, when his sword
  Has won the battle for the free,
Thy voice sounds like a prophet's word,
And in its hollow tones are heard
  The thanks of millions yet to be.

SECTION XXX.

VERY HIGH PITCH.

Very high pitch is the key appropriate for the expression of *ecstatic joy, rapturous delight, impassioned shouting, calling* and *commanding.*

Examples: I. Ecstatic Joy.

Very High Pitch, Thorough Stress, Impassioned Force, Pure Tone, Expulsive Form.

[From "Song of Valkrieur."—*Mrs. Hemans.*]

Lo, the mighty sun looks forth!
Arm, thou leader of the north!
Lo, the mists of twilight fly—
We must vanish, thou must die!

By the sword, and by the spear,
By the hand that knows not fear,
Sea-king, nobly shalt thou fall!
There is joy in Odin's hall!

II. Shouting.

Very High Pitch, Thorough Stress, Impassioned Force, Pure Tone, Expulsive Form.

[From "Prisoner for Debt."—*Whittier.*]

Go, ring the bells, and fire the guns,
And fling the starry banner out;
Shout "freedom" till your lisping ones
Give back their cradle-shout;
Let boasted eloquence declaim
Of honor, liberty, and fame;
Still let the poet's strain be heard,
With "glory" for each second word,
And every thing with breath agree
To praise "our glorious liberty."

III. Impassioned Command.

Very High Pitch, Thorough Stress, Impassioned Force, Pure Tone, Expulsive Form.

[From "Life Boat."—*Anon.*]

Quick! man the life-boat! See yon bark
That drives before the blast!
There's a rock ahead, the night is dark,
And the storm comes thick and fast.
Can human power, in such an hour,
Avert the doom that's o'er her?
Her mainmast's gone, but she still drives on
To the fatal reef before her.
The life-boat! Man the life-boat!

The ability to control the pitch of voice is one of the greatest accomplishments in Elocution. Without the power of readily accommodating the voice to the key demanded by the emotion, there can be no such thing as natural and impressive reading or speaking.

More public speakers fail from inability to control pitch than from any other cause. Instances are numerous of public speakers who, after the delivery of a few introductory sentences, allow the voice to rise an octave above the key demanded by the sentiment, and upon this unpleasant tone, without a change of more than one or two notes, speak for an hour at a time.

No one would listen willingly to a tune constructed with a change of only two or three notes. As in music, so in Elocution, a constant change in pitch is demanded. In speaking, not only does each separate word and syllable require a slight change in pitch, but often wide transitions are necessary to properly express the ever-varying sentiment.

Upon the different divisions of pitch all the previous attributes should be practiced.

SECTION XXXI.
MOVEMENT OF VOICE.

Movement of voice is the rapidity with which the sounds are uttered in continuous discourse.

The different rates of movement may be indicated by the terms Very Rapid, Rapid, Moderate, Slow, Very Slow.

Appropriate utterance demands control of every degree of movement from the slowest to the most rapid.

To acquire this power practice the following sentences, first in a moderate, then in a rapid, then in a slow, then in a very rapid, and lastly, in a very slow movement.

1. Now came still evening on.
2. Now fades the glimmering landscape from the sight.
3. O'er all the peaceful world the smile of heaven shall lie.

4. Wheel the wild dance till the morning break.

5. Haste thee, nymph, and bring with thee mirth and **youthful jollity.**

6. Now set the teeth and stretch the nostrils wide.

7. Here it comes sparkling,
   And there it lies darkling;
   Now smoking and frothing,
   Its tumult and wrath in,
   Till in this rapid race
     On which it is bent,
   It reaches the place
     Of its steep descent.

SECTION XXXII.
MODERATE MOVEMENT.

Moderate movement is appropriate for the delivery of *narrative, didactic* and *unimpassioned* thought in the form of scientific and literary lectures and introductions to speeches.

EXAMPLES: I. SIMPLE NARRATION.

Moderate Movement, Middle Pitch, Radical Stress, Moderate Force, Pure Tone, Expulsive Form.

[From "Destruction of Carthage."—*Anon.*]

The city and republic of Carthage were destroyed by the termination of the third Punic war, about one hundred and fifty years before Christ. The city was in flames during seventeen days, and the news of its destruction caused the greatest joy at Rome. The Roman Senate immediately appointed commissioners, not only to raze the walls of Carthage, but even to demolish and burn the very materials of which they were made, and in a few days that city, which had once been the seat of commerce, the model of magnificence, the common storehouse of the wealth of nations, and one of the most powerful States in the world, left behind no trace of its splendor, of its power, or even of its existence. The history of Carthage is one of the many proofs that we have of the transient nature of worldly glory, for of all her grandeur not a wreck remains. Her own walls, like the calm ocean that conceals forever the riches hid in its unsearchable abyss, now obscure all her magnificence.

II. Descriptive.

Moderate Movement, Middle Pitch, Radical Stress, Moderate Force, Pure Tone, Expulsive Form.

[From "Aspect of Egypt."—*Addison.*]

There cannot be a finer sight than Egypt at two seasons of the year; for if we ascend one of the pyramids in the months of July and August we behold, in the swollen waters of the Nile, a vast sea, in which numberless towns and villages appear, with several causeways leading from place to place, the whole interspersed with groves and fruit-trees, whose tops only are visible—all which forms a delightful prospect. This view is bounded by mountains and woods, which terminate, at the utmost distance the eye can discover, the most beautiful horizon that can be imagined. In winter, on the contrary, that is to say, in the months of January and February, the whole country is like one continuous scene of beautiful meadows, whose verdure, enameled with flowers, charms the eye. The spectator beholds on every side flocks and herds dispersed over all the plains, with infinite numbers of husbandmen and gardeners. The air is then perfumed by the great quantity of blossoms on the orange, lemon, and other trees, and is so pure that a wholesome or more agreeable is not to be found in the world, so that nature being then dead, as it were, in all other climates, seems to be alive only for so delightful an abode.

III. Introduction to Legal Speech.

Moderate Movement, Middle Pitch, Radical Stress, Moderate Force, Pure Tone, Expulsive Form.

[From "Reply to Wickham in Burr's Trial."—*Wirt.*]

In proceeding to answer the argument of the gentleman I will treat him with candor. If I misrepresent him it will not be intentionally. I will not follow the example which he has set me on a very recent occasion. I will endeavor to meet the gentleman's propositions in their full force, and to answer them fairly. I will not, as I am advancing toward them, with my mind's eye measure the height, breadth and power of the proposition. If I find it beyond my strength, halve it; if still beyond my strength, quarter it; if still necessary, subdivide it into eighths; and when, by this process, I have reduced it to the proper standard, take one of these sections and toss it with an air of elephantine strength and superiority. If I find myself capable of conducting, by a fair course of reasoning, any one of his propositions to an absurd conclusion, I will not begin by stating that absurd conclusion as the proposition itself which I am going to encounter. I will not, in commenting on the gentleman's authorities, thank the gentleman with sarcastic politeness for introducing them, declare that they conclude directly against him, read just so much of the authority as serves the purpose of that declaration, omitting that which contains the true point of the case, which makes against me; nor, if forced by a direct call to read that part also, will I content myself by running over it as rapidly and inarticulately as I can, throw down the book with a theatrical air, and exclaim, "Just as I said!" when I know it is just as I had not said.

SECTION XXXIII.
SLOW MOVEMENT.

Slow movement is appropriate for the expression of *solemn, serious, grave* and *devotional* thought.

EXAMPLES: I. SOLEMN AND SERIOUS THOUGHT.

Slow Movement, Low Pitch, Median Stress, Subdued Force, Pure Tone Effusive Form.

[From "Mountains of Life."—*Clark.*]

There's a land far away, 'mid the stars, we are told,
   Where they know not the sorrows of time;
Where the pure waters wander through valleys of gold,
   And life is a treasure sublime;
'Tis the land of our God, 'tis the home of the soul,
   Where the ages of splendor eternally roll;
Where the way-weary traveler reaches his goal,
   On the ever-green Mountains of Life.

II. GRAVE DIDACTIC.

Slow Movement, Low Pitch, Radical Stress, Moderate Force, Pure Tone Expulsive Form.

[From "Promises of Religion to the Young."—*Alison.*]

In every part of Scripture it is remarkable with what singular tenderness the season of youth is always mentioned, and what hopes are offered to the devotion of the young. It was at that age that God appeared unto Moses when he fed his flock in the desert, and called him to the command of his own people. It was at that age that he visited the infant Samuel, while he ministered in the temple of the Lord, "in days when the word of the Lord was precious, and when there was no open vision." It was at that age that his Spirit fe upon David, while he was yet the youngest of his father's sons, and when among the mountains of Bethlehem he fed his father's sheep.

It was at that age also that they brought young children unto Christ that he should touch them, and his disciples rebuked those that brought them. But when Jesus saw it he was much displeased, and said to them, "Suffer little children to come unto me, and forbid them not, for of such is the kingdom of heaven." If these, then, are the effects and promises of youth and piety, rejoice, O young man, in thy youth! rejoice in those days which are never to return, when religion comes to thee in all its charms, and when the God of nature reveals himself to thy soul, like the mild radiance of the morning sun when he rises amid the blessings of a grateful world.

III. Reverence and Devotion.

Slow Movement, Low Pitch, Median Stress, Moderate Force, Orotund, Effusive Form.

[From "The Groves, God's First Temples."—*Bryant.*]

     O God! when thou
Dost scare the world with tempests, set on fire
The heavens with falling thunderbolts, or fill,
With all the waters of the firmament,
The swift, dark whirlwind that uproots the woods
And drowns the villages; when, at thy call,
Uprises the great deep, and throws himself
Upon the continent, and overwhelms
Its cities; who forgets not, at the sight
Of these tremendous tokens of thy power,
His pride, and lays his strifes and follies by!
O from these sterner aspects of thy face
Spare me and mine; nor let us need the wrath
Of the mad, unchained elements to teach
Who rules them. Be it ours to meditate,
In these calm shades, thy milder majesty.
And to the beautiful order of thy works
Learn to conform the order of our lives.

SECTION XXXIV.
VERY SLOW MOVEMENT.

Very slow movement is appropriate for the expression of *profound reverence, deep solemnity, adoration, amazement, awe* and *horror.*

EXAMPLES: I. PROFOUND REVERENCE AND ADORATION

Very Slow Movement, Very Low Pitch, Median Stress, Energetic Force, Aspirate Orotund, Effusive Form.

[From "God."—*Derzhavin.*]

O thou Eternal One! whose presence bright
   All space doth occupy, all motion guide;
Unchanged through Time's all-devastating flight:
   Thou only God. There is no God beside.
Being above all beings. Mighty One,
   Whom none can comprehend, and none explore;
Who fillest existence with thyself alone;
   Embracing all, supporting, ruling o'er,
Being whom we call God, and know no more.

II. SUBLIMITY AND AWE.

Very Slow Movement, Very Low Pitch, Median Stress, Energetic Force, Aspirate-Pectoral Orotund, Effusive Form.

[From "Closing Year."—*Prentice.*]

               'Tis a time
For memory and for tears. Within the deep,
Still chambers of the heart, a specter dim,
Whose tones are like the wizard voice of Time,
Heard from the tomb of ages, points its cold
And solemn finger to the beautiful
And holy visions that have passed away,
And left no shadow of their loveliness
On the dead waste of life. That specter lifts
The coffin-lid of Hope, and Joy, and Love,
And, bending mournfully above the pale,
Sweet forms that slumber there, scatters dead flowers
O'er what has passed to nothingness.

III. AMAZEMENT, AWE AND HORROR.

Very Slow Movement, Very Low Pitch, Median Stress, Energetic Force, Aspirate-Pectoral Orotund, Effusive Form.

[From "Darkness."—*Byron.*]

               The world was void:
The populous and the powerful was a lump,
Seasonless, herbless, treeless, manless, lifeless;

A lump of death, a chaos of hard clay.
The rivers, lakes and ocean all stood still,
And nothing stirred within their silent depths.
Ships, sailorless, lay rotting on the sea,
And their masts fell down piecemeal: as they dropped
They slept on the abyss, without a surge,
The waves were dead; the tides were in their grave·
The moon, their mistress, had expired before;
The winds were withered in the stagnant air,
And the clouds perished: Darkness had no need
Of aid from them—she was the universe.

SECTION XXXV.

RAPID MOVEMENT.

Rapid movement is appropriate for the delivery of *animated, gay, joyous* thought and *impassioned* and *indignant emotion.* " It gives utterance to all *playful, humorous* and *mirthful* moods. It sometimes, on the other hand, gives its characteristic effect to *fear.*"

EXAMPLES: 1. ANIMATED.

Rapid Movement, High Pitch, Radical Stress, Energetic Force, Expulsive and Explosive Forms.

[From "Spirit of Poetry."—*Percival.*]

The world is full of poetry—the air
Is living with its spirit; and the waves
Dance to the music of its melodies,
And sparkle in its brightness. Earth is vailed
And mantled with its beauty; and the walls
That close the universe with crystal in
Are eloquent with voices that proclaim
The unseen glories of immensity,
In harmonies too perfect and too high
For aught but beings of celestial mold,
And speak to man, in one eternal hymn,
Unfading beauty and unyielding power.

II. Gay and Lively.

Rapid Movement, High Pitch, Radical Stress, Energetic Force, Pure Tone, Expulsive and Explosive Forms.

[From "Coquette Punished."—*Anon.*]

Ellen was fair, and knew it, too,
As other village beauties do,
　Whose mirrors never lie;
Secure of any swain she chose,
She smiled on half a dozen beaux,
And, reckless of a lover's woes,
She cheated these, and taunted those;
" For how could any one suppose
　A clown could take her eye ? "

III. Impassioned and Indignant Emotion.

Rapid Movement, High Pitch, Radical Stress, Impassioned Force, Orotund, Expulsive and Explosive Forms.

[From " Lochiel and the Seer."—*Campbell.*]

False wizard, avaunt! I have marshaled my clan,
Their swords are a thousand, their bosoms are one;
They are true to the last of their blood and their breath,
And like reapers descend to the harvest of death.
Then welcome be Cumberland's steed to the shock;
Let him dash his proud foam like a wave on the rock;
But woe to his kindred, and woe to his cause,
When Albin her claymore indignantly draws;
When her bonneted chieftains to victory crowd,
Clanranald the dauntless, and Moray the proud,
All plaided and plumed in their tartan array.

SECTION XXXVI

VERY RAPID MOVEMENT.

Very rapid movement is appropriate for the delivery of *ecstatic joy*, *lyric description* of *brilliant* and *exciting scenes.*

Examples: I. Ecstatic Joy.

Very Rapid Movement, Very High Pitch, Radical Stress, Impassioned Force, Pure Tone, Expulsive and Explosive Forms

[From "It Snows."—*Mrs. Hale.*]

"It snows," cries the schoolboy; "hurrah!" and his shout
  Is ringing through parlor and hall;
While swift as the wing of a swallow he's out,
  And his playmates have answered his call.
It makes the heart leap but to witness their joy;
  Proud wealth has no pleasure, I trow,
Like the rapture that throbs in the pulse of the boy
  As he gathers his treasures of snow.

II. Hurry and Commotion—Lyric Style.

Very Rapid Movement, Very High Pitch, Radical Stress, Impassioned Force, Pure Tone, Expulsive and Explosive Forms.

[From "Mazeppa."—*Byron.*]

Away, away, and on we dash!
Torrents less rapid and less rash.
Away, away, my steed and I,
  Upon the pinions of the wind,
  All human dwellings left behind:
We sped like meteors through the sky,
When with its crackling sound the night
Is checkered with the northern light:
From out the forest prance
A trampling troop—I see them come;
A thousand horse, and none to ride;
With flowing tail and flying mane,
Wide nostrils, never stretched by pain,
Mouths bloodless to the bit or rein,
And feet that iron never shod,
And flanks unscarred by spur or rod:
A thousand horse—the wild, the free,
Like waves that follow o'er the sea,
  Came thickly thundering on.
They stop, they start, they snuff the air,
Gallop a moment here and there,

> Approach, retire, wheel round and round,
> Then plunging back with sudden bound,
> They snort, they foam, neigh, swerve aside,
> And backward to the forest fly,
> By instinct, from a human eye.

Perfect command of every degree of movement is indispensable to the appropriate expression of the different forms of thought and emotion.

No defect more certainly kills the power of utterance than an improper rate of movement.

Ministers of the Gospel not unfrequently weary the patience of their audience by a slow, monotonous, tedious delivery. Lecturers and lawyers often mar the effect of a good discourse by a hurried and rapid utterance.

Schoolboy speaking is characterized by an unvarying movement.

"It is evident from the very nature of 'movement' that it must be an element of immense power in expression. The funeral march suggests to the ear its effect in music as associated with *awe*, *gloom* and *grief*, and the music of the dance reminds us of its power over the feelings of *gladness* and *exhilaration*. The grave psalm and the song of serious sentiment express, in their measured regularity, the adaptation of *gentle* and '*moderate movement*' to *tranquil* and *sedate* feeling.

"Similar effects in degree characterize the use of the voice in recitation and in reading. Appropriate elocution accommodates the movement of the voice to every mood of thought, from the *slowest*, *prolonged* and *lingering* utterance of *deep contemplation* and *profound awe* to the *swift* and *rapid* strains of *lyric rapture* and ecstasy. Every mood of mind has its appropriate 'movement,' or 'rate,' of utterance, as definitely expressed as its 'quality' of voice, its characteristic 'force,' or its peculiar 'pitch,' 'slide,' or 'wave.' Utterance, to be natural and effective, must have the genuine expression of its appropriate 'movement.' *Solemnity* cannot exist, to the ear, without *slowness*, nor *gayety* without *briskness* of utterance, *gravity* without *sedate* style, nor *animation* without a *lively* 'movement.'

"The power of 'movement,' in the elocution of a skilful reader or speaker, is indefinite, as we may observe in the difference between a schoolboy gabbling through his task, in haste to get rid of it, and a great tragedian, whose whole soul is rapt in the part of Cato uttering the soliloquy on immortality, or Hamlet musing on the great themes of duty, life and death.

"A command over the 'lively' and 'brisk movements' of the voice is not less important than the power of slow and solemn utterance. The style of reading which is most frequently introduced to enliven the evening circle at home requires of the reader the power to 'trip it as he goes' in the mood of *gay description, light satire, vivid dialogue* and *droll humor*.

"The three principal faults of 'movement,' which are exemplified in the common practice of reading, are *uniform slowness*, or, perhaps, a *drawling* style; *habitual rapidity*, which *prevents* all *deep* and *impressive* effect, and, perhaps, causes *indistinctness of enunciation;* a *uniform* '*moderate*' 'movement,' which never yields to any natural influence of emotion—so as to become appropriately expressive, and pass from *grave* to *gay*, or the reverse, by a change in the gait of the voice—but utters, automaton-like, all feelings in the same unmeaning and mechanical style, the voice marching on, with one uniform measured step, over all varieties of surface as regards the tenor of language and the subject."

SECTION XXXVII.
ACCIDENTS.

The attributes of voice having been sufficiently discussed, the attention of the student is now directed to those properties of utterance which may be appropriately termed *accidents*.

All the previously discussed elements, being essential to the delivery of any combination of words, have been denominated attributes; but the following being only employed at intervals in utterance, may or may not be exhibited in the delivery of every sentence, and hence are called accidents.

It will be observed that the accidents, except pauses, which are simply the absence of all attributes, are composed of two or more attributes; while the attributes themselves are original elements, and cannot therefore be resolved.

SECTION XXXVIII.
QUANTITY.

Quantity is the length of time occupied in the utterance of words and syllables. It might at first view appear that quantity is an attribute, since the utterance of any word or syllable occupies some time; but it must not be forgotten that form is the manner in which the sound is sent forth from the organs; that Effusive form is the sound sent forth gently from the organs, and therefore implies long quantity; that Explosive is the sound sent forth violently and abruptly, and hence necessitates short quantity. Again, Stress is an element of quantity.

Regarded as a separate element, it will be sufficient to discuss quantity under the divisions of *long* and *short*.

SECTION XXXIX.

LONG QUANTITY.

Long quantity is an indefinite prolongation in the utterance of *syllables* and *words*.

To cultivate long quantity practice the following words in the Effusive and Expulsive Forms, in Pure Tone and Orotund, with different degrees of Force, Stress and Pitch.

LONG QUANTITY—EXERCISE.

All,	arm,	ooze,	awe,
fool,	morn,	form,	poor,
always,	moon,	scorn,	star,
who,	roll,	wall,	hold,
noon,	own,	home,	blow,
roar,	ocean,	plume,	praise.

Long quantity is employed in the expression of *pathos, solemnity, sublimity, grandeur, reverence, adoration, shouting, calling, commanding,* and various other emotions and passions. The degree of prolongation will depend on the degree of emotion, the size of the audience, and other circumstances. Two or three illustrations will suffice, as quantity has been already illustrated under the attributes.

EXAMPLES: I. PATHOS.

Moderately Long Quantity, Slow Movement, Low Pitch, Median Stress Subdued Force, Pure Tone, Effusive Form.

[From "Missing."—*Anon.*]

Far away, through all the autumn
In a lonely, lonely glade,
In a dreary desolation
That the battle-storm has made,

With the rust upon his musket,
In the eve and in the morn,
In the rank gloom of the fern leaves,
Lies her noble, brave first-born.

II. Sublimity and Grandeur.

Very Long Quantity, Slow Movement, Low Pitch, Median Stress, **Energetic** *Force, Orotund, Effusive Form.*

[From "Bells."—*Poe.*]

Hear the tolling of the bells, iron bells!
What a world of solemn thought their monody compels!
In the silence of the night, how we shiver with affright
    At the melancholy menace of their tone!
For every sound that floats from the rust within their throats
    Is a groan.
And the people—ah, the people; they that dwell up in the steeple
    All alone,
And who tolling, tolling, tolling, in that muffled monotone,
Feel a glory in so rolling on the human heart a stone—
They are neither man nor woman, they are neither brute nor human,
    They are ghouls:
And their king it is who tolls; and he rolls, rolls, rolls, rolls
A pæan from the bells! and his merry bosom swells
With the pæan of the bells! and he dances and he yells;
Keeping time, time, time, in a sort of Runic rhyme,
    To the pæan of the bells, of the bells:
Keeping time, time, time, in a sort of Runic rhyme,
    To the tolling of the bells,
Of the bells, bells, bells, bells, bells, bells, bells—
To the moaning and the groaning of the bells.

III. Shouting and Calling.

Very Long Quantity, Slow Movement, High Pitch, Thorough Stress. Impassioned Force, Orotund, Effusive Form.

[From Satan's Call to his Legions.—*Milton.*]

    Princes! Potentates!
Warriors! The flower of heaven! once yours, now lost,
If such astonishment as this can seize eternal spirits.
Awake, arise, or be forever fallen!

SECTION XL.
SHORT QUANTITY.

Short quantity is the instantaneous utterance of *syllables* and *words*.

To obtain control of this element of delivery practice the following words in the Explosive Form, with Pure Tone and Orotund, and various degrees of Force, Stress and Pitch.

SHORT QUANTITY—EXERCISE.

Back,	beck,	neck,	duck,
hack,	pick,	sick,	tuck,
rap,	dip,	cup,	sup,
bat,	pit,	lip,	socket,
attack,	mutter,	tatter,	batter.

Short quantity is employed in the expression of *joy, gladness, excited command, anger, scorn, contempt, revenge, hate,* and other malignant passions.

EXAMPLES: I. ANGER AND THREATENING.

Short Quantity, Rapid Movement, High Pitch, Radical and Final Stress, Impassioned Force, Aspirate-Pectoral Orotund, Explosive Form.

[From Death to Satan.—*Milton.*]

Back to thy punishment,
False fugitive! and to thy speed add wings;
Lest with a whip of scorpions I pursue
Thy lingering, or, with one stroke of this dart,
Strange horror seize thee, and pangs unfelt before.

II. EXCITED COMMAND.

Short Quantity, Rapid Movement, High Pitch, Final Stress, Impassioned Force, Pure Tone, Explosive Form.

[From "Life-Boat."—*Anon.*]

Quick! man the life-boat! See yon bark,
That drives before the blast!
There's a rock ahead, the fog is dark,
And the storm comes thick and fast.

> Can human power, in such an hour,
> Avert the doom that's o'er her?
> Her mainmast's gone, but she still drives on
> To the fatal reef before her.
> The life-boat! Man the life-boat!

"The power and beauty of vocal 'expression' are necessarily dependent, to a great extent, on the command which a reader or speaker possesses over the element of 'quantity.' Poetry and eloquence derive their audible character from this source more than from any other. The music of verse is sacrificed unless the nicest regard be paid to 'quantity,' as the basis of rhythm and of meter, and, with the exception of the most exquisite strains of well-executed music, the ear receives no pleasure comparable to that arising from poetic feeling, embodied in the genuine melody of the heart, as it gushes from the expressive voice which has the power of

> "'Untwisting all the chains that tie
> The hidden soul of harmony.'

"Milton, in his Paradise Lost, affords innumerable examples of the majestic grandeur of long 'quantities' in epic verse, and without the just observance of these, the reading of the noblest passages in that poem becomes flat and dry. The same is true, still more emphatically, of the magnificent language of the poetic passages of Scripture, in those strains of triumph and of adoration which abound in the Book of Psalms and in the prophets.

"The necessity, on the other hand, of obeying the law of 'immutable quantity,' even in the grandest and most emphatic expression, is an imperative rule of elocution. A false, bombastic swell of voice never sounds so ridiculous as when the injudicious and unskillful reader or speaker attempts to interfere with the conditions of speech, and to prolong, under a false excitement of utterance, those sounds which nature has irrevocably determined short. We have this fault exemplified in the compound of bawling, drawling and redoubled 'wave' which some reciters contrive to crowd into the small space of the syllable *vic* in the conclusion of Moloch's war-speech,

"'Which if not victory is yet revenge.'

"The fierce intensity of emotion, in the true utterance of this syllable, brings it on the ear with an instantaneous *ictus* and tingling effect, resembling that of the lash of a whip applied to the organ. A similar case occurs in Shylock's fiendish half-shriek on the word *hip* in his exclamation referring to Antonio:

"'If I do catch him once upon the *hip*
I will feed fat the ancient grudge I bear him!'

"The sprawling, expanded utterance, which the style of rant preposterously endeavors to indulge on this word, causes the voice, as it were, to fall in pieces in the attempt, and to betray the falsity of the style which it affects.

"But it is in the chaste yet generous effect of the judicious prolongation and indulgence of '*mutable* quantities' that the skill of the elocutionist, and the power and truth of expression, are peculiarly felt. It is in these that the watchful analyst can trace at once the full soul and the swelling heart, which would impel the speaker to prolong indefinitely the tones of passion, to give 'ample scope' and verge enough to overflowing feeling, but no less surely the manly force of judgment, and the disciplined good taste, which forbid any display of mere sound in the utterance of earnest emotion."

SECTION XLI.
INFLECTIONS.

Inflections are changes in pitch through the concrete movement either upward or downward. These vary in degree according to the sentiment uttered.

The component elements of inflections are pitch and movement.

These will be discussed under the heads of rising and falling.

SECTION XLII.
RISING INFLECTION.

The **rising inflection** is an upward movement of the voice through the concrete change of pitch. This inflection may be made in various degrees, passing through different notes of the musical scale.

If a person, in the utterance of a sentence, is interrupted, there will be heard a slight rising slide running through the interval of the second of the musical scale, and known as a Rising Inflection of the Second, indicating incompleteness. A slight degree of surprise expressed in the utterance of the exclamation *Ah!* exhibits a Rising Inflection of the Third; a stronger expression of the same feeling will exhibit a Rising Inflection of the Fifth; and a very strong utterance of the emotion will illustrate a Rising Inflection of the Octave. These inflections do not have the exactness of the musical scale.

To cultivate the Rising Inflection practice the following sentences in all the different degrees described above.

RISING INFLECTION—EXERCISE.

1. Is there no retreat?
2. Did you say it was I?

3. Did you, sir, throw up a black crow?
4. Heard ye those loud contending waves?
5. Dare you insult me?
6. Will you pleasure me?
7. Shall I know your answer?

The Rising Inflection of the Second is used chiefly to suspend the sense in unimpassioned discourse.

EXAMPLES.

1. In the ancient republics of Greece and Rome,—
2. There are men who get one idea,—
3. We cannot honor our country,—
4. There is no one quality,—

The Rising Inflections of the Third and Fifth are used,

First, To ask a definite question, or one that can be answered by yes or no.

Second, To express different degrees of surprise, astonishment, or any ardent feeling in asking a question.

Third, To express the lively, joyous, playful emotions.

Fourth, To express the first member of words and phrases in pairs.

Fifth, To petition, beg, fawn, and flatter.

The above are by no means all the cases in which the rising inflections of the third and fifth are employed.

The degree of inflection can only be determined by the sentiment and emotion.

EXAMPLES: I. DEFINITE QUESTION.
Rising Inflection of Third and Fifth.

1. Is not forgiveness honorable to any man?
2. Is this the part of wise men?

3. Should I not have devoted myself entirely to the service of my country?

4. Can you think me capable of so vile a deed?

5. Are you aware of the discreditable reports in circulation about you?

6. What! looked he frowningly?

II. Astonishment, Surprise, Irony.
Rising Inflection, Third and Fifth.

1. Must I budge?
2. Must I crouch under your testy humor?
3. Must I observe you?
4. I an itching palm?
5. Cry aloud, for he is a god.
6. No doubt ye are the people, and wisdom will die with you.

III. Joyous, Lively Emotions.
Rising Inflection, Third and Fifth.

'Twas the night before Christmas, when all through the house
Not a creature was stirring, not even a mouse,
And mamma in her kerchief, and I in my cap,
Had just settled our brains for a long winter's nap,
When out on the lawn there rose such a clatter—
I sprang from the bed to see what was the matter.

IV. First Member of Pairs.
Rising Inflection, Third and Fifth.

For I am persuaded that neither death nor life, nor angels, nor principalities, nor powers, nor things present, nor things to come, nor height, nor depth, nor any other creature, shall be able to separate us from the love of God, which is in Christ Jesus our Lord.

V. Fawning, Flattering, Begging.
Rising Inflection, Third and Fifth.

1. Nay, I beseech you, sir, be not out with me.
2. I pray thee remember I have done thee worthy service; told

thee no lies, made no mistakings, served without grudge or grumblings.

2. Alas! what need you be so boisterous rough;
I will not struggle, I will stand stone still.
For Heaven's sake, Hubert, let me not be bound!
Nay, hear me, Hubert! drive these men away
And I will sit as quiet as a lamb;
I will not stir, nor wince, nor speak a word,
Nor look upon the irons angrily.

The Rising Inflection of the Octave is employed to express *intense surprise, wonder* and *astonishment.*

EXAMPLES—WONDER, SURPRISE, ASTONISHMENT.

Rising Inflection of Octave.

1. . . . Seems, madam?
Nay, it is; I know not seems.
2. Saw who?
My lord, the king, your father.
The king? My father?
3. Ecstasy.
4. Hath a dog money?

SECTION XLIII.

FALLING INFLECTION.

The **falling inflection** is a downward movement of the voice through the concrete change of pitch.

The falling, like the rising inflection, admits of various degrees.

If a person in reply to a question utters the word no, expressing a mild dissent, the voice will pass from the middle pitch downward, exhibiting a falling inflection of a second or third; when uttered so as to express stronger dissent it will commence on a higher pitch, and end in a downward slide of a fifth; and when uttered in a very strong or passionate dissent, the downward slide will run through a whole octave.

To acquire control of the falling inflection practice each of the following sentences in all the above described degrees.

EXERCISES.

1. By virtue we secure happiness.
2. All high truth is the union of two contradictories.
3. Crime and punishment grow out of one stem.
4. The mind, that does not converse with itself, is an idle wanderer.
5. Lowliness is the base of every virtue.
6. Trust men and they will be true to you.
7. I tell you, sir, I will not do it.
8. Go preach to the coward.

The Falling Inflection is used,

First, To express completion of thought.

Second, To express in different degrees positiveness, firmness, confidence, authority, declaration, determination, command, defiance, indignation, etc.

Third, To answer questions.

Fourth, To ask indefinite questions, or those beginning with relative pronouns or adverbs, and not admitting of an answer by yes or no.

Fifth, To give emphasis to words which otherwise would have the rising inflection.

EXAMPLES: I. COMPLETION OF THOUGHT.

Falling Inflection, Second and Third.

1. A wise son maketh a glad father, but a foolish son is the heaviness of his mother.
2. I come not here to talk.

3. It is natural for man to indulge in the illusions of hope.

4. It is my living sentiment.

5 Shakspeare was the greatest tragic writer.

6. Charity suffereth long, and is kind.

II. Positiveness, Confidence, Determination, etc.

Falling Inflection, Third, Fifth, and Octave.

1 The war must go on.

2. On such occasions I will place myself on the extreme boundary of my right, and bid defiance to the arm that would push me from it.

3. We shall not fail.

4. I am commissioned of heaven to perform this work.

5. It is my living sentiment, and, by the blessing of God, it shall be my dying sentiment, independence now and independence forever.

6. I cannot, my lords; I will not join in misfortune and disgrace.

7. Forward the Light Brigade.

8. Thy threats, thy mercies, I defy!
And give thee in thy teeth the lie!

III. Answer to Questions.

Falling Inflection, Third, Fifth, and Octave.

1. What would content you? Talent? No. Enterprise? No. Courage? No. Virtue? No. The men whom you would select should possess, not one, but all of these.

2. Are they Hebrews? So am I. Are they Israelites? So am I. Are they the seed of Abraham? So am I. Are they ministers of Christ? I am more.

3. Can honor set a leg? No. Or an arm? No. Or take away the grief of a wound? No. Honor hath no skill in surgery, then? No. What is honor? A word. What is that word honor? All. Who hath it? He that died on Wednesday. Doth he feel it? No. Doth he hear it? No. Is it insensible, then? Yes, to the dead.

But will it not live with the living? No. Why? Detraction will not suffer it.

4. With whom may Napoleon be compared? With Diogenes in acuteness of intellect, with Cæsar in ambition, and with Alexander in arms.

Was it ambition that induced Regulus to return to Carthage? No, but love of country, and respect for truth.

Wherein did Chatham surpass Burke? Not in argument, nor in the sublimity of his thoughts, nor yet in the richness and splendor of his diction, but in personal weight of character, and in the exterior graces and expressive power of the orator.

IV. Indefinite Questions.

Falling Inflection, Third, Fifth, and Octave.

1. Why reason ye these things in your hearts? ——
2. Who is here so base that he would be a bondman?
3. Why doth this man thus speak blasphemies?
4. What shall we do to inherit eternal life?
5. From whence hath this man these things?
6. Who hath warned you to flee from the wrath to come?
7. To what shall I liken the men of this generation
8. Can no support be offered? Can no encouragement be given?
9. But where is the iron-bound prisoner? Where?
   Ah! what is that flame which now bursts on his eye?

10. Who covered the earth with such a pleasing variety of fruits and flowers? Who gave them their delightful fragrance, and painted them with such exquisite colors? Who causeth the same water to whiten in the lily and blush in the rose? Do not these things prove the existence of a power infinitely superior to that of any finite being?

V. Emphatic Words.

Falling Inflection, Fifth and Octave.

1. If we fail it can be no worse with us.

2. I'd rather be a dog, and bay the moon, than such a Roman

3. I dare accusation.   I defy the honorable gentleman.

4. All this?   Ay, and more.

No element of utterance is more important in giving significance to speech than inflection.

It constitutes that part of modulation which renders expression addressed to the understanding intelligible.

In the reading and recitation of verse it is the proper management of the inflections that prevent monotony on the one hand, and chanting on the other.

"So important is a just mixture of inflections that the moment they are neglected our pronunciation becomes forceless and monotonous. If the sense of a sentence require the voice to adopt the rising inflection on any particular word, either in the middle or at the end of the phrase, variety and harmony demand the falling inflection on one of the preceding words; and, on the other hand, if emphasis, harmony, or a completion of sense, require the falling inflection on any word, the word immediately preceding almost always demands the rising inflection, so that these inflections of voice are in an order nearly alternate."

SECTION XLIV.
CIRCUMFLEX.

The **circumflex** is a combination of the two inflections on the same syllable or word. Sometimes the upward movement comes first, and sometimes the downward. Often more than two inflections are combined on the same word, so that a great variety of waves are possible in speech. Dr. Rush has actually enumerated one hundred and eighty varieties. An extended discussion of these would be of little practical advantage to the general student.

A few illustrations must suffice.

The Circumflex is employed chiefly in the expression of *irony, sarcasm, sneer, drollery,* etc.

Examples.

1. The atrocious crime of being a young man, which, with so much spirit and decency the gentleman has charged upon me, I shall neither attempt to palliate nor deny.

2. A second Daniel, a *Daniel,* Jew!
   Now, infidel, I have thee on the hip.
   A Daniel, still I say; a second Daniel!
   I thank thee, Jew, for teaching me that word.

3. Hath a dog money? Is it possible
   A cur can lend three thousand ducats?

4. Yet this is Rome, and we are Romans.

5. Yet Brutus says he was ambitious;
   And Brutus is an honorable man.

6. Has the gentleman done? Has he completely done?

The Circumflex is one of the most impressive elements of expression in the whole range of vocal effect.

Mockery, raillery, irony, and sarcasm cannot be given without it.

An intelligent and discriminating use of this element is indispensable, however, to its right effect.

Adopted too frequently and expressed too pointedly, it offends the ear.

SECTION XLV.

CADENCE.

Cadence is that dropping of the voice at the close of the sentence, which indicates that the sense is complete.

This is done by dropping the voice on the last three

syllables, either in the discrete or concrete movement, at least three full tones lower than that which prevailed in the body of the sentence.

The note to which the cadence falls, and the space through which it descends, will depend on the emotion of the sentiment.

In strong emotion the cadence is both abrupt and low, in gentle emotion it is gradual and moderate, while on unemotional thought it is slight.

No element of utterance more demands the watchful attention of the living teacher, or is more difficult for the pupil to acquire from books, than that of cadence.

Practice the following sentences with different degrees of cadence.

Examples.

1. I love it, I love it, and cannot tear
My soul from my mother's old arm-chair!

2. When the evening comes with its beautiful smile,
And our eyes are closing to slumber awhile,
May that "Greenwood" of soul be in sight!

3. The sorrow for the dead is the only sorrow from which we refuse to be divorced.

4. We'll all meet again in the morning.

5. In teaching me the way to live,
It taught me how to die.

6. He sinks into thy depths with bubbling groan,
Without a grave, unknelled, uncoffined, and unknown.

7. Be armed with courage against thyself, against thy passions, and against flatterers.

8. The true American patriot is ever a worshiper.

Perfect command of Cadence is a rare accomplishment. It is one of the distinguishing marks of excellence in the cultivated reader.

Pauses.

Pauses are supensions of the voice between words and sentences. No definite rules can be given to guide the reader or speaker in the use of pauses. Their length and frequency can be determined only by the sentiment.

Unimpassioned didactic thought demands but moderate pauses; gay, lively and joyous thought very short pauses; solemnity, sublimity, grandeur and reverence, long pauses; while impassioned thought may demand long or short pauses.

A pause should always be made before and after an emphatic word.

It will be hardly necessary to say that the pauses referred to are not indicated by the marks of punctuation. These may or may not harmonize with the rhetorical pauses.

Examples: I. Didactic Thought.

Moderate Pauses.

[From "Expression."—*Winthrop*.]

A woman's voice can tell a long history of sorrow in a single word. This wonderful instrument, our voice, alters its timbre with every note it yields, as the face changes with every look, until at last the dominant emotion is master, and gives quality to tone and character to expression. . . .

Every look, tone, gesture of a man is a symbol of his complete nature. If we apply the microscope severely enough we can discern the fine organism by which the soul sends itself out in every act of the being. And the more perfectly developed the creature the more significant, and yet the more mysterious, is every habit, and every motion mightier than habit, of body and soul.

II. Solemnity.

Long Pauses.

[From "Hymn to Intellectual Beauty."—*Shelley*.]

The day becomes more solemn and serene
    When noon is past; there is a harmony
    In autumn, and a luster in its sky,
Which through the summer is not heard nor seen,
As if it could not be, as if it had not been!
    Thus let thy power, which like the truth
    Of nature on my passive youth
Descended, to my onward life supply
    Its calm, to one who worships thee,
    And every form containing thee,
    Whom, Spirit, fair, thy spells did bind
To fear himself, and love all human kind.

III. Solemnity and Sublimity.

Very Long Pauses.

[From "Hamlet's Soliloquy."—*Shakspeare*.]

To be, or not to be, that is the question:
Whether 'tis nobler in the mind to suffer
The slings and arrows of outrageous fortune;
Or to take arms against a sea of troubles,
And, by opposing, end them? To die; to sleep;
No more: and, by a sleep, to say we end
The heart-ache, and the thousand natural shocks
That flesh is heir to—'tis a consummation
Devoutly to be wished. To die; to sleep;
To sleep! perchance to dream; ay, there's the rub;
For in that sleep of death what dreams may come,
When we have shuffled off this mortal coil,
Must give us pause: There's the respect,
That makes calamity of so long life:
For who would bear the whips and scorns of time,
The oppressor's wrong, the proud man's contumely,
The pangs of despised love, the law's delay,
The insolence of office, and the spurns
That patient merit of the unworthy takes,
When he himself might his quietus make

With a bare bodkin? Who would fardels bear
To grunt and sweat under a weary life;
But that the dread of something after death,
The undiscovered country, from whose bourn
No traveler returns—puzzles the will;
And makes us rather bear those ills we have,
Than fly to others that we know not of?
Thus conscience does make cowards of us all;
And thus the native hue of resolution
Is sicklied o'er with the pale cast of thought;
And enterprises of great pith and moment,
With this regard, their currents turn awry,
And lose the name of action.

IV. Animated.

Short Pauses.

[From "L'Allegro."—*Milton.*]

Straight mine eye hath caught new pleasures,
Whilst the landscape round it measures;
Russet lawns, and fallows gray,
Where the nibbling flocks do stray;
Mountains on whose barren breast
The laboring clouds do often rest:
Meadows trim with daisies pied:
Shallow brooks, and rivers wide:
Towers and battlements it sees
Bosom'd high in tufted trees,
Where perhaps some beauty lies,
The Cynosure of neighboring eyes.

V. Lively, Animated Description.

Very Short Pauses.

[From "How they Brought the Good News from Ghent to Aix."—*Browning.*]

I sprang to the stirrup, and Joris, and he:
I galloped, Dirck galloped, we galloped all three;
"God-speed!" cried the watch as the gate-bolts undrew;
"Speed!" echoed the wall to us galloping through;
Behind shut the postern, the light sank to rest,
And into the midnight we galloped abreast.

The careful observance of the "rhetorical" pause is one of the chief means of distinctness in the expression of thought. In *narration* and *description*, and in *plain didactic style*, it is equally important that the successive sounds of the voice should be relieved from each other in portions best adapted to present the component parts of the whole in a clear, distinct, impressive manner, according to their comparative length and importance. The thought or sentiment which is thus communicated falls on the ear with a definite and satisfactory succession of sounds, which the mind easily receives and appreciates. The parts being thus exactly given, each takes its own due weight, and at the same time enhances the effect of the whole. The result is that the communication is fully understood and makes its just impression.

Young readers in particular are often deficient in this most striking and impressive of all the effects of appropriate reading and recitation. It becomes, therefore, a matter of great moment in practice to cultivate the habit of watching the effect of full and long pauses introduced at appropriate places. Without these the most solemn passages of Scripture, and the poetry of Milton and of Young, produce no effect, comparatively, on the mind; while reading, aided by their "expressive silence," seems to be inspired with an unlimited power over the sympathies of the soul.

SECTION XLVII.
EMPHASIS.

Emphasis is a peculiar utterance given to words and phrases, by which they are rendered specially significant.

This may be given by an increase of Force or Stress, by a change in Quality, Form, Pitch, or Movement, or by a change in the combination of two or more of these attributes.

Variety and power of emphasis require control of all the previously discussed elements of utterance. The kind and degree of emphasis which is to be given can only be determined by the sentiment, and the occasion or circumstances of the delivery. Where the whole passage is of an earnest or impassioned character the emphatic words require greater prominence.

The highly-wrought emphasis of impassioned oratory would be wholly out of place in a parlor reading of the same speech, and in large audiences a much stronger emphasis is in place than in small ones.

"Emphasis is in speech what coloring is in painting. It admits of all possible degrees, and must, to indicate a particular degree of distinction, be more or less intense according to the ground word or current melody of the discourse."

An attentive analysis of Emphasis will discover the fact that in the utterance of any emphatic word or phrase no one mode of emphasis alone prevails, but that a greater or less combination of modes always exists. In Emphasis of Force, though Force may largely predominate as an element of Emphasis, still it will generally be combined with Stress and Pitch, and Emphasis of Pitch will be combined with Force and Stress.

The same will be equally true of all other modes. The following illustrations indicate the predominant mode of emphasis in each.

SECTION XLVIII.
EMPHASIS OF FORCE.

Emphasis of force is the utterance of certain words or phrases with an increase or decrease of the prevailing force. This style of emphasis is usually employed in unimpassioned discourse to direct special attention to certain words and phrases.

EXAMPLES.

1. The repose of the soul is *exercise*, not rest.
2. Study to show thyself a *man*.
3. I have been accused of *ambition* in presenting this measure.
4. I come not here *to talk*.
5. *Ignorance* is the mother of error.
6. *Learning* is wealth to the poor, and an *ornament* to the rich.

SECTION XLIX.
EMPHASIS OF STRESS.

Emphasis of stress is either the prevailing stress of the utterance intensified, or an entire change of Stress on certain words and phrases. "This is the most obvious and easy way of emphasizing, and, therefore, the most common, even where it is altogether inappropriate. Hence it is necessary to guard against the too frequent use of it." When judiciously employed, this form of emphasis is very significant.

EXAMPLES—RADICAL STRESS.

1. *Back* to thy punishment, false fugitive!
2. Be ready, gods, with all your thunderbolts!
   Dash him to pieces!
3. "*Tried* and *convicted traitor!*" Who says this!
4. *Banished* from Rome! what's banished but set *free*
   From daily contact of the things I loathe?

MEDIAN STRESS.

1. 'Tis heaven itself that points out an hereafter,
   And intimates eternity to man.
   Eternity! thou pleasing, dreadful thought!

2. What a piece of work is *man!*
How *noble* in reason! how *infinite* in faculties!
In *form* and *moving* how express and admirable!
In *action* how like an *angel!* In *apprehension* how like a god!

3. *O change! O wondrous change!*
Burst are the prison bars.

Final Stress.

1. Ye gods, it doth amaze me!
A man of such a *feeble* temper should
So get the start of the *majestic* world,
And bear the palm *alone*.

2. Thou *slave!* thou *wretch!* thou *coward!*

3. Let the consequences be what they will
I am *determined* to proceed.

Compound Stress.

1 *Arm! arm!* ye heavens, against these perjured kings!

2. A *widow* cries! be husband to me, heavens!

3. *Ecstasy!* My pulse as yours doth temperately keep time.

Thorough Stress.

1. *Revenge* is stamped upon my spear,
And *blood's* my battle cry.

2. I ask, Why not "traitor" unqualified by an epithet? I will tell him. It was because he *durst* not. It was the act of a *coward*, who raises his arm to strike, but has not courage to give the blow.

3. If ye are *beasts*, then stand here like fat oxen waiting for the butcher's knife; if ye are *men*, follow me.

4. *O Rome! Rome!* thou hast been a tender nurse to me

SECTION L.

EMPHASIS OF QUALITY.

Emphasis of quality is a change, on certain words and phrases, from the prevailing quality to that of some other.

This change is usually from a Pure Tone or Orotund to Aspirate, Pectoral, or Guttural. This is a very impressive form of emphasis.

EXAMPLES—ASPIRATE.

1. And then I cried for *vengeance*.

2. Give me liberty or give me *death*.

3. If I were an American, as I am an Englishman, while a foreign troop remained upon my country's shores I would never lay down my arms. *Never! never! never!*

4. A lowly knee to earth he bent; his father's hand he took. *What was there in its touch that all his fiery spirit shook?*

5. We are *slaves*.

PECTORAL QUALITY.

1. O that the slave had *forty thousand* lives!
My great revenge had stomach for them all.

2.   You souls of *geese*,
That bear the *shapes* of men, how have you run
From slaves that *apes* would beat!—*Pluto* and *hell!*
All hurt *behind; backs red*, and *faces pale*
With *flight* and *agued fear!* Mend, and *charge home.*
Or, by the *fires of heaven*, I'll leave the *foe*
And make my wars on *you: look to't. Come on.*

GUTTURAL QUALITY.

1. Whence and what art thou, *execrable* shape!

2. Thou stand'st at length before me undisguised,
Of all earth's groveling crew the most accursed.

Thou *worm!* thou *viper!* to thy native earth
Return! Away! Thou art too base for man
To tread upon. Thou *scum!* thou *reptile!*

SECTION LI.

EMPHASIS OF PITCH.

Emphasis of pitch is a sudden raising or lowering of pitch on certain words and phrases, either through the discrete or concrete movement.

Discrete Emphasis of Pitch is expressed by any variation on the emphatic word or phrase from the prevailing pitch.

EXAMPLES—DISCRETE MOVEMENT.

Very High Pitch.

1. Simpson came up with his face pale as ashes, and said, "Captain, the ship is on fire."
Then "*Fire! fire! fire!*" on shipboard.

2. *Hurrah, hurrah,* for Sheridan!
Hurrah, hurrah, for horse and man!

3. "*Charge!*" Trump and drum awoke,
Onward the bondmen broke;
Bayonet and saber-stroke
Vainly opposed their rush.

Very Low Pitch.

[From "The Oath."—*T. B. Read.*]

Ye freemen, how long will ye stifle
 The vengeance that justice inspires?
With treason how long will ye trifle
 And shame the proud name of your sires?
Out, out with the sword and the rifle
 In defense of your homes and your fires.

> The flag of the old Revolution
>   Swear firmly to serve and uphold,
> That no treasonous breath of pollution
>   Shall tarnish one star of its fold.
>   *Swear!*
> And hark, the deep voices replying,
> From the graves where your fathers are lying,
>   " *Swear, O swear!* "

The Concrete Emphasis of Pitch is expressed by the voice sliding either up or down on the emphatic word or phrase.

EXAMPLES—CONCRETE MOVEMENT.
Emphasis of the Rising Third.

This is the emphasis of simple interrogation, and is also employed to express the lower shades of emphatic distinction, as they occur in the diatonic melody.

1. Gavest thou the goodly wings to the *peacocks?* or wings and feathers unto the *ostrich?*
2. I love not *man* the less, but nature more, From these our interviews.
3. Yet *Brutus* says he was ambitious.

Emphasis of the Rising Fifth.

The examples which illustrate the two preceding forms may be used for illustration here by adding to the energy with which they are pronounced. The intervals of the fifth are of more rare occurrence than the third. The following additional examples must suffice.

Concrete.

1. Wouldst *thou* be *king?*
2. What though the field be lost? all is not *lost.*

NOTE.—When the emphatic rise, as in this last example, occurs on the last syllable or word of a declarative sentence, it must of course annul the cadence; so also if it occurs near the close.

Emphasis of the Rising Octave.

This is the most earnest expression of interrogative intonation, and is never used in grave discourse. Its appropriate expression is that of sneer or raillery. The rise is concrete when it occurs on long syllables; when on short or immutable syllables, it is formed by a change of radical pitch.

Concrete.

1.   Moneys is your suit.
What should I say to you? Should I not say,
Hath a *dog* money? Is it possible
A *cur* can lend three thousand ducats?

2. A king's son? *You* Prince of Wales?

Emphasis of Downward Third.

1. Does beauteous Tamar view, in this clear fount,
Herself, or *heaven?*

2. You are the *queen*, your husband's brother's wife.

Examples of Downward Fifth.

1. Seems, madam! nay, it *is*; I know not seems.

2. Before the sun, before the *heavens*, thou wert.

Example of Downward Octave.

Art thou that traitor *angel?* art thou *he*
Who first broke peace in heaven, and faith till then
Unbroken? and in proud rebellious arms,
Drew after him the third part of heaven's sons,
Conjured against the Highest? For which both *thou*
And they, outcast from God, are here condemned
To waste eternal days in *woe* and *pain*.
And reckonest thou thyself with spirits of heaven,
Hell-doomed, and breath'st defiance here, and scorn,
Where I reign King? and, to enrage thee more,
Thy King and *Lord*.

The Waves of the Voice are also often employed give emphasis, particularly in the expression of iro and scorn.

Examples—Waves.

1. O *upright judge!* Mark, Jew! *a learned judge!*

2. The *atrocious crime* of being a young man.

3. *O!* but he *paused upon* the brink!

SECTION LII.

EMPHASIS OF MOVEMENT.

Emphasis of movement is a sudden change, on certain words and phrases, from the prevailing movement.

Examples.

Slow Movement.

1. Not among the prisoners—*Missing!*
   That was *all* the message said.

2. "Cyrus Drew!"—*then a silence fell—*
   This time no answer followed the call.

Rapid Movement.

3. His person partook the character of his mind: *if the one never yielded in the cabinet, the other never bent in the field.* Nature had no obstacles that he did not surmount, space no opposition that he did not spurn; *and whether amid Alpine rocks, Arabian sands, or polar snows,* he seemed proof against peril, and empowered with ubiquity! The whole continent of Europe trembled at beholding the audacity of his designs and the miracle of their execution.

Great care will be required on the part of the public speaker to guard against too frequent emphasis. When there are many words in a passage strongly significant of emotion or passion, a temptation arises to load the delivery with emphasis.

It must be borne in mind that too frequent emphasis destroys the effect of emphasis, which consists essentially in distinguishing the most significant words and phrases from the others with which they stand immediately connected. Again, great care will be required to guard against the restriction of the voice to but one or two of the many modes of emphasis, and the excessive use of the particular mode employed, so that coloring becomes caricaturing.

"Many readers and speakers seem to have no practical notion of any other mode of emphasizing a word, but by throwing upon it a decided stress of voice, and their delivery is characterized by a perpetual occurrence of *ictus* upon *ictus*, stroke upon stroke, of heavy enunciation that soon wearies the ear, and at the same time fails of its designed effect. There being no distinction, there is, so far, no emphasis. A perfect command should be acquired over all the varieties of emphatic expression, so that without effort, as it were, spontaneously, the delivery shall proceed, colored, as the ever-varying shades of thought and feeling shall require, with correspondingly various modifications of the utterance.

"The other fault, of exaggerating every instance of emphatic expression, is not less common. Many seem to have no notion of degrees or shades of coloring in emphasis. To emphasize is ever to raise to a certain fixed degree of prominence in the delivery. They have no conception how a skillful painter brings out a feature by a single delicate stroke of his pencil, and when they wish to emphasize at all, they daub and caricature. Where a skillful speaker or reader will start the tear of his hearer by a single semitone or a tremor upon a single word, they rave and rant with violent labor of voice, and only stun or disgust at last instead of exciting an emotion. Trying to shade a parenthetical expression, such readers can only reduce the volume of voice to almost whispering notes, and lower the pitch a third or a fifth, to spring back again with a violent skip and an explosion upon the leading part of the expression, painfully jerking and rending the nerves of hearing, while yet they utterly fail of their object to exhibit the just relations of the thought."

SECTION LIII.
CLIMAX.

Climax is an utterance gradually increasing in intensity, and changing in pitch and movement. No definite rules can be given as to the degree of intensity or the changes in pitch and movement. Only the sentiment can determine this. Generally the changes will be from a middle or low to a high pitch, and from a moderate or slow to a rapid movement; yet this rule will often be reversed. Sometimes the Climax will be heightened by a change in the quality of voice, as in the eleventh example, in which each repetition of the word never demands a more aspirate quality. The Climax is employed in the delivery of those sentences only which rise as it were step by step in importance, dignity and force.

EXAMPLES.
Climax.

1. It is a religion by which to live, a religion by which to die; a religion that cheers in darkness, relieves in perplexity, and guides the inquirer to that blessed land "where the wicked cease from troubling, and the weary are at rest."

2. For I am persuaded, that neither death, nor life, nor angels, nor principalities, nor powers, nor things present, nor things to come, nor height, nor depth, nor any other creature, shall be able to separate us from the love of God, which is in Christ Jesus.

3. Add to your faith, virtue; and to virtue, knowledge; and to knowledge, temperance; and to temperance, patience; and to patience, godliness; and to godliness, brotherly kindness; and to brotherly kindness, charity.

4. Was that country a desert? No; it was rich and fertile, cultivated and populous. Friendship was its inhabitant; love was its inhabitant: liberty was its inhabitant; all bounded by the stream of the Rubicon.

5. Of all God made upright, and in their nostrils breathed a living soul, most prone, most earthy, most debased; of all that sell eternity for time, none bargain on so easy terms with death.

6. What a piece of work is man! How noble in reason! How infinite in faculties! In form and moving, how express and admirable! In action, how like an angel! In apprehension, how like a god!

7. I tell you, though you, though the whole world, though an angel from heaven, were to declare the truth of it, I would not believe it.

8. There is Boston, and Concord, and Lexington, and Bunker Hill, and there they will remain forever.

9. But every-where, spread all over in characters of living light, blazing on all its ample folds, as they float over the sea and over the land, and in every wind under the whole heaven, that other sentiment, dear to every American heart—Liberty and Union, now and forever, one and inseparable.

10. The battle, sir, is not to the strong alone; it is to the vigilant, the active, the brave.

11. If I were an American, as I am an Englishman, while a foreign troop remained in my country I never would lay down my arms; no, never, never, never.

12. I scorn to count what feelings, withered hopes, strong provocations, bitter, burning wrongs, I have within my heart's hot cells shut up to leave you in your lazy dignities.

13. Days, months, years, and ages shall circle away,
    And still the vast waters above thee shall roll;
  Earth loses thy pattern forever and ay;
    O sailor boy, sailor boy, peace to thy soul!

14.　　　　By your gracious patience
I will a round, unvarnished tale deliver
Of my whole course of love; what drugs, what charms,
What conjuration, and what mighty magic—
For such proceedings I am charged withal—
I won his daughter with.

15. The cloud-capt towers, the gorgeous palaces,
The solemn temples, the great globe itself,
Yea, all that it inherit, shall dissolve,
And, like the baseless fabric of a vision,
Leave not a rack behind.

16. When this fiery mass
　　Of living valor, rolling on the foe
And burning with high hope, shall molder cold and low

17. Let but the commons hear this testament,
(Which, pardon me, I do not mean to read,)
And they would go and kiss dead Cæsar's wounds,
And dip their napkins in his sacred blood—
Yea, beg a hair of him, for memory,
And, dying, mention it within their wills,
Bequeathing it as a rich legacy
Unto their issue.

18. Not such as swept along
By the full tide of power, the conqueror led
To crimson glory and undying fame.

19. Tell me I hate the bowl?
　　Hate is a feeble word:
I loathe, abhor; my very soul
　　With strong disgust is stirred
Whene'er I see, or hear, or tell
Of the dark beverage of hell.

20. Clarence has come! false, fleeting, perjured Clarence!

21. And Douglas, more, I tell thee here;
　　Here, in thy pitch of pride;
Here, in thy hold, thy vassals near:
　　I tell thee thou'rt defied.

SECTION LIV.

GROUPING.

Grouping is that nice modulation and adaptation of the voice to the sentiment expressed which renders the utterance not only more impressive, but more pleasing to the ear. It is the *sine qua non* of excellence in reading and speaking.

Without it success cannot be attained.

The public speaker may have perfect command of all other elements of utterance, yet if he fails in grouping he fails in that element which more than all others commands the attention of an audience.

Grouping is a term borrowed from painting, and is to reading and speaking what the adjustment of the figures is to the picture—that which gives beauty and expression to the whole.

As he is not regarded as the most skillful artist who can paint most perfectly each separate figure, but he who by his superior judgment and taste groups his figures into one harmonious picture; so he is not the best reader or speaker who possesses the most cultivated voice, or can most perfectly illustrate each separate element, but he who by his cultivated taste and judgment most pleasantly modulates his voice, and best adapts it to the sentiment he expresses.

To change the figure, command of Form, Force, Quality, Stress, Pitch, Movement, etc., are the flowers out of which the speaker is to weave the bouquet of delivery. It is upon this part, which may be termed the æsthetics of Elocution, that so many public speakers fail.

It is not sufficient that speaking be correct; it must be pleasing and impressive.

It was to perfect grouping that Booth studied thirty years the delivery of the Lord's Prayer, and then said that he did not know how to repeat it ; it was to perfect grouping that the elder Kean repeated the three words, "Was that thunder!" for an hour every night during a voyage of a month across the Atlantic Ocean, and it was the reward of his toil and the evidence of his success when the audience rose to their feet at his thrilling utterance of the words on the occasion of his first benefit in Drury Lane Theater, after his return to his native land ; it was to perfect grouping that Cicero traveled in foreign countries, and Demosthenes declaimed on the sea-shore; and it was the perfection of grouping that so distinguished the delivery of Clay, Everett, Phillips and Gough.

When the student shall have mastered all the previous elements he will then have begun, and only begun, the study of Elocution.

Upon no other part of the subject is it so difficult to give definite instruction.

Grouping consists, not in control of any one, but of all elements of utterance. It is not any particular blending, but an endless variety of blendings. It cannot be said of James E. Murdoch's reading (and he is perhaps the best reader in America) that as he groups so others should group, nor will he necessarily group the same selection twice in the same way.

Grouping is, in short, the exhibition of the same power that is displayed by the musical composer when he arranges the notes into a pleasing tune.

To illustrate: if the following verse be read with Effusive Form, Pure Tone, Subdued Force, Median Stress, Low Pitch, and Slow Movement, it will be read correctly, though it may not be read æsthetically.

Examples: I.

[From "Missing."]

Not among the suffering wounded,
Not among the peaceful dead,
Not among the prisoners—Missing:
That was all the message said.

Let the reading be grouped in the following manner, and it will not only be more impressive, but more pleasing to the ear:

Give the first line with Moderately Subdued Force, Median Stress, Low Pitch, and Slow Movement; the next line with less force and slower movement; the third line, to the word "missing," with more force, higher pitch, and faster movement than the first line was given; the word "missing" with more subdued force, lower pitch, and slower movement than the second line was given; the fourth line with more force, higher pitch, and faster movement than the second line, though not so great as the first line.

It must be borne in mind that all these changes must be under the general heads of Pure Tone, Effusive Form, Median Stress, Low Pitch, and Slow Movement, though in different degrees.

Now it is not claimed that this grouping is the only one, nor the best one; it is only presented as an illustration.

II.

[From "No Excellence Without Labor."—*Wirt.*]

The education, moral and intellectual, of every individual must be chiefly his own work. Rely upon it that the ancients were right—both in morals and intellect we give their final shape to our own characters, and thus become emphatically the architects of our own fortunes.

The above extract may be read correctly by giving it Expulsive Form, Pure Tone, Moderate Force, Radical Stress, Middle Pitch, Moderate Movement; still it might be very monotonous.

It may be grouped in the following manner:

Give the words, "The education," with the above attributes, in a moderate degree; upon the words "moral and intellectual" slightly reduce the force, lower the pitch, slow the movement and moderate the stress; give "of every individual" with about the same degree of force, stress, pitch and movement as "the education," though gradually increased; "must be" will require additional force and stress; "chiefly" should be dropped to about the same as "moral and intellectual" were given; "his own work" begin with nearly the same force, stress, pitch and movement as upon "must be," and close gently with the cadence. Give "Rely upon it that the ancients were right" with the attributes slightly increased from the close of the last sentence; "both in morals and intellect" will require less force, slower movement and lower pitch than "rely upon it the ancients were right;" "we give their final shape to our characters, and thus become" should begin with more force, higher pitch, and more decided stress than "rely upon it," etc., was begun, and these attributes should be gradually increased to the close of the word "become." "Emphatically," being an emphatic word, will require a decided increase of Force, Stress and elevation of Pitch, which should glide down on that word, through the concrete movement, at least a fifth. The Force, Stress and Movement should be a slight increase on what it was on "become," and then gradually diminish to the close, giving the complete cadence on the words "our own fortunes."

Illustrations of Grouping might be multiplied indefinitely, but this will be sufficient, it is hoped, to clearly present the idea. It will be here that the skill of the student of Elocution will be most severely tested. Only by a frequent analysis, similar to the above, of the delivery of passages can the highest success be attained. The results will richly compensate years of patient study and practice, and only thus can great results be obtained.

CHAPTER IV.

ACTION.

ACTION embraces all that part of delivery which addresses itself to the Eye, as distinguished from the Voice, or that part which appeals to the Ear. Considered as a just and elegant adaptation of every part of the body to the nature and import of the sentiment expressed, action has always been regarded as one of the most essential parts of oratory.

Its power, as Cicero observes, is much greater than that of words.

Demosthenes regarded action as the first, second, and third qualification of an orator. It is the language of nature in the strictest sense, and makes its way to the heart without the utterance of a single sound.

"Such, however, is the force of custom, that though we all confess the power and necessity of this branch of public speaking, we find few that are hardy enough to put it in practice. Some of our most accomplished speakers in the pulpit, senate, and bar are very faulty in their use of action, and it is remarkable that those who are excellent in every other part of oratory are very deficient in this. The truth is, though the reason of action in speaking is in the nature of things, the difficulty of acquiring the other requisites of an orator, and the still greater difficulty of attaining excellence in action, (which after all our pains is less esteemed than excellences of another kind ;) these seem to be the reasons why action is so little cultivated among us; to this we may add that, so different are national tastes in this particular, that hardly any two people agree in the just proportion of this so celebrated and essential quality of an orator. Perhaps the finished action of a Cicero or a Demosthenes would scarcely be borne in our times, though accompanied with every other excellence.

"But though the oratory of the moderns does not require all those various evolutions of gesture which were almost indispensable in the ancients, yet a certain degree of it must necessarily enter into the composition of every good speaker and reader. To be perfectly motionless while we are pronouncing words which require force and energy, is not only depriving them of their necessary support, but rendering them unnatural and ridiculous. A very vehement address pronounced without any motion but that of the lips and tongue would be a burlesque upon the meaning, and produce laughter; nay, so unnatural is this total absence of gesticulation, that it is not very easy to speak in this manner.

"As some action, therefore, must necessarily accompany our words, it is of the utmost consequence that this be such as is suitable and natural. No matter how little, if it be but akin to the words and passions, for if foreign to them, it counteracts and destroys the very intention of delivery. The voice and gesture must harmonize and be in keeping with each other, and if there is not a mutual understanding and relationship existing between them, discord must inevitably be the consequence. An awkward action, and such as is unsuitable to the words and passion, not only mars the effect of discourse, but is as painful to the eye as discord to the ear."

The true end of action is not to exhibit the body and

limbs, but to give power to the utterance; not to exhibit grace, but to convey explanation.

As there is a tone of voice appropriate for the utterance of every sentiment and emotion, so also there is an appropriate attitude of body and expression of countenance. "Thus," as Austin remarks, "anger threatens, affright starts, joy laughs and dances, but nature does not by any means suggest (except it may be to some chosen few) the most dignified or graceful expressions of the various passions."

These should be carefully studied and practiced, that we may accustom ourselves to the habit of assuming them easily in public. What Pope says of writing is equally true of action in oratory:

> "True ease in *action* comes from art, not chance:
> So those move easiest who have learned to dance."

Only by continued and frequent practice can the pupil hope to acquire ease, grace and power of gesture.

To present an analysis of action, and thus facilitate the work of the student of Elocution, is the object of this part of the work.

SECTION I.

POSITIONS OF FEET.

"The propriety of commencing this part of our subject with a consideration of the Feet and Lower Limbs will become obvious to the learner as we pass along. To the orator nothing is unimportant which contributes to the general impression he makes upon his audience, and this depends very materially on the dignity and grace of his movements. And what particularly concerns us to remark at this point, is that dignity and grace in the standing figure are known to depend on the positions of the lower limbs, which should be such as to give to the body both firmness of support and facility of movement. Mere firmness or stability can be secured when combined with every degree of awkwardness, and rude strength most frequently perhaps supports the weight of the body equally on both feet. Firmness and grace, however, are combined when the weight of the body is principally supported on one leg, and the other so placed as to preserve the balance of the body and keep it from tottering, at the same time that it is left free to move at will. Austin has remarked that this is the position adopted in the Apollo, the Antinous, and in other beautiful and well-executed statues. In this position the foot which supports the body is to be firmly planted, and the body so erect that a perpendicular line let fall from the center of the neck should pass through the heel of that foot. Either foot may thus support the body, and may be more or less advanced than the free foot, thus giving four positions, which are the principal ones suited to oratory. The conditions of all these are, first, that the feet are to be separated from each other only three or four inches; second, that the toes of the foot which supports the body, as well as of the other, should be turned moderately outward; and third, that the feet should be so placed that lines passing lengthwise through

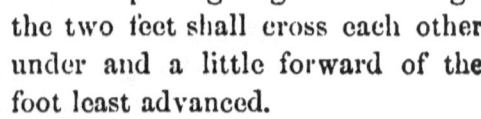

the two feet shall cross each other under and a little forward of the foot least advanced.

First Position.

FIRST POSITION.

In this position the left foot is firmly planted, and supports the weight of the body. The right is placed a little in advance, forming, with the left, nearly an angle of forty-five degrees, and resting lightly on the ball of the great toe. The right knee is slightly bent.

Second Position.

In the second position the weight of the body is supported by the right foot, which is planted firmly. The left is placed a little in advance, resting lightly on the ball of the great toe, and, with the right, forms nearly an angle of forty-five degrees. The left knee is slightly bent.

SECOND POSITION.

Third Position.

THIRD POSITION.

In this position the weight of the body is upon the right foot, which is placed in advance of the left. The toe of the left foot balances the body, which is thrown a little forward. The heel of the left foot is elevated about an inch, and swings in toward the right foot.

Fourth Position.

In the fourth position the weight rests upon the left foot, which is placed a little in advance. The toe of the right foot balances the body, the heel inclining in to the left foot. The body is inclined forward.

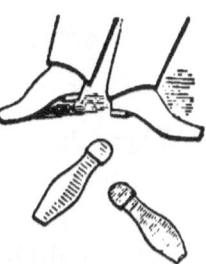

FOURTH POSITION.

SECTION II.

CHANGES IN POSITION.

The changes of position should be made as quietly as possible, and usually by placing either backward or forward the foot not supporting the weight of the body.

In the first part of a discourse but few changes of position should be made.

SECTION III.

POSITION OF BODY.

Oratory requires only the erect position of self-sustained dignity, and allows no marked deviation from this position.

To be more particular: the body of the speaker should be well balanced and sustained erect on the supporting limb; the head likewise should be sustained with manliness and grace. He should front his audience, presenting himself, as Quintilian expresses it, *æquo pectore*, and with his face as well as his breast directed to those whom he addresses. This perfectly erect position of the body and the head should, however, yield to every gesture of the arm.

SECTION IV.

POSITION OF THE ARMS IN REPOSE.

When the arms are not employed in gesture they should hang naturally by the side.

This position, however, too long sustained becomes tiresome and monotonous, and requires change. Where the circumstances are favorable the left hand may rest gently on a table or stand, the thumb may be placed in a watch-guard, or the fingers placed between the buttons of the vest. At times the left arm may be thrown behind the body. In various ways, the eye of the audience, as well as the monotony of the speaker, may be relieved by a nice adjustment of the body and arms.

SECTION V.

POSITIONS OF THE ARMS IN GESTURE.

First.—In gesticulation, the arm should be free and unconstrained, the action proceeding from the shoulder rather than the elbow. The elbow should be slightly curved and flexible.

Second.—The arm should be so moved that the hand will always describe curved lines instead of those which are straight and angular. The curve is the line of beauty, and grace in the action of the arm depends very materially on the observance of this principle.

Third.—The arm should not remain stationary even for a moment while out in gesticulation. It should either be kept moving preparatory to another gesture, or return to the side.

Fourth.—Gestures ordinarily should not be made at a greater angle than forty-five degrees from a horizontal line passing directly forward from the center of the breast.

Fifth.—In general there should be a point at which the gesture will terminate. This, in emphatic gesticulation, will be upon the word that demands the gesture, and just at the instant of the utterance of the accented part of the word. A mere swing of the arm, even though it describes a curved line ever so graceful, does not accomplish the important part of gesture.

Sixth.—The ease and grace of the motion of the arm will depend on the free use of the joints of the shoulder elbow and wrist. Without the free use of the wrist-joint particularly there can be no grace.

Seventh.—Preference in gesticulation should be given to the right arm. As a general rule, when the right hand is employed in gesture, the weight of the body should be on the left foot, the right advanced.

SECTION VI.

THE HAND.

The expressiveness of gesture depends largely on the hand. Next to the tones of the voice and the expressions of countenance, the hand has the greatest variety and power of expression. Sheridan says: "Every one knows that with the hands we can demand or promise, call, dismiss, threaten, supplicate, ask, deny, show joy, sorrow, detestation, fear, confession, penitence, admiration, respect, and many other things now in common use."

SECTION VII.

POSITIONS OF THE HAND.

The hand is prone when the palm is turned downward.

It is supine when the palm is turned upward.

It is vertical when the plane of the palm is perpendicular to the horizon, the fingers pointing upward.

The natural state of the fingers, when the arm is hanging freely by the side, or employed in unimpassioned gesture, is that in which the hand is fully open, with the forefinger nearly straight, and slightly separated from the middle finger; the middle finger is more bent, and rests partly on the third finger, which it gently touches; the little finger is still more bent, and slightly separated from the third finger; the thumb is withdrawn from the palm, and so placed that a line from the top of it will be a little above the line of the forefinger.

This arrangement of the fingers is observed in the Venus de Medicis, and other eminent specimens of both statuary and painting.

The position of the hand, as regards the palm, most suitable to be adopted by the public speaker in unimpassioned gesticulation, is that which presents an inclination from the supine of an angle of forty-five degrees, and accompanied with a slight bend of the wrist downward, in the direction of the little finger.

In emphatic or impassioned gesture the hand may be closed as it is brought down.

SECTION VIII.
ACCOMPANIMENTS OF GESTURE.*

1. *Body and Countenance.*—"The subordinate gesture is one of the accompaniments of the principal; but there are other accompaniments to be attended to. The movements of the lower limbs, of the body, and of the head, must all join in harmony with the principal gesture of the hand, otherwise the movement will be but a mere *imitation* of nature. And even though the body and limbs should move in perfect concert, while the countenance should remain unmoved and unexcited, the entire action would be but that of a well-contrived automaton. With all of these at perfect command, and employed in harmony with the diversified melodies of the voice, nothing can be wanting for the enforcement of either thought or feeling."

2. *Preparation and Termination of Gesture.*—"Every act of gesture consists of two parts—the preparatory and

---

* The following pages on gesture so nearly embody our own view that they have been copied almost entire from Caldwell's Practical Elocution.

the terminating movement. The last is that for which the gesture is made, and the former is but the preliminary movement, which of necessity precedes it. The *collected* state of the hand, for example, belongs exclusively to the preparatory part of gesture. Again, the hand cannot be brought downward in emphatic expression till it has been elevated. The elevation of the arm and hand, then, is the preparatory part of such a gesture. Though, in one sense, this is entirely a subordinate part of gesture, yet on it depend essentially the force as well as the grace of its termination. It must be executed neither too early, so as to leave the arm too long suspended; nor too late, so as to make the gesture short and hurried. It should appear easy and natural, be made in curved rather than in straight lines, and should seem to be prompted, as indeed it ought to be, by the rising thought."

3. *Transition of Gesture.*—" When the hand has once been brought into action in gesture, instead of dropping to the side, and then being brought up again for a similar purpose, it should generally remain in its position till relieved by the other hand, or till it passes into a state of preparation for a succeeding gesture. The term *transition* may be applied to the passing thus from any one gesture to another, whether from one principal gesture to another of the same hand, or from the gesture of one hand to that of the other. No rules for such transitions can be given. The term is, however, used in a sense more analogous with the same term as applied to the voice when it is made to refer to such changes as arise from transitions in the sentiment, whether they are sudden and abrupt, or more gradual, like those which take place in the regular progress of a discourse. At this point it need only be remarked, that these last-named

transitions of gesture should never be made, except when dictated by such transitions of thought and sentiment as call for corresponding changes in the vocal expression."

SECTION IX.
QUALITIES OF GESTURE.

The qualities on which the excellence of gesture depends are Simplicity, Propriety, Precision, Energy, Boldness, Variety, Grace, Magnificence.

These will be briefly noticed.

1. *Simplicity of Gesture* is perfectly free and unaffected, and appears to be the natural result of the situation and sentiments of the speaker, presenting evidence neither of studied variety nor of reserve. Its opposite is *affectation*.

2. *Propriety of Gesture* always indicates some obvious connection between the sentiment and the action. It implies the use of such gestures as are best suited to illustrate or to express the sentiment, and thus often calls into use the significant gestures. The opposite of this is *solecism* in gesture, implying the recurrence of false, contradictory, or unsuitable gestures.

3. *Precision of Gesture* arises from the just preparation, the due force, and the correct timing of the action. The stroke of the gesture must not only fall on the emphatic syllable, but its force must exactly suit the character of the sentiment and the speaker. This gives the same effect to action that neatness of articulation does to speech. The opposites are gestures which distract the attention, while they neither enforce nor illustrate the sentiment. Such are most of those which consist in a mere swing of the arm, while the stroke of the gesture is wanting.

4. *Energy of Gesture* consists in the firmness and decision of the whole action, and these depend very materially on the precision with which the stroke of the gesture is made to support the voice in marking the emphasis. Let bad habits be overcome, and a ready command of all the elements of gesture be acquired, then will energy of gesture be the necessary result of a clear head and a warm heart. Its opposites are *feebleness* and *indecision*.

5. *Boldness of Gesture* is exhibited in striking but unexpected positions, movements and transitions. It is the offspring of a daring self-confidence, which ventures to hazard any action which it is conceived may either illustrate or enforce. The courage thus to execute is valuable only when under the guidance of *good taste*. The opposite of this is *tameness*, which hazards nothing, is distrustful of its powers, and produces no great effect.

6. *Variety of Gesture* consists in the adapting of gesture to the condition and ever-varying sentiment of the speaker, so as to avoid a too frequent recurrence of the same gesture, or the same set of gestures. It is opposed both to *sameness* of gesture and to *mechanical variety*.

7. *Grace of Gesture* is the result of all other perfections, arising from a dignified self-possession of mind, and the power of personal exertion practiced into facility after the best models and according to the truest taste. This usually, therefore, depends more on art than on nature, and has more to do with pleasing the fancy than with producing conviction. It suggests not a single movement, but simply preserves the gestures employed for other purposes from all awkwardness. The opposites of this are *awkwardness*, *vulgarity* or *rusticity*.

Magnificence of Gesture is secured by perfect freedom of movement. The arm moves from the shoulder, and the hand is carried through an ample space. The head moves freely, the body is erect, and the step is free and firm. Opposed to these are *contracted gestures, constrained motions, short steps* and *doubtful* and *timid movements.*

SECTION X.

ADAPTATION OF GESTURE.

Gesticulation should correspond to the sentiments expressed by the words. Unimpassioned didactic thought will require but little gesture.

Descriptive thought will require more decided and various gesture.

Argumentative thought, stirring appeals, impassioned addresses will require bold, energetic and magnificent gesticulation.

Strong emotion, violent passion will require gestures corresponding to the feeling expressed. This can only be determined by a careful study of the passions.

The importance of a good carriage and a pleasing address in appearing before an audience cannot be overestimated.

It is from these the audience receive their first impressions of the speaker, and as their minds are not supposed to be occupied with any thing else, they are perfectly free to criticise his manner.

These movements, then, demand special attention. He should omit no proper mode of expressing respect for those before him, and thus bespeaking their favor. In general terms, so far as movement and gesture are concerned, the orator should present himself to the audience modestly, and without any show of self-confidence.

After taking his position before the audience the

speaker should make a very slight bow by a gentle bend of the whole body.

In many cases, as in the sacred desk, the bow should be omitted altogether.

Before leaving this part of the subject it may be well to call attention to some

Significant Gestures.

The Head and Face.

The hanging down of the head denotes shame or grief.
The holding of it up, pride or courage.
To nod forward implies assent;
To toss the head back, dissent.
The inclination of the head implies diffidence or languor.
The head is averted in dislike or horror.
It leans forward in attention.

The Eyes.

The eyes are raised in prayer.
They weep in sorrow.
They burn in anger.
They are downcast or averted in shame or grief.
They are cast on vacancy in thought.
They are cast in various directions in doubt and anxiety.

The Arms.

The placing of the hand on the head indicates pain or distress;
On the eyes, shame or sorrow;
On the lips, an injunction of silence;
On the breast, an appeal to conscience.
The hand is waved or flourished in joy or contempt.

Both hands are held supine, or they are applied or clasped in prayer.
Both are held prone in blessing.
They are clasped or wrung in affliction.
They are held forward and received in friendship.

The Body.

The body, held erect, indicates steadiness and courage;
Thrown back, pride;
Stooping forward, condescension or compassion;
Bending, reverence or respect;
Prostrate, the utmost humility or abasement.

The Lower Limbs.

The firm position of the lower limbs signifies courage obstinacy.
Bended knees indicate timidity or weakness.
The lower limbs advance in desire or courage.
They retire in aversion or fear;
Start, in terror;
Stamp, in authority or anger;
Kneel, in submission and prayer.

These are a few of the simple gestures which may be termed significant.

SECTION XI.

THE EYE AND COUNTENANCE.

The Countenance has the greatest power of expression, and the Eye is the most expressive of all the features.
So great is the facial power of expression that we can truly say "a speaking countenance." In the language of Quintilian, "This is the dominant power of expression. With this we supplicate; with this we threaten; with

this we soothe; with this we mourn; with this we rejoice; with this we triumph; with this we make our submissions; upon this the audience hang; upon this they keep their eyes fixed; this they examine and study even before a word is spoken; this it is which excites in them favorable or unfavorable emotions; from this they understand almost every thing; often it becomes more significant than any words."

It is said of Whitefield, the Prince of Pulpit Orators, His face was like a canvas, and upon it he painted every passion that stirs the human breast. It was at one moment terrific, as if all the furies were enthroned on that dark brow; and next, as by a dissolving view, there would come forth an angelic sweetness that savored of heaven.

"The expressive power of the eye is so great that it determines, in a manner, the expression of the whole countenance. Through it the soul makes its most clear and vivid manifestations of itself. Joy and grief, anger, pride, scorn, hatred, love, jealousy, pity; in a word, all the passions and emotions of the human heart in all their degrees and outer workings with each other, express themselves, with the utmost fullness and power, in the eyes.

"Even animals are susceptible of its power. The dog watches the eye of his master, and discovers from it, before a word is spoken, whether he is to expect a caress or apprehend chastisement.

"The lion cannot attack a man so long as the man looks him steadily in the eyes.

"In order that the speaker may avail himself of this great and mysterious power of expression he must not allow his eyes to become fixed upon his manuscript, nor to assume a vacant expression under the influence of the intellectual operation of invention or remembering, nor to wander around the walls of the audience-room, nor to follow the motions of the hands as if the speaker were looking at them. He must look at the audience, and scan their faces individually, in order to open a personal communication between himself and every one of them. He should not allow his eye to wander from the audience except when, by a glance, he indicates the direction of a gesture. Thus he will be enabled to command their attention and awaken their sympathy, and his eye will naturally express and convey to them all the passions and emotions of his own heart."

SECTION XII.
THE PASSIONS.*

It now remains to say something of those expressions of countenance which mark the passions and emotions of the speaker. A full description of each would far transcend the bounds of a work of this kind. Only a few can be noticed, and these but briefly.

"It should be remarked in passing that feeling cannot be expressed by words alone, or even by the tones of the voice. It finds its best, and ofttimes its only, expression in the flash of passion on the cheek, in the speaking eye, the contracted brow, the compressed lip, the heaving breast, the trembling frame, in the rigid muscle and the general bearing of the entire body; and when emotion or passion thus speaks, its language is often confined to no particular part of the body, but the living frame as a whole sympathizes in the action."

Aaron Hill, in his Essay on the Art of Acting, has made a bold attempt at such a description of the passions as may enable an actor or orator to adopt them mechanically, by showing that all the passions require

* The following pages, on the Passions, have been adapted from Walker's Elocution.

either a braced or relaxed state of the sinews, and a peculiar cast of the eye.

It is certain that all the passions, when violent, brace the sinews; grief which, when moderate, may be said to melt or relax the frame, when accompanied by anguish and bitter complainings becomes active and bracing. Pity seems never to rise to a sufficient degree of sorrow to brace the sinews, and anger, even in the slightest degree, seems to give a kind of tension to the voice and limbs. Thus Shakspeare has given us an admirable picture of this passion in its violence, and has made this violent tension of the sinews a considerable part of its composition.

> Now imitate the action of the tiger!
> Stiffen the sinews, summon up the blood;
> Lend fierce and dreadful aspect to the eye;
> Set the teeth close, and stretch the nostrils wide;
> Hold hard the breath, and bend up every spirit
> To its full height.

To this might be added that admirable picture of violent anger which Shakspeare puts in the mouth of Suffolk in the second part of Henry VI.:

> Would curses kill, as doth the mandrake's groan,
> I would invent as bitter, searching terms,
> As curst, as harsh, and horrible to hear,
> Delivered strongly through my fixed teeth,
> With full as many signs of deadly hate
> As lean-faced Envy in her loathsome cave.
> My tongue should stumble in mine earnest words,
> Mine eyes should sparkle like the beaten flint,
> Mine hair be fixed on end like one distract,
> Ay, every joint should seem to curse and ban;
> And even now my burdened heart would break,
> Should I not curse them.

Who can read these admirable descriptions of anger without feeling his whole frame braced, and his mind strongly tinctured with the passion delineated? How much is it to be regretted that so great a master of the passions as Shakspeare has not left us a description similar to this of every emotion of the soul! But though he has not described every other passion like this, he has placed them all in such marking points of view as enables us to see the workings of the human heart from his writings in a clearer and more affecting way than in any other of our poets; and perhaps the best description that could be given us of the passions in any language may be extracted from the epithets he has made use of.

SECTION XIII.
A PICTURE OF THE PASSIONS.
TRANQUILLITY.

Tranquillity appears by the composure of the countenance and general repose of the whole body, without the exertion of any one muscle. The countenance open, the forehead smooth, the eyebrows arched, the mouth not quite shut, and the eyes passing with an easy motion from object to object, but not dwelling long upon any one. To distinguish it, however, from insensibility it seems necessary to give it that cast of happiness which borders on cheerfulness.

CHEERFULNESS.

When joy is settled into a habit, or flows from a placid temper of mind, desiring to please and be pleased, it is called gayety, good humor, or cheerfulness. Cheerfulness adds a smile to tranquillity, and opens the mouth a little more.

Cheerfulness in Retirement.

Now, my co-mates and brothers in exile,
Hath not old custom made this life more sweet

Than that of painted pomp? Are not these woods
More free from peril than the envious court?
Here feel we but the penalty of Adam,
The season's difference; as the icy fang
And churlish chiding of the winter's wind,
Which, when it bites and blows upon my body
Even till I shrink with cold, I smile and say,
This is no flattery; these are counselors
That feelingly persuade me what I am.
Sweet are the uses of adversity,
That like a toad, ugly and venomous,
Wears yet a precious jewel in its head;
And this our life exempt from public haunts,
Finds tongues in trees, books in the running brooks,
Sermons in stones, and good in every thing.
— *As You Like It.*

MIRTH.

When joy arises from ludicrous or fugitive amusements in which others share with us it is called merriment or mirth.

Mirth or laughter opens the mouth horizontally, raises the cheeks high, lessens the aperture of the eyes, and, when violent, shakes and convulses the whole frame, fills the eyes with tears, and occasions holding the sides from the pain the convulsive laughter gives them.

Jaq. A fool, a fool! I met a fool i' the forest,
A motley fool; a miserable world!
As I do live by food, I met a fool;
Who laid him down and basked him in the sun,
And railed on lady Fortune, in good terms,
In good set terms, and yet a motley fool.
Good-morrow, fool, quoth I: No, sir, quoth he,
Call me not fool till heaven hath sent me fortune.
And then he drew a dial from his poke;
And looking on it with lack-luster eye,
Says, very wisely, It is ten o'clock.
Thus may we see, quoth he, how the world wags.
'Tis but an hour ago since it was nine,
And after an hour more 'twill be eleven;

And so from hour to hour we ripe and ripe,
And then from hour to hour we rot and rot,
And thereby hangs a tale. When I did hear
The motley fool thus moral on the time,
My lungs began to crow like chanticleer,
That fools should be so deep contemplative;
And I did laugh, *sans* intermission,
An hour by his dial. O noble fool!
A worthy fool! Motley's the only wear.

JOY.

A pleasing elation of mind on the actual or assured attainment of good, or deliverance from evil, is called joy.

Joy, when moderate, opens the countenance with smiles, and throws, as it were, a sunshine of delectation over the whole frame. When it is sudden and violent it expresses itself by clapping the hands, raising the eyes toward heaven, and giving such a spring to the body as to make it attempt to mount up as if it could fly. When joy is extreme, and goes into transport, rapture and ecstacy, it has a wildness of look and gesture that borders on folly, madness and sorrow.

Joy Expected.

Ah! Juliet, if the measure of thy joy
Be heaped like mine, and that thy skill be more
To blazon it, then sweeten with thy breath
This neighbor air, and let rich music's tongue
Unfold the imagined happiness that both
Receive in either by this dear encounter.
—*Romeo and Juliet.*

Joy Approaching to Transport.

Oh! joy, thou welcome stranger, twice three years
I have not felt thy vital beam, but now
It warms my veins, and plays about my heart;
A fiery instinct lifts me from the ground,
And I could mount.
—*Dr. Young's Revenge.*

PITY.

Pity is benevolence to the afflicted. It is a mixture of love for an object that suffers, and a grief that we are not able to remove those sufferings. It shows itself in a compassionate tenderness of voice, a feeling of pain in the countenance, and a gentle raising and falling of the hands and eyes, as if mourning over the unhappy object. The mouth is open, the eyebrows are drawn down, and the features contracted or drawn together.

Pity for a Departed Friend.

Alas! poor Yorick! I knew him, Horatio; a fellow of infinite jest, of most excellent fancy. He hath borne me on his back a thousand times, and now how abhorred in my imagination it is; my gorge rises at it. Here hung those lips that I have kissed I know not how oft. Where be your gibes now? Your gambols? Your songs? Your flashes of merriment, that were wont to set the table in a roar? Not one now to mock your own grinning! Quite chop-fallen! Now get thee to my lady's chamber, and tell her, let her paint an inch thick, to this favor she must come; make her laugh at that.—*Hamlet.*

HOPE.

Hope is a mixture of desire and joy agitating the mind and anticipating its enjoyment. It erects and brightens the countenance, spreads the arms and hands open as to receive the object of its wishes. The voice is plaintive and inclining to eagerness, the breath drawn inward more forcibly than usual in order to express our desires more strongly, and our earnest expectation of receiving the object of them.

Collins, in his Ode on the Passions, gives us a beautiful picture of

Hope.

But thou, O Hope! with eyes so fair,
What was thy delighted measure?
Still it whispered prómised pleasure,
And bade the lovely scenes at distance hail.

Still would her touch the strain prolong,
And from the rocks, the woods, the vale,
She called on Echo still through all her song;
And, where her sweetest theme she chose,
A soft responsive voice was heard at every close,
And Hope, enchanted, smiled, and waved her golden hair.

HATRED, AVERSION.

Hatred or aversion draws back the body as if to avoid the hated object, the hands at the same time thrown outspread as if to keep it off. The face is turned away from that side toward which the hands are thrown out, the eyes looking angrily and obliquely the same way the hands are directed; the eyebrows are contracted, the upper lip disdainfully drawn up, and the teeth set; the pitch of the voice is low, but loud and harsh, the tone chiding, unequal, surly and vehement.

Hatred Cursing the Object Hated.

Poison be their drink,
Gall, worse than gall, the daintiest meat they taste:
Their sweetest shade a grove of cypress trees,
Their sweetest prospects murdering basilisks,
Their softest touch as smart as lizards' stings,
Their music frightful as the serpent's hiss,
And boding screech-owls make the concert full;
All the foul terrors of dark-seated hell.
—*Henry VI.*

This seems Imitated by Dr. Young.

Why, get thee gone, horror and night go with thee.
Sisters of Acheron, go hand in hand,
Go dance about the bower and close them in;
And tell them that I sent you to salute them.
Profane the ground, and for th' ambrosial rose
And breath of jessamin, let hemlock blacken,
And deadly night-shade poison all the air:
For the sweet nightingale may ravens croak,
Toads pant, and adders rustle through the leaves:

May serpents, winding up the trees, let fall
Their hissing necks upon them from above,
And mingle hisses—such as I would give them.
—*The Revenge.*

Hatred of a Rival in Glory.

He is my bane, I cannot bear him;
One heaven and earth can never hold us both;
Still shall we hate, and with defiance deadly
Keep rage alive till one be lost for ever:
As if two suns should meet in one meridian,
And strive in fiery combat for the passage.
—*Rowe's Tamerlane.*

ANGER, RAGE, FURY.

When hatred and displeasure rise high suddenly from an apprehension of injury received, and perturbation of mind in consequence of it, it is called anger; and rising to a very high degree, and extinguishing humanity, it becomes rage and fury.

Anger, when violent, expresses itself with rapidity, noise, harshness, and sometimes with interruption and hesitation, as if unable to utter itself with sufficient force. It wrinkles the brow, enlarges and heaves the nostrils, strains the muscles, clinches the fist, stamps with the foot, and gives a violent agitation to the whole body. The voice assumes the highest tone it can adopt consistently with force and loudness, though sometimes, to express anger with uncommon energy, the voice assumes a low and forcible tone.

Anger and Scorn.

Thou den of drunkards with the blood of princes!
Gehenna of the waters! thou sea Sodom!
Thus I devote thee to the infernal gods!
Thee and thy serpent seed! Slave, do thine office!
Strike as I struck the foe! Strike as I would
Have struck those tyrants! Strike deep as my curse!
Strike, and but once.

A PICTURE OF THE PASSIONS.

Scorn and Violent Anger, Reproving.

Grace me no grace, nor uncle me no uncle;
I am no traitor's uncle; and that word—grace,
In an ungracious mouth is but profane.
Why have those banished and forbidden legs
Dared once to touch a dust of England's ground?
But more than why—why have they dared to march
So many miles upon her peaceful bosom;
Frightening her pale-faced villages with war,
And ostentation of despised arms?
Comest thou because the anointed king is hence?
Why, foolish boy, the king is left behind,
And in my loyal bosom lies his power.
Were I but now the lord of such hot youth
As when, brave Gaunt, thy father and myself
Rescued the Black Prince, that young Mars of men,
From forth the ranks of many thousand French;
O, then, how quickly should this arm of mine,
Now prisoner to the palsy, chastise thee,
And minister correction to thy fault!
—*Richard II.*

REVENGE.

Revenge is a propensity and endeavor to injure the offender, which is attended with triumph and exultation when the injury is accomplished. It expresses itself like malice, but more openly, loudly and triumphantly.

Determined Revenge.

I know not: if they speak but truth of her,
These hands shall tear her; if they wrong her honor
The proudest of them shall well hear it.
Time hath not yet so dried this blood of mine,
Nor age so eat up my invention,
Nor fortune made such havoc of my means,
Nor my bad life 'reft me so much of friends,
But they shall find awaked in such a kind,
Both strength of limb and policy of mind,
Ability in means, and choice of friends
To quit me of them thoroughly.
—*Much Ado about Nothing.*

Eager Revenge.

O I could play the woman with mine eyes,
And braggart with my tongue! But, gentle heaven,
Cut short all intermission: front to front,
Bring thou this fiend of Scotland and myself;
Within my sword's length set him; if he 'scape,
Heaven forgive him too!
—*Macbeth.*

REPROACH.

Reproach is settled anger or hatred, chastising the object of dislike by casting in his teeth the severest censures upon his imperfections or misconduct. The brow is contracted, the lip turned up with scorn, the head shaken, the voice low, as if abhorring, and the whole body expressive of aversion.

Reproaching with Want of Friendship.

You have done that you should be sorry for.
There is no terror, Cassius, in your threats;
For I am armed so strong in honesty,
That they pass me by as the idle wind
Which I respect not. I did send to you
For certain sums of gold, which you denied me,
For I can raise no money by vile means:
By heaven, I had rather coin my heart,
And drop my blood for drachmas, than to wring
From the hard hands of peasants their vile trash
By any indirection. I did send
To you for gold to pay my legions,
Which you denied me. Was that done like Cassius?
Should I have answered Caius Cassius so?
When Marcus Brutus grows so covetous,
To lock such rascal counters from his friends,
Be ready, gods, with all your thunderbolts;
Dash him to pieces!

Reproach with Want of Courage and Spirit.

Thou slave! thou wretch! thou coward!
Thou little valiant, great in villainy!

Thou ever strong upon the stronger side!
Thou fortune's champion, thou dost never fight
But when her humorous ladyship is by
To teach thee safety! Thou art perjured, too,
And sooth'st up greatness. What a fool art thou,
A ramping fool, to brag, and stamp, and sweat,
Upon my party! Thou cold-blooded slave,
Hast thou not spoke like thunder on my side?
Been sworn my soldier? bidding me depend
Upon thy stars, thy fortune, and thy strength?
And dost thou now fall over to my foes?
Thou wear a lion's hide? Doff it for shame,
And hang a calf's skin on those recreant limbs.

FEAR AND TERROR.

Fear is a mixture of aversion and sorrow, discomposing and debilitating the mind upon the approach or anticipation of evil. When this is attended with surprise and much discomposure it grows into terror and consternation.

Fear, violent and sudden, opens wide the eyes and mouth, shortens the nose, gives the countenance an air of wildness, covers it with deadly paleness, draws back the elbows parallel with the sides, lifts up the open hands, with the fingers spread, to the height of the breast, at some distance before it, so as to shield it from the dreadful object. One foot is drawn back behind the other, so that the body seems shrinking from the danger, and putting itself in a posture for flight. The heart beats violently, the breath is quick and short, and the whole body is thrown into a general tremor. The voice is weak and trembling, the sentences are short and the meaning confused and incoherent.

Terror of Evening and Night Described.
Light thickens; and the crow
Makes wing to the rooky wood;

Good things of day begin to droop and drouse;
While night's black agents to their prey do rouse
Thou marvel'st at my words; but hold thee still;
Things bad begun, make strong themselves by ill.
—*Macbeth.*

Fear from a Dreadful Object.

Angels and ministers of grace, defend us!
Be thou a spirit of health, or goblin damned,
Bring with thee airs from heaven, or blasts from hell,
Be thy intents wicked or charitable,
Thou com'st in such a questionable shape
That I will speak to thee. I'll call thee Hamlet,
King, father! Royal Dane: O answer me!
Let me not burst in ignorance.
—*Hamlet.*

Horror at a Dreadful Apparition.

How ill this taper burns! ha! who comes here?
I think it is the weakness of mine eyes
That shapes this monstrous apparition.
It comes upon me. Art thou any thing?
Art thou some god, some angel, or some devil,
That mak'st my blood cold, and my hair to stare.
Speak to me, what thou art!
—*Julius Cesar.*

Fear of being Discovered in Murder.

Alack! I am afraid they have awaked,
And 'tis not done! the attempt, and not the deed,
Confound us. Hark! I laid their daggers ready,
He could not miss them! Had he not resembled
My father as he slept I had done't!
—*Macbeth.*

SORROW.

Sorrow is a painful depression of spirit upon the deprivation of good or arrival of evil. When it is silent and thoughtful it is sadness; when long indulged, so as to prey upon and possess the mind, it becomes habitual, and grows into melancholy; when tossed by hopes and fears, it is distraction; when these are swallowed up by it, it settles into despair.

In moderate sorrow the countenance is dejected, the eyes are cast downward, the arms hang loose, sometimes a little raised, suddenly to fall again; the hands open, the fingers spread, and the voice plaintive, frequently interrupted with sighs. But when this passion is in excess it distorts the countenance, as if in agonies of pain; it raises the voice to the loudest complainings, and sometimes even to cries and shrieks; it wrings the hands, beats the head and breast, tears the hair, and throws itself on the ground, and, like other passions in excess, seems to border on frenzy.

Sadness.

In sooth, I know not why I am so sad.
It wearies me; you say it wearies you:
But how I caught it, found it, or came by it,
What stuff 'tis made of, whereof 'tis born,
I am to learn.
And such a want-wit sadness makes of me,
That I have much ado to know myself.

Silent Grief.

Seems, madam! nay, it is; I know not seems.
'Tis not alone my inky cloak, good mother,
Nor the dejected 'havior of the visage,
No, nor the fruitful river in the eye,
Together with all forms, modes, shows of grief,
That can denote me truly: these, indeed, seem,
For they are actions that a man might play;
But I have that within which passeth show;
These but the trappings and the suits of woe.

SNEER.

Sneer is ironical approbation, where, with a voice and countenance of mirth somewhat exaggerated, we cast the severest censures; it is hypocritical mirth and good humor, and differs from the real by the sly, arch, satirical tone of voice, look and gesture which accompany it

Scoffing at Supposed Cowardice.

Satan beheld their plight,
And to his mates thus in derision called:
O friends, why come not on these victors proud?
Erewhile they fierce were coming, and when we,
To entertain them fair with open front
And breast, (what could we more?) propounded terms
Of composition, straight they changed their minds,
Flew off, and into strange vagaries fell,
As they would dance; yet for a dance they seemed
Somewhat extravagant and wild, perhaps
For joy of offered peace; but I suppose,
If air proposals once again were heard,
We should compel them to a quick result.
—*Paradise Lost.*

SURPRISE, WONDER, AMAZEMENT, ASTONISHMENT.

An uncommon object produces wonder. If it appears suddenly it begets surprise, surprise continuing becomes amazement, and, if the object of wonder comes gently to the mind, and arrests the attention by its beauty or grandeur, it excites admiration, which is a mixture of approbation and wonder: so true is that observation of Dr Young in the tragedy of the Revenge:

Late time shall wonder that my joys shall raise,
For wonder is involuntary praise.

Wonder or amazement opens the eyes and makes them appear very prominent. It sometimes raises them to the skies, but more frequently fixes them on the object. The mouth is open, and the hands are held up nearly in the attitude of fear. The voice is at first low, but so emphatical that every word is pronounced slowly and with energy. When, by the discovery of something excellent in the object of wonder, the emotion may be called admiration, the eyes are raised, the hands lifted up or clapped together, and the voice elevated with expressions of rapture.

Surprise at Unexpected Events.

Gone to be married? gone to swear a peace?
False blood to false blood joined? gone to be friends?
Shall Lewis have Blanche, and Blanche those provinces?
It is not so: thou hast misspoke, misheard:
Be well advised, tell o'er thy tale again:
It cannot be! thou dost but say 'tis so!
What dost thou mean by shaking of thy head?
Why dost thou look so sadly on my son?
What means that hand upon that breast of thine?
Why holds thine eye that lamentable rheum,
Like a proud river peering o'er his bounds?
Be these sad signs confirmers of thy words?
Then speak again; not all thy former tale,
But this one word, whether thy tale be true.
—*King John.*

VEXATION.

Vexation, besides expressing itself by the looks, gestures, tone and restlessness of perplexity, adds to these complaint, fretting and remorse.

Vexation at Neglecting One's Duty.

O what a rogue and peasant slave am I!
Is it not monstrous, that this player here,
But in a fiction, in a dream of passion,
Could force his soul so to his own conceit,
That, from her working, all his visage wann'd:
Tears in his eyes, distraction in's aspect,
A broken voice, and his whole function suiting
With forms to his conceit? And all for nothing!
For Hecuba!
What's Hecuba to him, or he to Hecuba,
That he should weep for her?
—*Hamlet.*

SHAME.

Shame, or a sense of appearing to disadvantage before one's own fellow-creatures, turns away the face from the beholders, covers it with blushes, hangs the head, casts down the eyes, draws down and contracts the eyebrows. It either strikes the person dumb, or, if he attempts to say any thing in his own defense, causes his tongue to falter, confounds his utterance, and puts him upon making a thousand gestures and grimaces to keep himself in countenance; all which only heighten his confusion and embarrassment.

Shame at being Convicted of a Crime.

O my dread lord,
I should be guiltier than my guiltiness,
To think I can be undiscernible
When I perceive your grace, like power divine,
Hath looked upon my passes; then, good prince,
No longer session hold upon my shame,
But let my trial be mine own confession:
Immediate sentence, then, and sequent death,
Is all the grace I beg.
—*Measure for Measure.*

GRAVITY.

Gravity, or seriousness, as when the mind is fixed, or deliberating on some important subject, smooths the countenance, and gives it an air of melancholy; the eyebrows are lowered, eyes cast downward, the mouth almost shut, and sometimes a little contracted. The posture of the body and limbs is composed, and without much motion; the speech slow and solemn, the tone without much variety.

Grave Deliberation on War and Peace.

Fathers, we once again are met in council:
Cæsar's approach has summoned us together,

And Rome attends her fate from our resolves.
How shall we treat this bold aspiring man?
Success still follows him and backs his crimes:
Pharsalia gave him Rome. Egypt has since
Received his yoke, and the whole Nile is Cesar's.
Why should I mention Juba's overthrow,
Or Scipio's death? Numidia's burning sands
Still smoke with blood; 'tis time we should decree
What course to take: our foe advances on us,
And envies us even Libya's sultry deserts.
Fathers, pronounce your thoughts; are they still fixed,
To hold it out and fight it to the last?
Or are your hearts subdued at length, and wrought,
By time and ill success, to a submission?
Sempronius, speak.
   —Addison's Cato.

COMMANDING.

Commanding requires an air a little more peremptory, with a look a little severe or stern. The hand is held out and moved toward the person to whom the order is given, with the palm upward, and sometimes it is accompanied by a nod of the head to the person commanded. If the command be absolute, and to a person unwilling to obey, the right hand is extended and projected forcibly toward the person commanded.

Commanding Combatants to Fight.

We were born not to sue, but to command;
Which since we cannot do to make you friends,
Be ready, as your lives shall answer it,
At Coventry, upon St. Lambert's day;
There shall your swords and lances arbitrate
The swelling difference of your settled hate.
Since we cannot atone you, you shall see
Justice decide the victor's chivalry.
Lord Marshal, command our officers at arms
Be ready to direct these home alarms.
   —Richard II.

Trifling as the preceding selection of examples of passions may appear, it is presumed it will be for singularly useful to public speakers in general, and those in particular who are training themselves or being trained for the elegant, refined and dignified of public speaking.

PART II.

DEDUCTIONS.

CHAPTER I.

STYLES.

If the discussion of the principles under Part I, Chapter III, has been clearly apprehended, it will be readily perceived that the following thirteen styles are the logical deductions therefrom.

In some one of these styles, or a combination of two or more of them, with at times, in the expression of certain emotions and passions, the change of a single attribute, every form of thought and feeling may be appropriately and impressively delivered.

To attempt to read or speak in public without first determining the Form, Quality, Force, Stress, Pitch and Movement, the sentiment to be uttered should receive, will be as little likely to be crowned with success as would be the effort of one who should presume to sing in public without first determining the tune he would use or the notes composing that tune.

To assist the student, therefore, in determining the attributes of which each style is composed, the diagram on the following page is commended to his careful consideration.

A DIAGRAM OF THE STYLES OF UTTERANCE AND THEIR RESPECTIVE ATTRIBUTES.

Arranged by S. S. Hamill, September 7, 1862.

	Form of Voice.	Quality of Voice.	Force of Voice.	Stress of Voice.	Pitch of Voice.	Movement of Voice.
Pathetic	Effusive.	Pure Tone.	Subdued.	Median.	Low.	Slow and Very S.
Serious	Effusive.	Pure Tone.	Subdued.	Median.	Low.	Slow.
Tranquil	Effusive.	Pure Tone.	Moderate.	Median.	Middle.	Moderate.
Grave	Expulsive.	Pure Tone.	Moderate.	Unimp. Radical.	Low.	Moderate.
Didactic	Expulsive.	Pure Tone.	Moderate.	Unimp. Radical.	Middle.	Moderate.
Lively	Expulsive.	Pure Tone.	Mod. and En.	Unimp. Radical.	High.	Rapid.
Gay	Exp. and Expl.	Pure Tone.	Mod. and En.	Imp. Radical.	High.	Rapid.
Joyous	Exp. and Expl.	Pure Tone.	En. and Imp.	Imp. Radical.	High and Very H.	Rapid and Very R.
Sublime	Effusive.	Orotund.	Mod. and En.	Median.	Low and Very L.	Slow and Very S.
Oratorical	Exp. and Expl.	Orotund.	En. and Imp.	En. and Imp. Rad.	Middle and High.	Moderate.
Imp. Poetic	Exp. and Expl.	Orotund.	En. and Imp.	Thorough.	Middle and High.	Moderate and Rapid.
Shouting	Expulsive.	Orotund.	En. and Imp.	Thorough.	High and Very H.	Moderate and Slow.
Vehement	Explosive.	Oro., Asp. and Gutt.	Impassioned.	Imp. Radical.	High and Low.	Moderate and Rapid.

SECTION I.

EXPLANATION.

In the following classification of selections it is not claimed that every word, or even every line of each selection, can only be uttered, appropriately, in the style under which it is classed, but that the selection as a whole belongs under that style.

It not unfrequently will happen that a selection will begin in one style and close in another; nay more, the different lines of a single verse may belong under as many different styles.

As there is a grouping belonging to each style, which consists in the nice modulation of the voice on the attributes belonging to that style, so in the reading of any selection, the delivery of any lecture, speech, or oration, there is a grouping of the delivery, as a whole, which consists in changing the *style* of utterance to suit the varying sentiment expressed.

It is this command of every style and the ability to change at pleasure which so distinguishes the delivery of the accomplished speaker from that of the untrained novice.

CHAPTER II.

PATHETIC STYLE.

The Pathetic Style is appropriate for the delivery of that form of thought which, in a quiet and tranquil manner, is designed to move the tender emotions—as grief, sorrow, sadness, etc.

The Death-Bed.
Thomas Hood.

1. We watched her breathing through the night,
    Her breathing, soft and low,
   As in her breast the wave of life
    Kept heaving to and fro.

2. So silently we seemed to speak,
    So slowly moved about,
   As we had lent her half our powers
    To eke her living out.

3. Our very hopes belied our fears,
    Our fears our hopes belied;
   We thought her dying when she slept,
    And sleeping when she died.

4. For when the morn came, dim and sad,
    And chill with early showers,
   Her quiet eyelids closed—she had
    Another morn than ours.

The Pauper's Death-Bed.
Mrs. Southey.

1. Tread softly; bow the head,
    In reverent silence bow;
   No passing bell doth toll;
    Yet an immortal soul
   Is passing now.

2. Stranger! however great,
     With lowly reverence bow;
   There's one in that poor shed,
   One by that paltry bed—
     Greater than thou.

3. Beneath that beggar's roof,
     Lo! Death doth keep his state·
   Enter; no crowds attend;
   Enter; no guards defend
     This palace-gate.

4. That pavement, damp and cold,
     No smiling courtiers tread;
   One silent woman stands,
   Lifting with meager hands
     A dying head.

5. No mingling voices sound:
     An infant wail alone,
   A sob suppressed; again
   That short, deep gasp—and then
     The parting groan!

6. O change! O wondrous change!
     Burst are the prison-bars:
   This moment there, so low,
   So agonized—and now
     Beyond the stars!

7. O change! stupendous change!
     There lies the soulless clod;
   The sun eternal breaks,
   The new immortal wakes—
     Wakes with his God.

My Mother's Bible

G. P. Morris.

1. This book is all that's left me now
     Tears will unbidden start;
   With faltering lip and throbbing brow
     I press it to my heart;

    For many generations past,
        Here is our family tree;
    My mother's hands this Bible clasped;
        She, dying, gave it me.

2. Ah! well do I remember those
      Whose names these records bear,
    Who round the hearth-stone used to close
      After the evening prayer;
    And speak of what these pages said,
      In tones my heart would thrill;
    Though they are with the silent dead,
      Here are they living still.

3. My father read this holy book
      To brothers, sisters, dear:
    How calm was my dear mother's look,
      Who loved God's word to hear.
    Her aged face—I see it yet,
      As thronging memories come!
    Again that little group is met
      Within the halls at home!

4. Thou truest friend man ever knew,
      Thy constancy I've tried;
    When all were false I found thee true,
      My counselor and guide.
    The mines of earth no treasure give
      That could this volume buy:
    In teaching me the way to live,
      It taught me how to die.

THE OLD ARM CHAIR.
Eliza Cook.

1. I love it! I love it! and who shall dare
    To chide me for loving that old arm chair?
    I've treasured it long as a sainted prize,
    I've bedewed it with tears and embalmed it with sighs,
    'Tis bound by a thousand bands to my heart,
    Not a tie will break, not a link will start;
    Would you know the spell? a mother sat there;
    And a sacred thing is that old arm chair.

2. In childhood's hour I lingered near
That hallowed seat with a listening ear,
To the gentle words that mother could give,
To fit me to die and teach me to live:
She told me shame would never betide,
With truth for my creed, and God for my guide
She taught me to lisp my earliest prayer
As I knelt beside that old arm chair.

3. I sat and watched her many a day
When her eyes grew dim, and her locks were gray,
And I almost worshiped her when she smiled
And turned from her Bible to bless her child:
Years rolled on, but the last one sped,
My idol was shattered, my earth-star fled!
I felt how much the heart can bear,
When I saw her die in that old arm chair.

4. 'Tis past! 'tis past! but I gaze on it now
With quivering lip and throbbing brow;
'Twas there she nursed me, 'twas there she died,
And memory still flows with lava tide.
Say it is folly, and deem me weak,
As the scalding drops start down my cheek:
But I love it! I love it! and cannot tear
My soul from my mother's old arm chair!

The Burial of Arnold.
N. P. Willis.

1. Ye've gathered to your place of prayer
    With slow and measured tread:
Your ranks are full, your mates all there
    But the soul of one has fled.
He was the proudest in his strength,
    The manliest of ye all;
Why lies he at that fearful length,
    And ye around his pall?

2. Ye reckon it in days since he
    Strode up that foot-worn aisle,
With his dark eye flashing gloriously,
    And his lip wreathed with a smile.

O had it been but told you then
　To mark whose lamp was dim,
From out yon rank of fresh-lipped men,
　Would ye have singled him?

3. Whose was the sinewy arm which flung
　　Defiance to the ring?
　Whose laugh of victory loudest rung,
　　Yet not for glorying?
　Whose heart, in generous deed and thought
　　No rivalry might brook,
　And yet distinction claiming not?
　　There lies he—go and look!

4. On now, his requiem is done,
　　The last deep prayer is said;
　On to his burial, comrades, on,
　　With the noblest of the dead.
　Slow, for it presses heavily;
　　It is a man ye bear!
　Slow, for our thoughts dwell wearily
　　On the noble sleeper there.

5. Tread lightly, comrades, ye have laid
　　His dark locks on his brow;
　Like life, save deeper light and shade,
　　We'll not disturb them now.
　Tread lightly, for 'tis beautiful,
　　That blue-veined eyelid's sleep,
　Hiding the eye death left so dull,
　　Its slumber we will keep.

6. Rest now, his journeying is done,
　　Your feet are on his sod;
　Death's chain is on your champion,
　　He waiteth here his God.
　Ay, turn and weep, 'tis manliness
　　To be heart-broken here,
　For the grave of earth's best nobleness
　　Is watered by the tear.

The Last Footfall.

Anonymous.

1. There is often sadness in the tone,
    And a moisture in the eye,
  And a trembling sorrow in the voice,
    When we bid a last good-by.
  But sadder far than this, I ween,
    O sadder far than all!
  Is the heart-throb with which we strain
    To catch the last footfall.

2. The last press of a loving hand,
    Will cause a thrill of pain
  When we think, "O should it prove that we
    Shall never meet again."
  And as lingeringly the hands unclasp,
    The hot, quick drops will fall;
  But bitterer are the tears we shed,
    When we hear the last footfall.

3. We never felt how dear to us
    Was the sound we loved full well,
  We never knew how musical,
    Till its last echo fell:
  And till we heard it pass away
    Far, far beyond recall,
  We never thought what grief 'twould be
    To hear the last footfall!

4. And years and days that long are passed,
    And the scenes that seemed forgot,
  Rush through the mind like meteor-light
    As we linger on the spot;
  And little things that were as nought,
    But now will be our all,
  Come to us like an echo low
    Of the last, the last footfall.

ANNABEL LEE.
Edgar Allan Poe.

1. It was many, full many a year ago,
    In a kingdom by the sea,
   That a maiden lived, whom you may know
    By the name of Annabel Lee;
   And this maiden lived with no other thought
    Than to love and be loved by me.

2. I was a child, and she was a child,
    In this kingdom by the sea;
   But we loved with a love that was more than love,
    I and my Annabel Lee:
   With a love the wingéd seraphs of heaven
    Coveted her and me.

3. And this was the reason that long ago,
    In this kingdom by the sea,
   A wind blew out of a cloud, chilling
    My beautiful Annabel Lee:
   So that her highborn kinsman came
    And bore her away from me,
   To shut her up in a sepulcher,
    In this kingdom by the sea.

4. The angels not half so happy in heaven,
    Went envying her and me;
   Yes, that was the reason, as all men know,
    In this kingdom by the sea,
   That the wind came out of the cloud by night,
    Chilling and killing my Annabel Lee.

5. But our love was stronger by far than the love
    Of those who were older than we—
    Of many far wiser than we;
   And neither the angels above in heaven,
    Nor the demons down under the sea,
   Can ever dissever my soul from the soul
    Of the beautiful Annabel Lee.

6. For the moon never beams without bringing me d:
    Of the beautiful Annabel Lee:
   And the stars never rise but I feel the bright eyes
    Of the beautiful Annabel Lee;

And so all the night tide I lie down by the side
Of my darling, my darling, my life and my bride,
  In the sepulcher there by the sea,
  In her tomb by the sounding sea.

The Bridge of Sighs.
Thomas Hood.

1. One more unfortunate,
    Weary of breath,
   Rashly importunate,
    Gone to her death!

2. Take her up tenderly,
    Lift her with care;
   Fashioned so slenderly,
    Young, and so fair.

3. Look at her garments
   Clinging like cerements;
    Whilst the wave constantly
   Drips from her clothing.
    Take her up instantly,
   Loving, not loathing.

4. Touch her not scornfully;
   Think of her mournfully,
   Gently and humanly,
    Not of the stains of her;
    All that remains of her
   Now is pure womanly.

5. Make no deep scrutiny
   Into her mutiny
    Rash and undutiful:
   Past all dishonor,
   Death has left on her
    Only the beautiful.

6. Still, for all slips of hers,
    One of Eve's family;
   Wipe those poor lips of hers,
    Oozing so clammily.

7. Loop up her tresses,
       Escaped from the comb,
   Her fair auburn tresses;
       Whilst wonderment guesses
   Where was her home?

8. Who was her father?
       Who was her mother?
   Had she a sister?
       Had she a brother?
   Or was there a dearer one
   Still, and a nearer one
       Yet, than all others?

9. Alas! for the rarity
   Of Christian charity
       Under the sun!
   O it was pitiful!
   Near a whole city full,
       Home she had none.

10. Sisterly, brotherly,
    Fatherly, motherly,
        Feelings had changed;
    Love, by harsh evidence,
    Thrown from its eminence;
    Even God's providence
        Seeming estranged.

11. Where the lamps quiver
        So far in the river,
    With many a light
    From window and casement,
    From garret to basement,
    She stood with amazement,
        Houseless by night.

12. The bleak wind of March
        Made her tremble and shiver;
    But not the dark arch,
        Or the black flowing river:
    Mad from life's history,
    Glad to death's mystery,
        Swift to be hurled—
    Anywhere, anywhere
        Out of the world!

13. In she plunged boldly,
　　　No matter how coldly
　　　　　The rough river ran;
　　　Over the brink of it,
　　　Picture it, think of it,
　　　　　Dissolute man!
　　　　　*　　*　　*　　*

14. Take her up tenderly,
　　　　　Lift her with care;
　　　Fashioned so slenderly,
　　　　　Young, and so fair.

15. Ere her limbs frigidly,
　　　Stiffen too rigidly,
　　　　　Decently, kindly,
　　　Smooth and compose them,
　　　And her eyes, close them,
　　　　　Staring so blindly;
　　　Dreadfully staring
　　　　　Through muddy impurity,
　　　As when with the daring,
　　　Last look of despairing
　　　　　Fixed on futurity.

16. Perishing gloomily,
　　　Spurred by contumely,
　　　Burning insanity
　　　　　Into the rest;
　　　Cross her hands humbly,
　　　As if praying dumbly,
　　　　　Over her breast.

17. Owning her weakness,
　　　　　Her ill behavior,
　　　And leaving, with meekness,
　　　　　Her sins to her Saviour.

The Grave of the Beloved.
Washington Irving.

1. The sorrow for the dead is the only sorrow from which we refuse to be divorced. Every other wound we seek to heal, every other affliction to forget, but this wound we consider our duty to keep

open; this affliction we cherish and brood over in solitude. Where is the mother that would willingly forget the infant that perished like a blossom from her arms, though every recollection is a pang? Where is the child that would willingly forget the most tender of parents, though to remember be but to lament? Who, even in the hour of agony, would forget the friend over whom he mourns? Who, even when the tomb is closing upon the remains of her he most loved, and he feels his heart, as it were, crushed in the closing of its portal, would accept consolation that was to be bought by forgetfulness? No, the love which survives the tomb is one of the noblest attributes of the soul. If it has its woes it has likewise its delights, and when the overwhelming burst of grief is calmed into the gentle tear of recollection, when the sudden anguish and the convulsive agony over the present ruins of all that we most loved is softened away into pensive meditation on all that it was in the days of its loveliness, who would root out such a sorrow from the heart? Though it may sometimes throw a passing cloud even over the bright hour of gayety, or spread a deeper sadness over the hour of gloom, yet who would exchange it even for the song of pleasure or the burst of revelry? No, there is a voice from the tomb sweeter than song; there is a recollection of the dead to which we turn even from the charms of the living. O the grave! the grave! It buries every error, covers every defect, extinguishes every resentment. From its peaceful bosom spring none but fond regrets and tender recollections. Who can look down upon the grave even of an enemy and not feel a compunctious throb that even he should have warred with the poor handful of earth that lies moldering before him!

2. The grave of those we loved—what a place for meditation! There it is that we call up in long review the whole history of virtue and gentleness, and the thousand endearments lavished upon us almost unheeded in the daily intercourse of intimacy; there it is that we dwell upon the tenderness, the solemn, awful tenderness of the parting scene; the bed of death with all its stifled griefs; its noiseless attendants; its mute, watchful assiduities; the last testimonies of expiring love; the feeble, faltering, thrilling (O how thrilling!) pressure of the hand; the last fond look of the glazing eye turning upon us even from the threshold of existence; the faint, faltering accents struggling in death to give one more assurance of affection! Ay, go to the grave of buried love and meditate! There settle the account with thy conscience for every past benefit unrequited, every past endearment unregarded of that being who can never never never return to be soothed by thy contrition!

3. If thou art a child, and hast ever added a sorrow to the soul, or a furrow to the silvered brow of an affectionate parent; if thou art a husband, and hast ever caused the fond bosom that ventured its whole happiness in thy arms to doubt one moment of thy kindness or thy truth; if thou art a friend, and hast ever wronged in thought, word, or deed, the spirit that generously confided in thee; if thou art a lover, and hast ever given one unmerited pang to that true heart that now lies cold and still beneath thy feet; then be sure that every unkind look, every ungracious word, every ungentle action, will come thronging back upon thy memory and knocking dolefully at thy soul; then be sure that thou wilt lie down sorrowing and repentant on the grave, and utter the unheard groan and pour the unavailing tear; more deep, more bitter, because unheard and unavailing.

4. Then weave thy chaplet of flowers and strew the beauties of nature about the grave; console thy broken spirit if thou canst with these tender yet futile tributes of regret, but take warning by the bitterness of this thy contrite affliction over the dead, and be more faithful and affectionate in the discharge of thy duties to the living.

CHAPTER III.

SERIOUS STYLE.

The Serious Style is appropriate for the delivery of that form of thought which, in a quiet and tranquil manner, is designed to lead out the mind in a solemn strain.

NEARER HOME.
Phebe Cary.

1. One sweetly solemn thought
      Comes to me o'er and o'er;
   I'm nearer my home to-day
      Than I ever have been before.

2. Nearer my Father's house,
      Where the many mansions be;
   Nearer the great white throne,
      Nearer the crystal sea;

3. Nearer the bound of life,
      Where we lay our burdens down;
   Nearer leaving the cross,
      Nearer gaining the crown.

4. But the waves of that silent sea
      Roll dark before my sight,
   That brightly the other side
      Break on a shore of light.

5. O, if my mortal feet
      Have almost gained the brink,
   If it be I am nearer home
      Even to-day than I think,

6. Father, perfect my trust,
      Let my spirit feel in death
   That her feet are firmly set
      On the Rock of a living faith.

The Heavenly Canaan
Watts.

1. There is a land of pure delight,
    Where saints immortal reign;
   Eternal day excludes the night,
    And pleasures banish pain.

2. There everlasting spring abides,
    And never-fading flowers;
   Death, like a narrow sea, divides
    This heavenly land from ours.

3. Sweet fields, beyond the swelling flood,
    Stand dressed in living green:
   So to the Jews fair Canaan stood,
    While Jordan rolled between.

4. But timorous mortals start and shrink,
    To cross this narrow sea;
   And linger, trembling, on the brink,
    And fear to launch away.

5. O! could we make our doubts remove,
    Those gloomy doubts that rise,
   And see the Canaan that we love
    With unbeclouded eyes,

6. Could we but climb where Moses stood
    And view the landscape o'er,
   Not Jordan's stream, nor death's cold flood,
    Should fright us from the shore.

In the Other World.
H. Beecher Stowe.

1. It lies around us like a cloud,
    A world we do not see;
   Yet the sweet closing of an eye
    May bring us there to be.

2. Its gentle breezes fan our cheek;
    Amid our worldly cares
   Its gentle voices whisper love,
    And mingle with our prayers.

3. Sweet hearts around us throb and beat,
   Sweet helping hands are stirred,
   And palpitates the vail between
   With breathings almost heard.

4. The silence—awful, sweet, and calm—
   They have no power to break;
   For mortal words are not for them
   To utter or partake.

5. So thin, so soft, so sweet they glide,
   So near to press they seem,
   They seem to lull us to our rest,
   And melt into our dream.

6. And in the hush of rest they bring,
   'Tis easy now to see
   How lovely, and how sweet a pass
   The hour of death may be.

7. To close the eye, and close the ear
   Wrapped in a trance of bliss,
   And gently dream in loving arms—
   To swoon to that—from this.

8. Scarce knowing if we wake or sleep,
   Scarce asking where we are,
   To feel all evil sink away,
   All sorrow and all care.

9. Sweet souls around us! watch us still,
   Press nearer to our side;
   Into our thoughts, into our prayers,
   With gentle helpings glide.

10. Let death between us be as naught,
    A dried and vanished stream—
    Your joy be the reality,
    Our suffering life the dream.

If We Knew.
Anonymous.

1. If we knew the woe and heartache
    Waiting for us down the road,
   If our lips could taste the wormwood,
    If our backs could feel the load;
   Would we waste the day in wishing
    For a time that ne'er can be?
   Would we wait with such impatience
    For our ships to come from sea?

2. If we knew the baby fingers,
    Pressed against the window pane,
   Would be cold and stiff to-morrow,
    Never trouble us again;
   Would the bright eyes of our darling
    Catch the frown upon our brow?
   Would the print of rosy fingers
    Vex us then as they do now?

3. Ah, these little ice-cold fingers!
    How they point our memories back
   To the hasty words and actions
    Strewn along our backward track!
   How these little hands remind us,
    As in snowy grace they lie,
   Not to scatter thorns, but roses,
    For our reaping by and by.

4. Strange we never prize the music
    Till the sweet-voiced bird has flown;
   Strange that we should slight the violets
    Till the lovely flowers are gone;
   Strange that summer skies and sunshine
    Never seem one-half so fair
   As when winter's snowy pinions
    Shake their white down in the air.

5. Lips from which the seal of silence
    None but God can roll away,
   Never blossomed in such beauty
    As adorns the mouth to-day;

And sweet words that freight our memory
    With their beautiful perfume,
Come to us in sweeter accents
    Through the portals of the tomb

2. Let us gather up the sunbeams,
    Lying all around our path;
Let us keep the wheat and roses,
    Casting out the thorns and chaff;
Let us find our sweetest comfort
    In the blessings of to-day;
With the patient hand removing
    All the briers from our way.

Forty Years Ago.

I've wandered to the village, Tom,
    I've sat beneath the tree,
Upon the school-house play-ground,
    That sheltered you and me;
But none were left to greet me, Tom,
    And few were left to know,
Who played with us upon that green
    Just forty years ago.

2. The grass was just as green, Tom,
    Barefooted boys at play
Were sporting, just as we did then,
    With spirits just as gay.
But the master sleeps upon the hill,
    Which, coated o'er with snow,
Afforded us a sliding-place
    Some forty years ago.

3. The old school-house is altered some,
    The benches are replaced
By new ones, very like the same
    Our jack-knives had defaced;
But the same old bricks are in the wall,
    And the bell swings to and fro,
Its music's just the same, dear Tom,
    'Twas forty years ago.

4. The boys were playing some old game
   Beneath that same old tree;
   I do forget the name just now—
   You've played the same with me
   On that same spot; 'twas played with knives,
   By throwing so and so;
   The loser had a task to do
   There forty years ago.

5. The river's running just as still;
   The willows on its side
   Are larger than they were, Tom;
   The stream appears less wide;
   But the grape-vine swing is missed now,
   Where once we played the beau,
   And swung our sweethearts—pretty girls—
   Just forty years ago.

6. The spring that bubbled 'neath the hill,
   Close by the spreading beech,
   Is very low; 'twas once so high
   That we could scarcely reach;
   And kneeling down to take a drink,
   Dear Tom, I started so,
   To think how very much I've changed
   Since forty years ago.

7. Near by that spring, upon an elm,
   You know I cut your name,
   Your sweetheart's just beneath it, Tom,
   And you did mine the same.
   Some heartless wretch has peeled the bark;
   'Twas dying sure, but slow,
   Just as she died whose name you cut
   There forty years ago.

8. My lids have long been dry, Tom,
   But tears came in my eyes;
   I thought of her I loved so well,
   Those early broken ties.

I visited the old church-yard,
  And took some flowers to strow
Upon the graves of those we loved
  Just forty years ago.

9. Some are in the church-yard laid,
  Some sleep beneath the sea;
But none are left of our old class
  Excepting you and me.
And when our time shall come, Tom,
  And we are called to go,
I hope we'll meet with those we loved
  Some forty years ago.

The Mountains of Life.

J. G. Clark.

1. There's a land far away, 'mid the stars, we are told,
Where they know not the sorrows of time;
Where the pure waters wander through valleys of gold,
And life is a treasure sublime:
'Tis the land of our God, 'tis the home of the soul,
Where the ages of splendor eternally roll,
Where the way-weary traveler reaches his goal,
On the ever-green Mountains of Life.

2. Our gaze cannot soar to that beautiful land,
But our visions have told of its bliss,
And our souls by the gale of its gardens are fanned
When we faint in the desert of this;
And we sometimes have longed for its holy repose,
When our spirits were torn with temptations and woes,
And we've drank from the tide of the river that flows
From the ever-green Mountains of Life.

3. O the stars never tread the blue heavens at night
But we think where the ransomed have trod,
And the day never smiles from his palace of light
But we feel the bright smile of our God.
We are traveling homeward through changes and gloom,
To a kingdom where pleasures unceasingly bloom,
And our guide is the glory that shines through the tomb,
From the ever-green Mountains of Life.

The Isle of Long Ago.
B. F. Taylor.

1. O a wonderful stream is the river Time,
    As it runs through the realm of tears,
   With a faultless rhythm and a musical rhyme,
   And a boundless sweep and a surge sublime,
    As it blends with the Ocean of Years.

2. How the winters are drifting, like flakes of snow,
    And the summers like buds between,
   And the year in the sheaf, so they come and they go,
   On the river's breast, with its ebb and flow,
    As it glides in the shadow and sheen.

3. There's a magical isle up the river Time,
    Where the softest of airs are playing;
   There's a cloudless sky and a tropical clime,
   And a song as sweet as a vesper chime,
    And the Junes with the roses are straying.

4. And the name of that Isle is the Long Ago,
    And we bury our treasures there;
   There are brows of beauty and bosoms of snow;
   There are heaps of dust—but we loved them so!
    There are trinkets and tresses of hair;

5. There are fragments of song that nobody sings,
    And a part of an infant's prayer;
   There's a lute unswept, and a harp without strings;
   There are broken vows and pieces of rings,
    And the garments she used to wear.

6. There are hands that are waved when the fairy shore
    By the mirage is lifted in air,
   And we sometimes hear through the turbulent roar
   Sweet voices we heard in the days gone before,
    When the wind down the river is fair.

7. O remembered for aye, be the blessed Isle,
    All the day of our life until night;
   When the evening comes with its beautiful smile,
   And our eyes are closing to slumber awhile,
    May that "Greenwood" of Soul be in sight!

God the True Source of Consolation.
Thomas Moore.

1. O Thou who driest the mourner's tear,
   How dark this world would be,
   If, when deceived and wounded here,
   We could not fly to thee!

2. The friends who in our sunshine live
   When winter comes are flown,
   And he who has but tears to give
   Must weep those tears alone.

3. But Thou wilt heal the broken heart,
   Which, like the plants that throw
   Their fragrance from the wounded part,
   Breathes sweetness out of woe.

4. When joy no longer soothes or cheers,
   And e'en the hope that threw
   A moment's sparkle o'er our tears,
   Is dimmed and vanished too.

5. O who could bear life's stormy doom!
   Did not thy wing of love
   Come brightly wafting through the gloom
   Our peace-branch from above!

6. Then sorrow touched by thee grows bright
   With more than rapture's ray,
   As darkness shows us worlds of light
   We never saw by day.

Gratitude.
Addison.

1. When all thy mercies, O my God,
   My rising soul surveys,
   Transported with the view, I'm lost
   In wonder, love and praise.

2. Unnumbered comforts to my soul
   Thy tender care bestowed,
Before my infant heart conceived
   From whom those comforts flowed.

3. When in the slippery paths of youth
   With heedless steps I ran,
Thine arm, unseen, conveyed me safe,
   And led me up to man.

4. Ten thousand thousand precious gifts
   My daily thanks employ;
Nor is the least a cheerful heart,
   That tastes those gifts with joy.

5. Through every period of my life,
   Thy goodness I'll pursue;
And after death, in distant worlds,
   The glorious theme renew.

6. Through all eternity, to thee
   A joyful song I'll raise:
But O! eternity's too short
   To utter all thy praise!

OVER THE RIVER.

Miss Priest.

1. Over the river they beckon to me;
   Loved ones, who have passed to the further side
The gleam of their snowy robes I see—
   But their voices are lost in the dashing tide.
There was one with ringlets of sunny gold,
   And eyes the reflection of heaven's own blue;
He passed in the twilight gray and cold,
   And the pale mist hid him from mortal view.
We saw not the angels who met him there,
   The gates of the city we could not see—
Over the river, over the river,
   My brother stands waiting to welcome me.

2. Over the river the boatman pale
    Carried another, our household pet;
Her brown curls waved in the gentle gale,
    Darling Minnie! I see her yet.
She crossed on her bosom her dimpled hands,
    And fearlessly entered the phantom bark;
We felt it glide from the silver sands,
    And all our sunshine grew strangely dark.
We know she is safe on the further side,
    Where all the angels and ransomed be—
Over the river, the mystic river,
    Our household pet is waiting for me.

3. For none return from those quiet shores
    Who pass with the boatman cold and pale;
We hear the dip of their golden oars,
    We catch a glimpse of their snowy sail;
And lo! they have passed from our yearning heart,
    They have crossed the stream, and are gone for aye—
We may not sunder the vail apart,
    That hides from our vision the gates of day.
We only know that their barks no more
    Will glide with us o'er life's stormy sea;
But somewhere, I know, on that unseen shore,
    They watch and beckon and wait for me.

4. And I sit and think, when the sunset's gold
    Is flushing river and hill and shore,
I shall one day stand by the water cold
    And list to the sound of the boatman's oar.
I shall catch a gleam of the snowy sail,
    I shall hear the boat as it nears the strand,
I shall pass with the boatman cold and pale
    To the better shore of the spirit-land.
I shall know the loved who have gone before,
    And joyfully sweet will the meeting be—
When over the river, the peaceful river,
    The angel of Death shall carry me.

CHAPTER IV.
TRANQUIL STYLE.

The Tranquil Style is appropriate for the delivery of quiet, calm thought.

RAIN ON THE ROOF.
Coates Kinney.

1. When the humid shadows hover over all the starry spheres,
And the melancholy darkness gently weeps in rainy tears,
What a joy to press the pillow of a cottage chamber bed,
And to listen to the patter of the soft rain overhead.

2. Every tinkle on the shingles has an echo in the heart,
And a thousand dreamy fancies into busy being start;
And a thousand recollections weave their bright hues into woof,
As I listen to the patter of the soft rain on the roof.

3. Now in fancy comes my mother, as she used to years agone,
To survey the infant sleepers ere she left them till the dawn.
O! I see her bending o'er me, as I list to the refrain
Which is played upon the shingles by the patter of the rain.

4. Then my little seraph sister, with her wings and waving hair,
And her bright-eyed cherub brother—a serene, angelic pair—
Glide around my wakeful pillow with their praise or mild reproof,
As I listen to the murmur of the soft rain on the roof.

5. And another comes to thrill me with her eyes' delicious blue,
I forget, as gazing on her, that her heart was all untrue;
I remember that I loved her with a rapture kin to pain,
While my heart's quick pulses vibrate to the patter of the rain.

6. There is naught in art's bravuras that can work with such a spell,
In the spirit's pure, deep fountains, whence the holy passions well,
As that melody of nature—that subdued, subduing strain
Which is played upon the shingles by the patter of the rain!

NIGHT.
Shelley.

How beautiful this night! The balmiest sigh,
Which vernal zephyrs breathe in evening's ear,
Were discord to the speaking quietude
That wraps this moveless scene. Heaven's ebon vault,
Studded with stars unutterably bright,
Through which the moon's unclouded grandeur rolls,
Seems like a canopy which love has spread
To curtain her sleeping world. Yon gentle hills,
Robed in a garment of untrodden snow;
Yon darksome rocks, whence icicles depend—
So stainless, that their white and glittering spires
Tinge not the moon's pure beam; yon castled steep,
Whose banner hangeth o'er the time-worn tower
So idly, that rapt fancy deemeth it
A metaphor of peace; all form a scene
Where musing solitude might love to lift
Her soul above this sphere of earthliness;
Where silence, undisturbed, might watch alone,
So cold, so bright, so still.

THE LIGHT-HOUSE.
Moore.

1. The scene was more beautiful far to my eye
    Than if day in its pride had arrayed it:
   The land-breeze blew mild, and the azure-arched sky
    Looked pure as the Spirit that made it:
   The murmur rose soft, as I silently gazed
    On the shadowy waves' playful motion,
   From the dim distant hill, till the light-house fire blazed
    Like a star in the midst of the ocean.

2. No longer the joy of the sailor-boy's breast
    Was heard in his wildly-breathed numbers;
   The sea-bird had flown to her wave-girdled nest,
    The fisherman sunk to his slumbers:
   One moment I looked from the hill's gentle slope,
    All hushed was the billows' commotion,
   And o'er them the light-house looked lovely as hope,
    That star of life's tremulous ocean.

3. The time is long past, and the scene is afar,
　　Yet, when my head rests on its pillow,
　Will memory sometimes rekindle the star
　　That blazed on the breast of the billow:
In life's closing hour, when the trembling soul flies,
　　And death stills the heart's last emotion,
O then may the seraph of mercy arise,
　　Like a star on eternity's ocean!

Musings.
Amelia.

1. I wandered out one summer-night,
　　'Twas when my years were few,
　The wind was singing in the light,
　　And I was singing too;
　The sunshine lay upon the hill,
　　The shadow in the vale,
　And here and there a leaping rill
　　Was laughing on the gale.

2. One fleecy cloud upon the air
　　Was all that met my eyes;
　It floated like an angel there
　　Between me and the skies;
　I clapped my hands and warbled wild
　　As here and there I flew,
　For I was but a careless child,
　　And did as children do.

3. The waves came dancing o'er the sea
　　In bright and glittering bands,
　Like little children, wild with glee,
　　They linked their dimpled hands—
　They linked their hands, but ere I caught
　　Their sprinkled drops of dew,
　They kissed my feet, and, quick as thought,
　　Away the ripples flew.

4. The twilight hours, like birds, flew by,
　　As lightly and as free;
　Ten thousand stars were in the sky,
　　Ten thousand on the sea;

For every wave with dimpled face,
   That leaped upon the air,
Had caught a star in its embrace,
   And held it trembling there.

5. The young moon, too, with upturned sides,
   Her mirrored beauty gave,
And, as a bark at anchor rides,
   She rode upon the wave;
The sea was like the heaven above,
   As perfect and as whole,
Save that it seemed to thrill with love
   As thrills th' immortal soul.

6. The leaves, by spirit-voices stirred,
   Made murmurs on the air,
Low murmurs, that my spirit heard
   And answered with a prayer;
For 'twas upon that dewy sod,
   Beside the moaning seas,
I learned at first to worship God,
   And sing such strains as these.

7. The flowers, all folded to their dreams,
   Were bowed in slumber free,
By breezy hills and murmuring streams,
   Where'er they chanced to be;
No guilty tears had they to weep,
   No sins to be forgiven;
They closed their leaves and went to sleep
   'Neath the blue eye of heaven.

8. No costly robes upon them shone,
   No jewels from the seas,
Yet Solomon upon his throne,
   Was ne'er arrayed like these;
And just as free from guilt and art
   Were lovely human flowers,
Ere sorrow set her bleeding heart
   On this fair world of ours.

9. I heard the laughing wind behind
   A-playing with my hair;
The breezy fingers of the wind—
   How cool and moist they were!

I heard the night-bird warbling o'er
    Its soft enchanting strain;
I never heard such sounds before,
    And never shall again.

10. Then wherefore weave such strains as these,
    And sing them day by day,
When every bird upon the breeze
    Can sing a sweeter lay?
I'd give the world for their sweet art,
    The simple, the divine;
I'd give the world to melt one heart
    As they have melted mine.

The Rainbow.
Amelia.

1. I sometimes have thoughts in my loneliest hours,
That lie on my heart like the dew on the flowers,
Of a ramble I took one bright afternoon,
When my heart was as light as a blossom in June;
The green earth was moist with the late fallen showers,
The breeze fluttered down and blew open the flowers,
While a single white cloud, to its haven of rest,
On the white wing of peace, floated off in the west.

2. As I threw back my tresses to catch the cool breeze,
That scattered the rain-drops and dimpled the seas,
Far up the blue sky a fair rainbow unrolled
Its soft-tinted pinions of purple and gold.
'Twas born in a moment, yet, quick as its birth,
It had reached the uttermost ends of the earth,
And, fair as an angel, it floated as free,
With a wing on the earth and a wing on the sea.

3. How calm was the ocean! how gentle its swell!
Like a woman's soft bosom, it rose and it fell,
While its light sparkling waves, stealing laughingly o'er,
When they saw the fair rainbow, knelt down on the shore.
No sweet hymn ascended, no murmur of prayer,
Yet I felt that the spirit of worship was there,
And bent my young head in devotion and love,
'Neath the form of the angel that floated above.

4. How wide was the sweep of its beautiful wings!
How boundless its circle! how radiant its rings!
If I looked on the sky, 'twas suspended in air;
If I looked on the ocean, the rainbow was there;
Thus forming a girdle as brilliant and whole
As the thoughts of the rainbow that circled my soul.
Like the wing of the Deity, calmly unfurled,
It bent from the cloud and encircled the world.

5. There are moments, I think, when the spirit receives
Whole volumes of thought on its unwritten leaves,
When the folds of the heart in a moment unclose,
Like the innermost leaves from the heart of a rose.
And thus, when the rainbow had passed from the sky,
The thoughts it awoke were too deep to pass by;
It left my full soul, like the wing of a dove,
All fluttering with pleasure, and fluttering with love.

6. I know that each moment of rapture or pain
But shortens the links of life's mystical chain;
I know that my form, like that bow from the wave,
Must pass from the earth and lie cold in the grave;
Yet O! when death's shadows my bosom encloud,
When I shrink at the thought of the coffin and shroud,
May Hope, like the rainbow, my spirit enfold
In her beautiful pinions of purple and gold.

CHAPTER V.
GRAVE STYLE.

The Gráve Style is appropriate for the delivery of solemn and serious thought of a didactic character. Doctrinal and practical sermons come largely under this style.

The Inspiration of the Bible.
Edward Winthrop.

1. Such is the intrinsic excellence of Christianity that it is adapted to the wants of all, and it provides for all, not only by its precepts and by its doctrines, but also by its evidence.

2. The poor man may know nothing of history, or science, or philosophy; he may have read scarcely any book but the Bible; he may be totally unable to vanquish the skeptic in the arena of public debate; but he is, nevertheless, surrounded by a panoply which the shafts of infidelity can never pierce.

3. You may go to the home of the poor cottager, whose heart is deeply imbued with the spirit of vital Christianity; you may see him gather his little family around him. He expounds to them the wholesome doctrines and principles of the Bible, and if they want to know the evidence upon which he rests his faith of the divine origin of his religion, he can tell them upon reading the book which teaches Christianity he finds not only a perfectly true description of his own natural character, but in the provisions of this religion a perfect adaptation to all his needs.

4. It is a religion by which to live, a religion by which to die; a religion which cheers in darkness, relieves in perplexity, supports in adversity, keeps steadfast in prosperity, and guides the inquirer to that blessed land where "the wicked cease from troubling, and the weary are at rest."

5. We entreat you, therefore, to give the Bible a welcome, a cordial reception; obey its precepts, trust its promises, and rely implicitly upon that Divine Redeemer whose religion brings glory to God in the highest, and on earth, peace and good will to men.

6. Thus will you fulfill the noble end of your existence, and the great God of the universe will be your father and your friend; and when the last mighty convulsion shall shake the earth and the sea

and the sky, and the fragments of a thousand barks, richly freighted with intellect and learning, are scattered on the shores of error and delusion, your vessel shall in safety outride the storm, and enter in triumph the haven of eternal rest.

Goodness of God.

1. The light of nature, the works of creation, the general consent of nations, in harmony with divine revelation, attest the being, the perfections and the providence of God. Whatever cause we have to lament the frequent inconsistency of human conduct with this belief, yet an avowed atheist is a monster that rarely makes his appearance. God's government of the affairs of the universe, an acknowledgment of his active, superintending providence over that portion of it which constitutes the globe we inhabit is rejected, at least theoretically, by very few.

2. That a superior, invisible power is continually employed in managing and controlling by secret, imperceptible, irresistible means all the transactions of the world, is so often manifested in the disappointment as well as in the success of our plans, that blind and depraved must our minds be to deny what every day's transactions so fully prove. The excellence of the divine character, especially in the exercise of that goodness toward his creatures which is seen in the dispensation of their daily benefits, and in overruling occurring events, to the increase of their happiness, is equally obvious.

3. Do we desire evidence of these things? Who is without them in the experience of his own life? Who has not reason to thank God for the success which has attended his exertions in the world? Who has not reason to thank him for defeating plans, the accomplishment of which it has been afterward seen would have resulted in injury or ruin? Who has not cause to present him the unaffected homage of a grateful heart for the consequences of events apparently the most unpropitious, and for his unquestionable kindness in the daily supply of needful mercies?

Access to God.
James Hamilton.

1. However early in the morning you seek the gate of access, you find it already open; and the midnight moment when you find yourself in the sudden arms of death, the winged prayer can bring an instant Saviour near. And this wherever you are. It needs not that you ascend some special Pisgah or Moriah. It needs not that you should enter some awful shrine, or pull off your shoes on some holy ground.

2. Could a memento be reared on every spot from which an acceptable prayer has passed away, and upon which a prompt answer has come down, we should find Jehovah-shammah, "the Lord has been here," inscribed on many a cottage hearth and many a dungeon floor. We should find it not only in Jerusalem's proud temple, and David's cedar galleries, but in the fisherman's cottage by the brink of Gennesareth, and in the chamber where Pentecost began.

3. Whether it be the field where Isaac went to meditate, or the rocky knoll where Jacob lay down to sleep, or the brook where Israel wrestled, or the den where Daniel gazed on lions and the lions gazed on him, on the hill-side where the Man of sorrows prayed all night, we should still discern the prints of the ladder's feet let down from heaven—the landing-place of mercies, because the starting-point of prayer. And all this whatsoever you are.

4. It needs no saints, no proficient in piety, no adept in eloquent language, no dignity of earthly rank. It needs but a blind beggar, a loathsome lazar. It needs but a penitent publican or a dying thief. And it needs no sharp ordeal, no costly passport, no painful expiation, to bring you to the mercy-seat. The Saviour's merit—the name of Jesus, priceless as they are, cost the sinner nothing. They are freely put at his disposal, and instantly and constantly he may make use of them. This access to God in every place, at every moment, without any price or personal merit, is it not a privilege?

Infidelity Tested.

1. We might ask the patrons of infidelity, what fury impels them to attempt the subversion of Christianity? Is it that they have discovered a better system? To what virtues are their principles favorable? Or is there one which Christians have not carried to a higher than any of which their party can boast? Have they discovered a more excellent rule of life or a better hope in death, than that which the Scriptures suggest? Above all, what are the pretensions on which they rest their claims to be the guides of mankind, or which embolden them to expect we should trample on the experience of ages, and abandon a religion which has been attested by a train of miracles and prophecies in which millions of our forefathers have found a refuge in every trouble and consolation in the hour of death; a religion which has been adorned with the highest sanctity of character and splendor of talents, which enrolls among its disciples the names of Bacon, Newton, and Locke, the glory of their species, and to which these illustrious men were proud to dedicate the last and best fruits of their immortal genius.

2. If the question at issue is to be decided by argument, nothing can be added to the triumph of Christianity; if by an appeal to authority, what have our adversaries to oppose to these great names? Where are the infidels of such pure, uncontaminated morals, unshaken probity, and extended benevolence, that we should be in no danger of being seduced into impiety by their example? Into what obscure recesses of misery, into what dungeons have their philanthropists penetrated, to lighten the fetters and relieve the sorrows of the helpless captive? What barbarous tribes have their apostles visited? What distant climes have they explored, encompassed with cold, nakedness and want, to diffuse principles of virtue and the blessings of civilization? Or will they choose to waive their pretensions to this extraordinary, and in their eyes eccentric species of benevolence, and rest their character on their political exploits; on their efforts to reanimate the virtues of a sinking State, to restrain licentiousness, to calm the tumult of popular fury; and, by inculcating the spirit of justice, moderation and pity for fallen greatness, to mitigate the inevitable horrors of revolution? Our adversaries will, at least, have the discretion, if not the modesty, to recede from the test.

3. More than all, their infatuated eagerness, their parricidal zeal to extinguish a sense of Deity, must excite astonishment and horror. Is the idea of an almighty and perfect ruler unfriendly to any passion which is consistent with innocence, or an obstruction to any design which is not shameful to avow?

4. Eternal God! on what are thy enemies intent? What are those enterprises of guilt and horror, that, for the safety of their performers, require to be enveloped in a darkness which the eye of Heaven must not pierce? Miserable men! proud of being the offspring of chance; in love with universal disorder; whose happiness is involved in the belief of there being no witness to their designs, and who are at ease only because they suppose themselves inhabitants of a forsaken and fatherless world!

Religion the Only Basis of Society.
W. E. Channing.

1. Few men suspect, perhaps no man comprehends, the extent of the support given by religion to every virtue. No man, perhaps, is aware how much our moral and social sentiments are fed from this fountain; how powerless conscience would become without the belief of a God; how palsied would be human benevolence were there not the sense of a higher benevolence to quicken and sustain it; how suddenly the whole social fabric would quake, and with what a

fearful crash it would sink into hopeless ruin, were the ideas of a Supreme Being, of accountableness, and of a future life, to be utterly erased from every mind.

2. And let men thoroughly believe that they are the work and sport of chance; that no superior intelligence concerns itself with human affairs; that all their improvements perish forever at death; that the weak have no guardian, and the injured no avenger; that there is no recompense for sacrifices to uprightness and the public good; that an oath is unheard in heaven; that secret crimes have no witness but the perpetrator; that human existence has no purpose, and human virtue no unfailing friend; that this brief life is every thing to us, and death is total, everlasting extinction; once let them thoroughly abandon religion, and who can conceive or describe the extent of the desolation which would follow!

3. We hope, perhaps, that human laws and natural sympathy would hold society together. As reasonably might we believe, that, were the sun quenched in the heavens, our torches would illuminate and our fires quicken and fertilize the creation. What is there in human nature to awaken respect and tenderness if man is the unprotected insect of a day? And what is he more, if atheism be true?

4. Erase all thought and fear of God from a community, and selfishness and sensuality would absorb the whole man. Appetite, knowing no restraint, and suffering having no solace or hope, would trample in scorn on the restraints of human laws. Virtue, duty, principle, would be mocked and spurned as unmeaning sounds. A sordid self-interest would supplant every other feeling, and man would become, in fact, what the theory of atheism declares him to be —a companion for brutes.

The Promises of Religion to the Young.
Alison.

1. In every part of Scripture it is remarkable with what singular tenderness the season of youth is always mentioned, and what hopes are offered to the devotion of the young. It was at that age that God appeared unto Moses when he fed his flock in the desert, and called him to the command of his own people. It was at that age he visited the infant Samuel, while he ministered in the temple of the Lord, " in days when the word of the Lord was precious, and when there was no open vision." It was at that age that his Spirit fell upon David, while he was yet the youngest of his father's sons, and when among the mountains of Bethlehem he fed his father's sheep.

2. It was at that age also that they brought young children unto

Christ that he should touch them, and his disciples rebuked those that brought them. But when Jesus saw it he was much displeased, and said to them, "Suffer little children, and forbid them not, to come unto me, for of such is the kingdom of heaven." If these, then, are the effects and promises of youth and piety, rejoice, O young man, in thy youth! rejoice in those days which are never to return, when religion comes to thee in all its charms, and when the God of nature reveals himself to thy soul, like the mild radiance of the morning sun when he rises amid the blessings of a grateful world.

3. If already devotion hath taught thee her secret pleasures; if, when nature meets thee in all its magnificence or beauty, thy heart humbleth itself in adoration before the hand which made it, and rejoiceth in the contemplation of the wisdom by which it is maintained; if, when revelation unvails her mercies and the Son of God comes forth to give peace and hope to fallen man, thine eye follows with astonishment the glories of his path and pours at last over his cross those pious tears which it is a delight to shed; if thy soul accompanieth him in his triumph over the grave, and entereth on the wings of faith into that heaven "where he sat down at the right hand of the Majesty on High," and seeth the "society of angels and of the spirits of just men made perfect," and listeneth to the "everlasting song which is sung before the throne;" if such are the meditations in which thy youthful hours are passed, renounce not, for all that life can offer thee in exchange, these solitary joys. The world which is before thee—the world which thine imagination paints in such brightness—has no pleasures to bestow which can compare with these; and all that its boasted wisdom can produce has nothing so acceptable in the sight of heaven as this pure offering of thy infant soul.

4. In these days "the Lord himself is thy shepherd, and thou dost not want. Amid the green pastures and by the still waters" of youth he now makes "thy soul to repose." But the years draw nigh when life shall call thee to its trials; the evil days are on the wing when "thou shalt say thou hast no pleasure in them;" and as thy steps advance, "the valley of the shadow of death opens," through which thou must pass at last. It is then thou shalt know what it is to "remember thy Creator in the days of thy youth." In these days of trial or of awe "his Spirit shall be with thee," and thou shalt fear no ill; and amid every evil that surrounds thee "he shall restore thy soul. His goodness and mercy shall follow thee all the days of thy life;" and when at last "the silver cord is loosed, thy spirit shall return to God who gave it, and thou shalt dwell in the house of the Lord forever."

CHAPTER VI.

DIDACTIC STYLE.

The Didactic Style is appropriate for the delivery of those forms of thought which are simply designed to instruct either in the form of narration, description, or scientific and literary lectures.

Introductions to speeches and orations generally require the Didactic Style.

Cheerfulness.

1. There is no one quality that so much attaches man to his fellow-man as cheerfulness. Talents may excite more respect, and virtue more esteem, but the respect is apt to be distant and the esteem cold. It is far otherwise with cheerfulness. It endears a man to the heart, not the intellect or the imagination. There is a kind of reciprocal diffusiveness about this quality that recommends its possessor by the very effect it produces. There is a mellow radiance in the light it sheds on all social intercourse which pervades the soul to a depth that the blaze of intellect can never reach.

2. The cheerful man is a double blessing—a blessing to himself and to the world around him. In his own character his good nature is the clear blue sky of his own heart, on which every star of talent shines out more clearly. To others he carries an atmosphere of joy and hope and encouragement wherever he moves. His own cheerfulness becomes infectious, and his associates lose their moroseness and their gloom in the amber-colored light of the benevolence he casts around him.

3. It is true that cheerfulness is not always happiness. The face may glow in smiles while the heart "runs in coldness and darkness below," but cheerfulness is the best external indication of happiness that we have, and it enjoys this advantage over almost every other good quality, that the counterfeit 's as valuable to society as the

reality. It answers as a medium of public circulation fully as well as the true coin.

4. A man is worthy of all praise, whatever may be his private griefs, who does not intrude them on the happiness of his friends, but constantly contributes his quota of cheerfulness to the general public enjoyment. "Every heart knows its own bitterness," but let the possessor of that heart take heed that he does not distill it into his neighbor's cup, and thus poison his felicity.

5. There is no sight more commendable and more agreeable than a man whom we know fortune has dealt with badly smothering his peculiar griefs in his own bosom, and doing his duty in society with an unruffled brow and a cheerful mien. It is a duty which society has a right to demand—a portion of that great chain which binds humanity together, the links of which every one should preserve bright and unsullied.

6. It may be asked, What shall that man do whose burdens of grief are heavy, and made still heavier by the tears he has shed over them in private; shall he leave society? Certainly, until he has learned to bear his own burden. Shall he not seek the sympathy of his friends? He had better not. Sympathy would only weaken the masculine strength of mind which enables us to endure. Besides, sympathy unsought for is much more readily given, and sinks deeper in its healing effects into the heart. No, no, cheerfulness is a duty which every man owes. Let him faithfully discharge the debt.

Be Comprehensive.

1. Talk to the point, and stop when you reach it. The faculty which some possess of making one idea cover a quire of paper is despicable. To fill a volume upon nothing is a credit to nobody, though Chesterfield wrote a very clever poem upon nothing.

2 There are men who get one idea into their heads, and but one, and they make the most of it. You can see it and almost feel it in their presence. On all occasions it is produced till it is worn as thin as charity. They remind you of a twenty-four pounder discharging at a humming-bird. You hear a tremendous noise, see a volume of smoke, but you look in vain for the effects. The bird is scattered to atoms.

3. Just so with the idea. It is enveloped in a cloud, and lost amid the rumbling of words and flourishes. Short letters, sermons speeches and paragraphs are favorites with us. Commend us to the young man who wrote to his father, "Dear sir, I am going to get

married;" and also to the old gentleman, who replied, "Dear son, go ahead."

4. Such are the men for action. They do more than they say. The half is not told in their cases. They are worth their weight in gold for every purpose of life, and are men every-where prized.

Hamlet's Advice to the Players.
Shakspeare.

Speak the speech, I pray you, as I pronounced it to you, trippingly on the tongue; but if you mouth it, as many of our players do, I had as lief the town-crier had spoken my lines. And do not saw the air too much with your hands, but use all gently, for in the very torrent, tempest, and, as I may say, whirlwind of your passion, you must beget a temperance that will give it smoothness.

O it offends me to the soul to hear a robustious, periwig-pated fellow tear a passion to tatters, to very rags, to split the ears of the groundlings, who (for the most part) are capable of nothing but inexplicable dumb shows and noise. Pray you avoid it.

Be not too tame either, but let your own discretion be your tutor. Suit the action to the word, the word to the action, with this special observance, that you overstep not the modesty of nature, for any thing so overdone is from the purpose of playing, whose end is to hold, as it were, the mirror up to nature, to show virtue her own feature, scorn her own image, and the very age and body of the times their form and pressure.

Now this overdone, or come tardy off, though it may make the unskillful laugh, cannot but make the judicious grieve, the censure of which one must, in your allowance, outweigh a whole theater of others. O there be players that I have seen play, and heard others praise, and that highly — not to speak it profanely — that neither having the accent of Christian nor the gait of Christian, pagan, nor man, have so strutted and bellowed that I have thought some of Nature's journeymen had made men and not made them well, they imitated humanity so abominably.

Industry and Eloquence.
Wirt.

1. In the ancient republics of Greece and Rome oratory was a necessary branch of a finished education. A much smaller propor-

tion of the citizens were educated than among us, but of these a much larger number became orators. No man could hope for distinction or influence and yet slight this art. The commanders of their armies were orators as well as soldiers, and ruled as well by their rhetorical as by their military skill. There was no trusting with them, as with us, to a natural facility or the acquisition of an accidental fluency by occasional practice.

2. They served an apprenticeship to the art. They passed through a regular course of instruction in schools; they submitted to long and laborious discipline; they exercised themselves frequently both before equals and in the presence of teachers, who criticised, reproved, rebuked, excited emulation, and left nothing undone which art and perseverance could accomplish.

3. The greatest orators of antiquity, so far from being favored by natural tendencies, except, indeed, in their high intellectual endowments, had to struggle against natural obstacles, and, instead of growing up spontaneously to their unrivaled eminence, they forced themselves forward by the most discouraging artificial process.

4. Demosthenes combated an impediment in speech and an ungainliness of gesture which at first drove him from the forum in disgrace. Cicero failed at first through weakness of lungs and an excessive vehemence of manner which wearied the hearers and defeated his own purpose. These defects were conquered by study and discipline. He exiled himself from home, and during his absence in various lands passed not a day without a rhetorical exercise, seeking the masters who were most severe in criticism as the surest means of leading him to the perfection at which he aimed.

5. Such, too, was the education of their other great men. They were all, according to their ability and station, orators; orators, not by nature or accident, but by education, formed in strict process of rhetorical training.

6. The inference to be drawn from these observations is, that if so many of those who received an accomplished education became accomplished orators, because to become so was one purpose of their study, then it is in the power of a much larger proportion among us to form ourselves into creditable and accurate speakers. The inference should not be denied until proved false by experiment.

7. Let this art be made an object of attention; 'et young men train themselves to it faithfully and long, and if any of competent talents and tolerable science be found at last incapable of expressing themselves in continued and connected discourse, so as to answer the ends of public speaking, then, and not till then, let it be said that a pecul-

ral talent or natural aptitude is requisite, the want of which must render effort vain; then, and not till then, let us acquiesce in this indolent and timorous notion, which contradicts the whole testimony of antiquity and all the experience of the world.

No Excellence Without Labor.
Wirt.

1. The education, moral and intellectual, of every individual must be chiefly his own work. Rely upon it that the ancients were right; both in morals and intellect we give their final shape to our own characters, and thus become emphatically the architects of our own fortunes. How else could it happen that young men who have had precisely the same opportunities should be continually presenting us with such different results, and rushing to such opposite destinies? Difference of talent will not solve it, because that difference very often is in favor of the disappointed candidate.

2. You shall see issuing from the walls of the same college, nay, sometimes from the bosom of the same family, two young men, of whom the one shall be admitted to be a genius of high order, the other scarcely above the point of mediocrity; yet you shall see the genius sinking and perishing in poverty, obscurity and wretchedness, while, on the other hand, you shall observe the mediocre plodding his slow but sure way up the hill of life, gaining steadfast footing at every step, and mounting at length to eminence and distinction, an ornament to his family, a blessing to his country. Now, whose work is this? Manifestly their own. They are the architects of their respective fortunes.

3. The best seminary of learning that can open its portals to you can do no more than afford you the opportunity of instruction; but it must depend at last on yourselves whether you will be instructed or not, or to what point you will push your instruction. And of this, be assured, I speak from observation a certain truth: there is no excellence without great labor. It is the fiat of fate, from which no power of genius can absolve you.

4. Genius unexerted is like the poor moth that flutters around a candle till it scorches itself to death. If genius be desirable at all it is only of that great and magnanimous kind which, like the condor of South America, pitches from the summit of Chimborazo above the clouds, and sustains itself at pleasure in that empyreal region with an energy rather invigorated than weakened by the effort.

5. It is this capacity for high and long-continued exertion, t[…] vigorous power of profound and searching investigation, this careeri[…] and wide-spreading comprehension of mind, and those long reacl[…] of thought that

> "... pluck bright honor from the pale-faced moon,
> Or dive into the bottom of the deep,
> Where fathom line could never touch the ground,
> And drag up drownèd honor by the locks."

This is the prowess and these the hardy achievements which are[…] enroll your names among the great men of the earth.

Advice to a Young Lawyer.
Judge Story.

1. Whene'er you speak, remember every cause
   Stands not on eloquence, but stands on laws;
   Pregnant in matter, in expression brief,
   Let every sentence stand with bold relief;
   On trifling points nor time nor talents waste,
   A sad offense to learning and to taste;
   Nor deal with pompous phrase, nor e'er suppose
   Poetic flights belong to reasoning prose.

2. Loose declamation may deceive the crowd,
   And seem more striking as it grows more loud;
   But sober sense rejects it with disdain,
   As naught but empty noise, and weak as vain.

3. The froth of words, the schoolboy's vain parade
   Of books and cases—all his stock in trade—
   The pert conceits, the cunning tricks and play
   Of low attorneys, strung in long array,
   The unseemly jest, the petulant reply,
   That chatters on, and cares not how or why,
   Strictly avoid—unworthy themes to scan,
   They sink the speaker and disgrace the man;
   Like the false lights by flying shadows cast,
   Scarce seen when present, and forgot when past.

4. Begin with dignity; expound with grace
   Each ground of reasoning in its time and place·
   Let order reign throughout, each topic touch,
   Nor urge its power too little nor too much;

Give each strong thought its most attractive view,
In diction clear and yet severely true,
And as the arguments in splendor grow,
Let each reflect its light on all below;
When to the close arrived, make no delays
By petty flourishes or verbal plays,
But sum the whole in one deep, solemn strain,
Like a strong current hastening to the main.

MODULATION.
Lloyd.

1. 'Tis not enough the voice be sound and clear,
'Tis modulation that must charm the ear.
That voice all modes of passion can express
Which marks the proper word with proper stress;
But none emphatic can that speaker call
Who lays an equal emphasis on all.
Some o'er the tongue the labored measures roll,
Slow and deliberate as the parting toll;
Point every stop, mark every pause so strong,
Their words, like stage processions, stalk along

2. All affectation but creates disgust,
And e'en in speaking we may seem too just.
In vain for them the pleasing measure flows
Whose recitation runs it all to prose;
Repeating what the poet sets not down,
The verb disjointing from its favorite noun,
While pause and break and repetition join
To make a discord in each tuneful line.

3. Some placid natures fill the allotted scene.
With lifeless drawls, insipid and serene;
While others thunder every couplet o'er,
And almost crack your ears with rant and roar.
More nature oft, and finer strokes are shown
In the low whisper than tempestuous tone;
And Hamlet's hollow voice and fixed amaze
More powerful terror to the mind conveys
Than he who, swollen with impetuous rage,
Bullies the bulky phantom of the stage.

4. He who in earnest studies o'er his part,
   Will find true nature cling about his heart.
   The modes of grief are not included all
   In the white handkerchief and mournful drawl;
   A single look more marks the internal woe
   Than all the windings of the lengthened O!
   Up to the face the quick sensation flies,
   And darts its meaning from the speaking eyes:
   Love, transport, madness, anger, scorn, despair,
   And all the passions, all the soul is there.

Don't Run in Debt.
Eliza Cook.

1. Don't run in debt—never mind, never mind
     If the clothes are faded and torn;
   Fix 'em up, make 'em do, it is better by far,
     Than to have the heart weary and worn.
   Who'll love you more for the set of your hat,
     Or your ruff, or the tie of your shoe,
   The style of your vest, or your boots or cravat,
     If they know you're in debt for the new?

2. There's no comfort, I tell you, in walking the street
     In fine clothes if you know you're in debt,
   And feel that perchance you some tradesman may meet,
     Who will sneer, "They're not paid for yet."

3. Good friends, let me beg of you, don't run in debt;
     If the chairs and the sofa are old,
   They will fit your backs better than any new set,
     Unless they are paid for with gold.
   If the house is too small, draw the closer together;
     Keep it warm with a hearty good-will;
   A big one unpaid for, in all kinds of weather,
     Will send to your warm heart a chill.

4. Don't run in debt—dear girls, take a hint,
     If the fashions have changed since last season,
   Old nature is out in the very same tint,
     And old nature, we think, has some reason.

But just say to your friend that you cannot afford
   To spend time to keep up with the fashion;
That your purse is too light, and your honor too bright,
   To be tarnished with such silly passion.

5 Gents, don't run in debt—let your friends, if they can
   Have fine houses, and feathers, and flowers,
But, unless they are paid for, be more of a man
   Than to envy their sunshiny hours.
If you've money to spare I have nothing to say—
   Spend your dollars and dimes as you please,
But mind you, the man who his note has to pay,
   Is the man who is never at ease.

6. Kind husband, don't run in debt any more;
   'Twill fill your wife's cup of sorrow
To know that a neighbor may call at your door
   With a bill you must settle to-morrow.
O take my advice! it is good! it is true!
   (But lest you may some of you doubt it,)
I'll whisper a secret, now seeing 'tis you:
   I have tried it, and know all about it.

7. The chain of a debtor is heavy and cold,
   Its links all corrosion and rust;
Gild it o'er as you will, it is never of gold
   Then spurn it aside with disgust.

QUERIES.

1. Is it any body's business
   If a gentleman should choose
To wait upon a lady
   If the lady don't refuse?
Or, to speak a little plainer,
   That the meaning all may know
Is it any body's business
If a lady has a beau?

2. Is it any body's business
   When that gentleman may call,
Or when he leaves the lady,
   Or if he leaves at all?

Or is it necessary
  That the curtain should be drawn,
To save from further trouble
  The outside lookers-on?

3. Is it any body's business
    But the lady's, if her beau
  Rides out with other ladies,
    And doesn't let her know?
  Is it any body's business
    But the gentleman's, if she
  Accepts another escort,
    Where he doesn't chance to be?

4. Is a person on the sidewalk,
    Whether great or whether small,
  Is it any body's business
    Where that person means to call?
  Or if you see a person,
    As he's calling anywhere,
  Is it any of your business
    What his business may be there?

5. The substance of our query,
    Simply stated, would be this:
  Is it any body's business
    What another's business is?
  If it is, or if it isn't,
    We would really like to know:
  For we're certain, if it isn't,
    There are some who make it so.

CHAPTER VII.

LIVELY STYLE.

The Lively Style is appropriate for the delivery of animated narration, animated description, animated thought of every kind in which the feeling does not rise to impassioned emotion.

The Personality and Uses of a Laugh.

1. I would be willing to choose my friend by the quality of his laugh, and abide the issue. A glad, gushing outflow—a clear, ringing, mellow note of the soul, as surely indicates a genial and genuine nature as the rainbow in the dew-drop heralds the morning sun, or the frail flower in the wilderness betrays the zephyr-tossed seed of the parterre.

2. A laugh is one of God's truths. It tolerates no disguises. Falsehood may train its voice to flow in softest cadences, its lips to wreathe into smiles of surpassing sweetness, its face

" .... to put on
That look we trust in ;"

But its laugh will betray the mockery. Who has not startled and shuddered at the hollow " he-he-he ! " of some velvet-voiced Mephistopheles, whose sinuous fascinations, without this note of warning, this premonitory rattle—might have bound the soul with a strong spell ?

3. Leave nature alone. If she is noble, her broadest expression will soon tone itself down to fine accordance with life's earnestness; if she is base, no silken interweavings can keep out of sight her ugly head of discord. If we put a laugh into strait-jacket and leading-strings it becomes an abortion ; if we attempt to refine we destroy its pure, mellifluent ring; if we suppress a laugh it struggles and dies on the heart, and the place where it lies is apt ever after to be weak and vulnerable. No, laugh truly, as you would speak truly, and both the inner and the outer man will rejoice. A full, spontaneous outburst opens all the delicate valves of being, and glides, a subtle oil, through all its complicated mechanism.

4. Laugh heartily if you would keep the dew of your youth. There is no need to lay our girlhood and boyhood so doggedly down

upon the altar of sacrifice as we toil up life's mountain. Dear, innocent children, lifting their dewy eyes and fair foreheads to the benedictions of angels, prattling and gamboling because it is a great joy to live, should flit like sunbeams among the stern-faced and stalwart. Young men and maidens should walk with strong, elastic tread and cheerful voices among the weak and uncertain. White hairs should be no more the insignia of age, but the crown of ripe and perennial youth.

5. Laugh for your beauty. The joyous carry a fountain of light in their eyes, and round into rosy dimples, where the echoes of gladness play at "hide and go seek." Your "lean and hungry Cassius" is never betrayed into a laugh, and his smile is more cadaverous than his despair.

6. Laugh if you would live. He only exists who drags his days after him like a massive chain, asking sympathy with uplifted eyebrows and weak utterance, as the beggar asks alms. Better die, for your own sake and the world's sake, than to pervert the uses and graces and dignities of life.

7. Make your own sunshine and your own music, keep your heart open to the smile of the good Father, and brave all things.

"Care to our coffin adds a nail, no doubt,
And every grin so merry draws one out."

PADDLE YOUR OWN CANOE.
Mrs. Sarah T. Bolton.

1. Voyager upon life's sea,
    To yourself be true;
   And where'er your lot may be,
    Paddle your own canoe.
   Never, though the winds may rave,
    Falter nor look back,
   But upon the darkest wave
    Leave a shining track.

2. Nobly dare the wildest storm,
    Stem the hardest gale;
   Brave of heart and strong of arm,
    You will never fail.
   When the world is cold and dark,
    Keep an end in view,
   And toward the beacon mark
    Paddle your own canoe.

3. Every wave that bears you on
    To the silent shore,
From its sunny source has gone
    To return no more:
Then let not an hour's delay
    Cheat you of your due;
But while it is called to-day,
    Paddle your own canoe.

4. If your birth denied you wealth,
    Lofty state and power,
Honest fame and hardy health
    Are a better dower;
But if these will not suffice,
    Golden gain pursue,
And to win the glittering prize,
    Paddle your own canoe.

5. Would you wrest the wealth of fame
    From the hand of fate;
Would you write a deathless name,
    With the good and great;
Would you bless your fellow-men?
    Heart and soul imbue
With the holy task, and then
    Paddle your own canoe.

6. Would you crush the tyrant wrong
    In the world's fierce fight?
With a spirit brave and strong,
    Battle for the right;
And to break the chains that bind
    The many to the few—
To enfranchise slavish mind,
    Paddle your own canoe.

7. Nothing great is lightly won,
    Nothing won is lost;
Every good deed nobly done
    Will repay the cost.
Leave to Heaven, in humble trust,
    All you will to do;
But if you succeed, you must
    Paddle your own canoe.

I'm With You Once Again.
G. P. Morris.

1. I'm with you once again, my friends;
   No more my footsteps roam;
 Where it began my journey ends,
   Amid the scenes of home.
 No other clime has skies so blue,
   Or streams so broad and clear;
 And where are hearts so warm and true
   As those that meet me here?

2. Since last, with spirits wild and free,
   I pressed my native strand,
 I've wandered many miles at sea,
   And many miles on land:
 I've seen fair regions of the earth
   With rude commotion torn,
 Which taught me how to prize the worth
   Of that where I was born.

3. In other countries, when I heard
   The language of my own,
 How fondly each familiar word
   Awoke an answering tone!
 But when our woodland songs were sung
   Upon a foreign mart,
 The vows that faltered on the tongue
   With rapture filled my heart.

4. My native land, I turn to you
   With blessing and with prayer,
 Where man is brave and woman true,
   And free as mountain air.
 Long may our flag in triumph wave
   Against the world combined,
 And friends a welcome, foes a grave,
   Within our borders find.

A Psalm of Life.
Longfellow.

1 Tell me not, in mournful numbers,
   Life is but an empty dream!
 For the soul is dead that slumbers,
   And things are not what they seem

2. Life is real! Life is earnest!
    And the grave is not its goal:
  "Dust thou art, to dust returnest,"
    Was not written of the soul.

3. Not enjoyment, and not sorrow,
    Is our destined end or way,
  But to act, that each to-morrow
    Find us further than to-day.

4. Art is long, and time is fleeting,
    And our hearts, though stout and brave,
  Still, like muffled drums, are beating
    Funeral marches to the grave.

5. In the world's broad field of battle,
    In the bivouac of life,
  Be not like dumb, driven cattle;
    Be a hero in the strife.

6. Trust no future, howe'er pleasant;
    Let the dead past bury its dead;
  Act; act in the living present;
    Heart within, and God o'erhead.

7. Lives of great men all remind us
    We can make our lives sublime,
  And departing, leave behind us
    Footprints on the sands of time;

8. Footprints that perhaps another,
    Sailing o'er life's solemn main,
  A forlorn and shipwrecked brother,
    Seeing, shall take heart again.

9. Let us, then, be up and doing
    With a heart for any fate;
  Still achieving, still pursuing,
    Learn to labor and to wait.

CHAPTER VIII.
GAY STYLE.

THE Gay Style is appropriate for the delivery of m[ost] joyous thought. Dramatic scenes, sketches of life manners, vivid delineations of character, all demand Gay Style.

SPRING.
Bryant.

1. Is this a time to be gloomy and sad,
    When our mother Nature laughs around,
  When even the deep blue heavens look glad,
    And gladness breathes from the blossoming ground?

2. The clouds are at play in the azure space,
    And their shadows at play on the bright green vale;
  And here they stretch to the frolic chase,
    And there they roll on the easy gale.

3. And look at the broad-faced sun, how he smiles
    On the dewy earth that smiles on his ray,
  On the leaping waters and gay young isles;
    Ay, look, and he'll smile thy gloom away.

YOUNG LOCHINVAR.
Scott.

1. O, young Lochinvar is come out of the west!
  Through all the wide border his steed was the best;
  And save his good broadsword he weapon had none;
  He rode all unarmed, and he rode all alone.
  So faithful in love, and so dauntless in war,
  There never was knight like the young Lochinvar.

2. He staid not for brake, and he stopped not for stone;
  He swam the Eske river, where ford there was none;
  But ere he alighted at Netherby gate
  The bride had consented, the gallant came late

  ... laggard in love, and a dastard in war,
  ... to wed the fair Ellen of brave Lochinvar.

 ... boldly he entered the Netherby hall,
 'Mong bridesmen, and kinsmen, and brothers, and all.
 Then spoke the bride's father, his hand on his sword,
 (For the poor craven bridegroom said never a word,)
 " O come ye in peace here, or come ye in war,
 Or to dance at our bridal, young Lord Lochinvar ? "

4. " I long wooed your daughter, my suit you denied;
 Love swells like the Solway, but ebbs like its tide;
 And now am I come, with this lost love of mine,
 To lead but one measure, drink one cup of wine.
 There be maidens in Scotland, more lovely by far,
 That would gladly be bride to the young Lochinvar."

5. The bride kissed the goblet, the knight took it up,
 He quaffed off the wine, and he threw down the cup:
 She looked down to blush, and she looked up to sigh,
 With a smile on her lips and a tear in her eye.
 He took her soft hand ere her mother could bar,
 " Now tread we a measure," said young Lochinvar.

6. So stately his form, and so lovely her face,
 That never a hall such a galliard did grace;
 While her mother did fret, and her father did fume,
 And the bridegroom stood dangling his bonnet and plume,
 And the bride-maidens whispered, " 'Twere better by far
 To have matched our fair cousin with young Lochinvar."

7. One touch to her hand, and one word in her ear
 When they reached the hall-door, and the charger stood near·
 So light to the croup the fair lady he swung,
 So light to the saddle before her he sprung,
 " She is won! we are gone—over bank, bush, and scaur—
 They'll have swift steeds that follow," quoth young Lochinvar

8 There was mounting 'mong Græmes of the Netherby clan,
 Forsters, Fenwicks, and Musgraves, they rode and they ran;
 There was racing and chasing on Cannobie Lee,
 But the lost bride of Netherby ne'er did they see.
 So daring in love, and so dauntless in war,
 Have ye e'er heard of gallant like young Lochinvar ?

Let Us Try to be Happy.

1. Let us try to be happy! We may if we will
Find some pleasures in life to o'erbalance the ill;
There was never an evil, if well understood,
But what, rightly managed, would turn to a good.
If we were but as ready to look to the light
As we are to sit moping because it is night,
We should own it a truth, both in word and in deed,
That who tries to be happy is sure to succeed.

2. Let us try to be happy! Some shades of regret
Are sure to hang round which we cannot forget;
There are times when the lightest of spirits must bow
And the sunniest face wear a cloud on its brow.
We must never bid feelings, the purest and best,
To lie blunted and cold in our bosom at rest;
But the deeper our own griefs the greater our need
To try to be happy lest other hearts bleed.

3. O try to be happy! It is not for long
We shall cheer on each other by counsel or song;
If we make the best use of our time that we may,
There is much we can do to enliven the way;
Let us only in earnestness each do our best,
Before God and our conscience, and trust for the rest;
Still taking this truth, both in word and in deed,
That who tries to be happy is sure to succeed.

Coquette Punished.

1. ~~Ellen~~ was fair, and knew it, too,
As other village beauties do,
Whose mirrors never lie;
Secure of any swain she chose,
She smiled on half a dozen beaux,
And, reckless of a lover's woes,
She cheated these and taunted those,
"For how could any one suppose
A clown could take her eye?".

2. But whispers through the village ran,
That ~~Roger~~ was the ~~happy~~ man
The maid designed to bless;

For, wheresoever moved the fair,
The youth was, like her shadow, there,
And rumor boldly matched the pair,
   For village folks will guess.

3. Edgar did love, but was afraid
To make confession to the maid,
   So bashful was the youth:
Certain to meet a kind return,
He let the flame in secret burn,
Till from his lips the maid should learn
   Officially the truth.

4. At length one morn to take the air,
The youth and maid, in one-horse chair,
   A long excursion took.
Edgar had nerved his bashful heart
The sweet confession to impart,
For ah! suspense had caused a smart
   He could no longer brook.

5. He drove, nor slackened once his reins,
Till Hempstead's wide-extended plains
   Seemèd joined to skies above:
Nor house, nor tree, nor shrub was near
The rude and dreary scene to cheer,
Nor soul within ten miles to hear,
And still poor Edgar's silly fear
   Forbade to speak of love.

6. At last one desperate effort broke
The bashful spell, and Edgar spoke
   With most persuasive tone;
Recounted past attendance o'er,
And then, by all that's lovely, swore
That he would love forever more,
   If she'd become his own.

7. The maid in silence heard his prayer,
Then, with a most provoking air,
   She tittered in his face;
And said, "'Tis time for you to know
A lively girl must have a beau,
Just like a reticule—for show;
And at her nod to come and go;

8. "Your penetration must be dull
To let a hope within your skull
    Of matrimony spring.
Your wife? ha! ha! upon my word,
The thought is laughably absurd
As any thing I ever heard—
    I never dreamed of such a thing!"

9. The lover sudden dropp'd his rein
When on the center of the plain;
    "The linch-pin's out!" he cried;
"Be pleased one moment to alight,
Till I can set the matter right,
    That we may safely ride,"

10. He said, and handed out the fair;
Then laughing, cracked his whip in air,
And wheeling round his horse and chair,
Exclaimed, "Adieu, I leave you there
    In solitude to roam."
"What mean you, sir?" the maiden cried,
"Did you invite me out to ride,
To leave me here without a guide?
    Nay, stop, and take me home."

11. "What! take you home!" exclaimed the beau;
"Indeed, my dear, I'd like to know
How such a hopeless wish could grow,
    Or in your bosom spring.
What! take home! ha! ha! upon my word,
The thought is laughably absurd
As any thing I ever heard—
    I never dreamed of such a thing!"

RHYME OF THE RAIL.
Saxe.

1. Singing through the forests,
    Rattling over ridges,
Shooting under arches,
    Rumbling over bridges;

GAY STYLE.

Whizzing through the mountains,
  Buzzing o'er the vale,
Bless me! this is pleasant,
  Riding on the rail.

2. Men of different stations
    In the eye of fame,
  Here are very quickly
    Coming to the same;
  High and lowly people,
    Birds of every feather,
  On a common level,
    Traveling together.

3. Gentlemen in shorts,
    Looming very tall;
  Gentlemen at large,
    Talking very small;
  Gentlemen in tights,
    With a loose-ish mien;
  Gentlemen in gray,
    Looking rather green,

4. Gentlemen quite old
    Asking for the news;
  Gentlemen in black,
    In a fit of blues;
  Gentlemen in claret,
    Sober as a vicar;
  Gentlemen in tweed,
    Dreadfully in liquor.

5. Stranger on the right
    Looking very sunny,
  Obviously reading
    Something rather funny.
  Now the smiles are thicker—
    Wonder what they mean?
  Faith, he's got the Knicker-
    bocker Magazine!

6. Stranger on the left
    Closing up his peepers;
  Now he snores amain,
    Like the Seven Sleepers.

At his feet a volume
    Gives the explanation,
How the man grew stupid
    From "association!"

7. Ancient maiden lady
       Anxiously remarks,
   That there must be peril
       'Mong so many sparks;
   Roguish-looking fellow,
       Turning to the stranger,
   Says it's his opinion
       She is out of danger.

8. Woman with her baby,
       Sitting vis-a-vis;
   Baby keeps a-squalling,
       Woman looks at me;
   Asks about the distance,
       Says it's tiresome talking,
   Noises of the cars
       Are so very shocking.

9. Market woman, careful
       Of the precious casket,
   Knowing eggs are eggs,
       Tightly holds her basket;
   Feeling that a smash,
       If it come, would surely
   Send her eggs to pot
       Rather prematurely.

10. Singing through the forests,
        Rattling over ridges,
    Shooting under arches,
        Rumbling over bridges;
    Whizzing through the mountains,
        Buzzing o'er the vale;
    Bless me! this is pleasant,
        Riding on the rail.

CHAPTER IX.

JOYOUS STYLE.

The Joyous Style is appropriate for the delivery of static mirth, joy and light and playful humor.
Many of the scenes and passages of Shakspeare, Scott ving and Cowper demand the Joyous Style.

GUNEOPATHY.
Sawe.

1. I saw a lady yesterday,
   A regular M. D.,
   Who'd taken from the Faculty
   Her medical degree;
   And I thought if ever I was sick
   My doctor she should be.

2. I pity the deluded man
   Who foolishly consults
   Another man, in hopes to find
   Such magical results
   As when a pretty woman lays
   Her hand upon his pulse!

3. I had a strange disorder once,
   A kind of chronic chill,
   That all the doctors in the town,
   With all their vaunted skill,
   Could never cure, I'm very sure,
   With powder nor with pill;

4. I don't know what they called it
   In their pompous terms of art,
   Nor if they thought it mortal
   In such a vital part;
   I only know 'twas reckoned
   "Something icy round the heart."

5. A lady came, her presence brought
   The blood into my ears.
   She took my hand, and something like
   A fever now appears.
   Great Galen! I was all aglow,
   Though I'd been cold for years!

6. Perhaps it isn't every case
   That's fairly in her reach,
   But should I e'er be ill again
   I fervently beseech
   That I may have, for life or death,
   A lady for my "leech!"

MERCUTIO'S HUMOROUS DESCRIPTION OF QUEEN MAB.
Shakspeare.

O then I see Queen Mab hath been with you!
                                            She comes
In shape no bigger than an agate stone
On the forefinger of an alderman,
Drawn by a team of little atomies
Athwart men's noses as they lie asleep:
Her wagon spokes made of long spinners' legs;
The cover of the wings of grasshoppers;
The traces of the smallest spider's web;
The collars of the moonshine's watery beams;
Her whip of cricket's bone; the lash of film;
Her wagoner a small gray-coated gnat,
Not half so big as a round little worm
Pricked from the lazy finger of a maid;
Her chariot is an empty hazelnut,
Made by the joiner squirrel, or old grub,
Time out of mind the fairies' coach-makers.
And in this state she gallops night by night
Through lover's brains, and then they dream of love;
On courtiers' knees, that dream on court'sies straight·
O'er lawyers' fingers, who straight dream on fees;
O'er ladies' lips, who straight on kisses dream.
Sometimes she gallops o'er a courtier's nose,
And then dreams he of smelling out a suit;

And sometimes comes she with a tithe-pig's tail,
Tickling a parson's nose as he lies asleep,
Then dreams he of another benefice;
Sometimes she driveth o'er a soldier's neck,
And then dreams he of cutting foreign throats,
Of breaches, ambuscadoes, Spanish blades,
And healths five fathoms deep; and then anon
Drums in his ear, at which he starts and wakes;
And, being thus frighted, swears a prayer or two,
And sleeps again.

CHAPTER X.

SUBLIME STYLE.

The Sublime Style is appropriate for the delivery of those forms of thought which in a quiet way, express sublimity, grandeur, reverence, adoration, devotion, awe amazement, etc.

In Memoriam—A. Lincoln.
Mrs. Emily J. Bugbee.

1. There's a burden of grief on the breezes of spring,
And a song of regret from the bird on its wing;
There's a pall on the sunshine and over the flowers,
And a shadow of graves on these spirits of ours;
For a star hath gone out from the night of our sky,
On whose brightness we gazed as the war-cloud rolled by;
So tranquil and steady and clear were its beams,
That they fell like a vision of peace on our dreams.

2. A heart that we knew had been true to our weal,
And a hand that was steadily guiding the wheel;
A name never tarnished by falsehood or wrong,
That had dwelt in our hearts like a soul-stirring song;
Ah, that pure, noble spirit has gone to its rest,
And the true hand lies nerveless and cold on his breast·
But the name and the memory, these never will die,
But grow brighter and dearer as ages go by.

3. Yet the tears of a nation fall over the dead,
Such tears as a nation before never shed,
For our cherished one fell by a dastardly hand,
A martyr to truth and the cause of the land;
And a sorrow has surged, like the waves to the shore
When the breath of the tempest is sweeping them o'er;
And the heads of the lofty and lowly have bowed
As the shaft of the lightning sped out from the cloud.

SUBLIME STYLE.

4. Not gathered, like Washington, home to his rest,
When the sun of his life was far down in the west:
But stricken from earth in the midst of his years,
With the Canaan in view, of his prayers and his tears.
And the people, whose hearts in the wilderness failed,
Sometimes, when the stars of their promise had paled,
Now stand by his side on the mount of his fame,
And yield him their hearts in a grateful acclaim.

5. Yet there on the mountain our leader must die,
With the fair land of promise spread out to his eye;
His work is accomplished, and what he has done
Will stand as a monument under the sun;
And his name, reaching down through the ages of time,
Will still through the years of eternity shine,
Like a star sailing on through the depths of the blue,
On whose brightness we gaze every evening anew.

6. His white tent is pitched on the beautiful plain,
Where the tumult of battle comes never again,
Where the smoke of the war-cloud ne'er darkens the air,
Nor falls on the spirit a shadow of care.
The songs of the ransomed enrapture his ear,
And he heeds not the dirges that roll for him here;
In the calm of his spirit, so strange and sublime,
He is lifted far over the discords of time.

7. Then bear him home gently, great son of the West!
'Mid her fair blooming prairies lay Lincoln to rest,
From the nation who loved him she takes to her trust,
And will tenderly garner the consecrate dust.
A Mecca his grave to the people shall be,
And a shrine evermore for the hearts of the free.

BREAK! BREAK! BREAK!

Tennyson.

1. Break, break, break,
    On thy cold gray stones, O sea!
    And I would that my tongue could utter
        The thoughts that arise in me.

2. O well for the fisherman's boy
　　That he shouts with his sister at play!
　O well for the sailor lad
　　That he sings in his boat on the bay!

3. And the stately ships go on
　　To their haven under the hill;
　But O for the touch of a vanished hand!
　　And the sound of a voice that is still.

4. Break, break, break,
　　At the foot of thy crags, O sea!
　But the tender grace of a day that is dead
　　Will never come back to me.

God.

Derzhavin.

1. O thou eternal One! whose presence bright
　　All space doth occupy, all motion guide;
　Unchanged through time's all devastating flight!
　　Thou only God—there is no God beside!
　Being above all beings! Mighty One,
　　Whom none can comprehend and none explore;
　Who fill'st existence with thyself alone,
　　Embracing all, supporting, ruling o'er;
　　Being whom we call God, and know no more!

2. In its sublime research philosophy
　　May measure out the ocean deep, may count
　The sands or the sun's rays; but God! for thee
　　There is no weight nor measure; none can mount
　Up to thy mysteries; Reason's brightest spark,
　　Though kindled by thy light, in vain would try
　To trace thy counsels, infinite and dark;
　　And thought is lost ere thought can soar so high,
　　Even like past moments in eternity.

3. Thou from primeval nothingness didst call
　　First chaos, then existence; Lord, on thee
　Eternity hath its foundation; all
　　Sprung forth from thee—of light, joy, harmony,

Sole origin—all life, all beauty thine;
  Thy word created all, and doth create;
Thy splendor fills all space with rays divine;
  Thou art and wert and shalt be! Glorious! Great!
Light-giving, life-sustaining Potentate!

4. Thy chains the unmeasured universe surround—
  Upheld by thee, by thee inspired with breath!
Thou the beginning with the end hast bound,
  And beautifully mingled life and death!
As sparks mount upward from the fiery blaze,
  So suns are born, so worlds spring forth from thee·
And as the spangles in the sunny rays
  Shine round the silver snow, the pageantry
Of heaven's bright army glitters in thy praise.

5. A million torches, lighted by thy hand,
  Wander unwearied through the blue abyss—
They own thy power, accomplish thy command,
  All gay with life, all eloquent with bliss.
What shall we call them? Piles of crystal light—
  A glorious company of golden streams—
Lamps of celestial ether burning bright—
  Suns lighting systems with their joyous beams?
But thou to these art as the noon to night.

6. Yes, as a drop of water in the sea,
  All this magnificence in thee is lost:
What are ten thousand worlds compared to thee?
  And what am I then? Heaven's unnumbered host,
Though multiplied by myriads, and arrayed
  In all the glory of sublimest thought,
Is but an atom in the balance, weighed
  Against thy greatness—is a cipher brought
  Against infinity! What am I then? Naught!

7. Naught! But the effluence of thy light divine,
  Pervading worlds, hath reached my bosom too;
Yes, in my spirit doth thy spirit shine
  As shines the sunbeam in a drop of dew.
Naught! But I live, and on hope's pinions fly
  Eager toward thy presence; for in thee
I live and breathe and dwell; aspiring high,

Even to the throne of thy divinity.
I am, O God! and surely thou must be.

8. Thou art—directing, guiding all—thou art!
Direct my understanding then to thee;
Control my spirit, guide my wandering heart;
Though but an atom 'midst immensity,
Still I am something, fashioned by thy hand.
I hold a middle rank 'twixt heaven and earth,
On the last verge of mortal being stand,
Close to the realms where angels have their birth
Just on the boundaries of the spirit-land!

9. The chain of being is complete in me,
In me is matter's last gradation lost,
And the next step is spirit—Deity!
I can command the lightning, and am dust!
A monarch and a slave, a worm, a god!
Whence came I here, and how? so marvelously
Constructed and conceived? unknown! this clod
Lives surely through some higher energy;
For from itself alone it could not be!

10. Creator, yes. Thy wisdom and thy word
Created me. Thou source of life and good.
Thou spirit of my spirit, and my Lord,
Thy light, thy love, in their bright plenitude
Filled me with an immortal soul, to spring
Over the abyss of death, and bade it wear
The garments of eternal day, and wing
Its heavenly flight beyond this little sphere,
Even to its source—to thee—its Author there.

11. O thoughts ineffable! O visions blest!
Though worthless our conceptions all of thee,
Yet shall thy shadowed image fill our breast,
And waft its homage to thy Deity.
God! thus alone my lowly thoughts can soar,
Thus seek thy presence—Being wise and good!
'Midst thy vast works admire, obey, adore;
And when the tongue is eloquent no more
The soul shall speak in tears of gratitude.

God's First Temples.
Bryant.

1. The groves were God's first temples. Ere man learned
To hew the shaft, and lay the architrave,
And spread the roof above them, ere he framed
The lofty vault, to gather and roll back
The sound of anthems, in the darkling wood,
Amidst the cool and silence, he knelt down
And offered to the Mightiest solemn thanks
And supplication. For his simple heart
Might not resist the sacred influences
That, from the stilly twilight of the place,
And from the gray old trunks, that, high in heaven,
Mingled their mossy boughs, and from the sound
Of the invisible breath, that swayed at once
All their green tops, stole over him, and bowed
His spirit with the thought of boundless Power
And inaccessible Majesty. Ah, why
Should we, in the world's riper years, neglect
God's ancient sanctuaries, and adore
Only among the crowd, and under roofs
That our frail hands have raised? Let me, at least,
Here, in the shadow of the aged wood,
Offer one hymn; thrice happy, if it find
Acceptance in his ear.

2.   Father, thy hand
Hath reared these venerable columns: thou
Didst weave this verdant roof. Thou didst look down
Upon the naked earth, and forthwith rose
All these fair ranks of trees. They in thy sun
Budded, and shook their green leaves in thy breeze,
And shot toward heaven. The century-living crow,
Whose birth was in their tops, grew old and died
Among their branches, till at last they stood,
As now they stand, massy and tall and dark,
Fit shrine for humble worshiper to hold
Communion with his Maker.

3.   Here are seen
No traces of man's pomp or pride; no silks
Rustle, no jewels shine, nor envious eyes

Encounter; no fantastic carvings show
The boast of our vain race to change the form
Of thy fair works. But thou art here; thou fillest
The solitude. Thou art in the soft winds
That run along the summits of these trees
In music; thou art in the cooler breath,
That, from the inmost darkness of the place,
Comes, scarcely felt; the barky trunks, the ground,
The fresh, moist ground, are all instinct with thee.

4. Here is continual worship; nature here,
In the tranquillity that thou dost love,
Enjoys thy presence. Noiselessly around,
From perch to perch the solitary bird
Passes; and yon clear spring, that, 'midst its herbs,
Wells softly forth, and visits the strong roots
Of half the mighty forest, tells no tale
Of all the good it does.

5.   Thou hast not left
Thyself without a witness, in these shades,
Of thy perfections. Grandeur, strength and grace
Are here to speak of thee. This mighty oak—
By whose immovable stem I stand, and seem
Almost annihilated—not a prince,
In all the proud old world beyond the deep,
Ere wore his crown as loftily as he
Wears the green coronal of leaves with which
Thy hand has graced him. Nestled at his root
Is beauty, such as blooms not in the glare
Of the broad sun. That delicate forest flower,
With scented breath, and looks so like a smile,
Seems, as it issues from the shapeless mold,
An emanation of the indwelling life,
A visible token of the upholding love,
That are the soul of this wide universe.

6. My heart is awed within me when I think
Of the great miracle that still goes on,
In silence, round me—the perpetual work
Of thy creation, finished, yet renewed
Forever. Written on thy works I read
The lesson of thy own eternity.

Lo! all grow old and die; but see, again,
How, on the faltering footsteps of decay,
Youth presses—ever gay and beautiful youth—
In all its beautiful forms. These lofty trees
Wave not less proudly that their ancestors
Molder beneath them.

7.   O there is not lost
One of earth's charms: upon her bosom yet,
After the flight of untold centuries,
The freshness of her far beginning lies,
And yet shall lie. Life mocks the idle hate
Of his arch enemy Death; yea, seats himself
Upon the sepulcher, and blooms and smiles,
And of the triumphs of his ghastly foe
Makes his own nourishment. For he came forth
From thine own bosom, and shall have no end.

8. There have been holy men who hid themselves
Deep in the woody wilderness, and gave
Their lives to thought and prayer, till they outlived
The generation born with them, nor seemed
Less aged than the hoary trees and rocks
Around them; and there have been holy men
Who deemed it were not well to pass life thus.
But let me often to these solitudes
Retire, and, in thy presence, re-assure
My feeble virtue. Here, its enemies,
The passions, at thy plainer footsteps, shrink,
And tremble, and are still.

9.   O God, when thou
Dost scare the world with tempests, set on fire
The heavens with falling thunderbolts, or fill,
With all the waters of the firmament,
The swift, dark whirlwind, that uproots the woods
And drowns the villages; when, at thy call,
Uprises the great deep, and throws himself
Upon the continent, and overwhelms
Its cities; who forgets not, at the sight
Of these tremendous tokens of thy power,
His pride, and lays his strifes and follies by!
O from these sterner aspects of thy face

Spare me and mine; nor let us need the wrath
Of the mad, unchained elements, to teach
Who rules them. Be it ours to meditate,
In these calm shades, thy milder majesty,
And to the beautiful order of thy works
Learn to conform the order of our lives.

The Closing Year.
Prentice.

1. 'Tis midnight's holy hour, and silence now
Is brooding, like a gentle spirit, o'er
The still and pulseless world. Hark! on the winds
The bell's deep tones are swelling—'tis the knell
Of the departed year. No funeral train
Is sweeping past; yet, on the stream and wood,
With melancholy light, the moonbeams rest
Like a pale, spotless shroud; the air is stirred
As by a mourner's sigh; and on yon cloud,
That floats so still and placidly through heaven,
The spirits of the seasons seem to stand,
Young Spring, bright Summer, Autumn's solemn form,
And Winter with his aged locks, and breathe,
In mournful cadences, that come abroad
Like the far wind-harp's wild and touching wail,
A melancholy dirge o'er the dead year,
Gone from the earth forever.

2.   'Tis a time
For memory and for tears. Within the deep,
Still chambers of the heart, a specter dim,
Whose tones are like the wizard voice of Time,
Heard from the tomb of ages, points its cold
And solemn finger to the beautiful
And holy visions that have passed away,
And left no shadow of their loveliness
On the dead waste of life. That specter lifts
The coffin-lid of Hope and Joy and Love,
And, bending mournfully above the pale,
Sweet forms, that slumber there, scatters dead flowers
O'er what has passed to nothingness.

3.   The year
Has gone, and with it many a glorious throng
Of happy dreams. Its mark is on each brow,
Its shadow in each heart. In its swift course
It waved its scepter o'er the beautiful—
And they are not. It laid its pallid hand
Upon the strong man—and the haughty form
Is fallen, and the flashing eye is dim.
It trod the hall of revelry, where thronged
The bright and joyous—and the tearful wail
Of stricken ones is heard, where erst the song
And reckless shout resounded.

4   It passed o'er
The battle-plain, where sword and spear and shield
Flashed in the light of mid-day—and the strength
Of serried hosts is shivered, and the grass,
Green from the soil of carnage, waves above
The crushed and moldering skeleton. It came,
And faded like a wreath of mist at eve;
Yet, ere it melted in the viewless air,
It heralded its millions to their home
In the dim land of dreams.

5.   Remorseless Time!
Fierce spirit of the glass and scythe! what power
Can stay him in his silent course, or melt
His iron heart to pity? On, still on
He presses, and forever. The proud bird,
The condor of the Andes, that can soar
Through heaven's unfathomable depths, or brave
The fury of the northern hurricane,
And bathe his plumage in the thunder's home.
Furls his broad wings at nightfall, and sinks down
To rest upon his mountain crag; but Time
Knows not the weight of sleep or weariness,
And night's deep darkness has no chain to bind
His rushing pinions.

6   Revolutions sweep
O'er earth, like troubled visions o'er the breast
Of dreaming sorrow; cities rise and sink,
Like bubbles on the water; fiery isles

Spring blazing from the ocean, and go back
To their mysterious caverns; mountains rear
To heaven their bald and blackened cliffs, and bow
Their tall heads to the plain; new empires rise,
Gathering the strength of hoary centuries,
And rush down like the Alpine avalanche,
Startling the nations, and the very stars,
Yon bright and burning blazonry of God,
Glitter awhile in their eternal depths,
And, like the Pleiad, loveliest of their train,
Shoot from their glorious spheres, and pass away,
To darkle in the trackless void: yet Time—
Time, the tomb-builder, holds his fierce career,
Dark, stern, all-pitiless, and pauses not
Amid the mighty wrecks that strew his path,
To sit and muse, like other conquerors,
Upon the fearful ruin he has wrought.

Morning Hymn to Mont Blanc.
Coleridge.

1. Hast thou a charm to stay the morning star
   In his steep course? so long he seems to pause
   On thy bald, awful head, O sovereign Blanc!
   The Arve and Aveiron at thy base
   Rave ceaselessly; but thou, most awful form!
   Risest forth from thy silent sea of pines,
   How silently! Around thee and above
   Deep is the air and dark, substantial black,
   An ebon mass: methinks thou piercest it,
   As with a wedge! But when I look again,
   It is thine own calm home, thy crystal shrine,
   Thy habitation from eternity!

2. O dread and silent mount! I gazed upon thee,
   Till thou, still present to the bodily sense,
   Didst vanish from my thought: entranced in prayer
   I worshiped the Invisible alone.
   Yet like some sweet, beguiling melody,
   So sweet, we know not we are listening to it,
   Thou, the meanwhile, wast blending with my thoughts,

SUBLIME STYLE.

    Yea, with my life, and life's own secret joy—
    Till the dilating soul, enrapt, transfused,
    Into the mighty vision passing—there,
    As in her natural form, swelled vast to Heaven.

3. Awake, my soul! not only passive praise
    Thou owest—not alone these swelling tears,
    Mute thanks and secret ecstasy. Awake,
    Voice of sweet song! Awake, my heart, awake!
    Green vales and icy cliffs all join my hymn.
    Thou first and chief, sole sovereign of the vale!
    O, struggling with the darkness all the night,
    And visited all night by troops of stars,
    Or when they climb the sky, or when they sink:
    Companion of the morning-star at dawn,
    Thyself, earth's rosy star, and of the dawn
    Co-herald! wake, O wake, and utter praise.
    Who sank thy sunless pillars deep in earth?
    Who filled thy countenance with rosy light?
    Who made thee parent of perpetual streams?

4. And you, ye five wild torrents fiercely glad!
    Who called you forth from night and utter death,
    From dark and icy caverns called you forth,
    Down those precipitous, black, jagged rocks,
    Forever shattered and the same forever?
    Who gave you your invulnerable life,
    Your strength, your speed, your fury, and your joy,
    Unceasing thunder and eternal foam?
    And who commanded, and the silence came,
    "Here let the billows stiffen, and have rest?"

5. Ye ice-falls! ye that from the mountain's brow
    Adown enormous ravines slope amain—
    Torrents, methinks, that heard a mighty voice,
    And stopped at once amid their maddest plunge!
    Motionless torrents! silent cataracts!
    Who made you glorious as the gates of heaven
    Beneath the keen full moon? Who bade the sun
    Clothe you with rainbows? Who with living flowers
    Of loveliest blue, spread garlands at your feet?
    "God!" let the torrents, like a shout of nations,
    Answer, and let the ice-plains echo, "God!"

6. "God!" sing, ye meadow-streams, with gladsome voice!
Ye pine-groves, with your soft and soul-like sounds!
And they, too, have a voice, yon piles of snow,
And in their perilous fall shall thunder, "God!"
Ye living flowers that skirt the eternal frost!
Ye wild goats sporting round the eagle's nest!
Ye eagles, playmates of the mountain storm!
Ye lightnings, the dread arrows of the clouds!
Ye signs and wonders of the elements!
Utter forth "God!" and fill the hills with praise.

7. Once more, hoar mount, with thy sky-pointing peak,
Oft from whose feet the avalanche, unheard,
Shoots downward, glittering through the pure serene,
Into the depth of clouds that vail thy breast,
Thou, too, again, stupendous mountain! thou,
That, as I raise my head, awhile bowed down
In adoration, upward from thy base
Slow traveling, with dim eyes suffused with tears,
Solemnly seemest, like a vapory cloud,
To rise before me—rise, O ever rise!
Rise, like a cloud of incense, from the earth.
Thou kingly spirit throned among the hills,
Thou dread embassador from earth to heaven,
Great hierarch! tell thou the silent sky,
And tell the stars, and tell yon rising sun,
Earth, with her thousand voices, praises God.

CHAPTER XI.

ORATORICAL STYLE.

The Oratorical Style is appropriate for the delivery of speeches, senatorial, political and judicial, orations and sermons, in which the object is not only to enlighten the understanding, but to influence the will and arouse the emotions and passions.

Reply to Mr. Wickham in Burr's Trial, 1807.
William Wirt.

1. In proceeding to answer the argument of the gentleman, I will treat him with candor. If I misrepresent him, it will not be intentional. I will not follow the example which he has set me on a very recent occasion. I will endeavor to meet the gentleman's propositions in their full force, and to answer them fairly. I will not, as I am advancing toward them, with my mind's eye measure the height, breadth and power of the proposition; if I find it beyond my strength, halve it; if still beyond my strength, quarter it; if still necessary, subdivide it into eights; and when, by this process, I have reduced it to the proper standard, take one of these sections and toss it with an air of elephantine strength and superiority. If I find myself capable of conducting, by a fair course of reasoning, any one of his propositions to an absurd conclusion, I will not begin by stating that absurd conclusion as the proposition itself which I am going to encounter. I will not, in commenting on the gentleman's authorities, thank the gentleman, with sarcastic politeness, for introducing them, declare that they conclude directly against him, read just so much of the authority as serves the purpose of that declaration, omitting that which contains the true point of the case, which makes against me; nor, if forced by a direct call to read that part also, will I content myself by running over it as rapidly and inarticulately as I can, throw down the book with a theatrical air, and exclaim, "Just as I said!" when I know it is just as I had not said.

2. I know that, by adopting these arts, I might raise a laugh at the gentleman's expense; but I should be very little pleased with myself if I were capable of enjoying a laugh procured by such means. I know, too, that, by adopting such arts, there will always be those standing around us who have not comprehended the whole merits of the legal discussion, with whom I might shake the character of the gentleman's science and judgment as a lawyer. I hope I shall never be capable of such a wish; and I had hoped that the gentleman himself felt so strongly that proud, that high, aspiring and ennobling magnanimity, which I had been told conscious talents rarely fail to inspire, that he would have disdained a poor and fleeting triumph gained by means like these.

Aristocracy.
Robert R. Livingston.

1. The gentleman, who has so copiously declaimed against all declamation, has pointed his artillery against the rich and great. We are told that in every country there is a natural aristocracy, and that this aristocracy consists of the rich and the great. Nay, the gentleman goes further, and ranks in this class of men the wise, the learned, and those eminent for their talents or great virtues. Does a man possess the confidence of his fellow-citizens for having done them important services? He is an aristocrat. Has he great integrity? He is an aristocrat. Indeed, to determine that one is an aristocrat, we need only to be assured that he is a man of merit. But I hope we may have such. So sensible am I of that gentleman's talents, integrity and virtue, that we might at once hail him the first of the nobles, the very prince of the Senate.

2. But whom, in the name of common sense, would the gentleman have to represent us? Not the rich, for they are sheer aristocrats. Not the learned, the wise, the virtuous; for they are all aristocrats! Whom then? Why, those who are not virtuous; those who are not wise; those who are not learned; these are the men to whom alone we can trust our liberties! He says further, we ought not to choose aristocrats, because the people will not have confidence in them. That is to say, the people will not have confidence in those who best deserve and most possess their confidence. He would have his government composed of other classes of men. Where will he find them? Why, he must go forth into the highways and pick up the rogue and the robber. He must go to the hedges and the ditches

and bring in the poor, the blind and the lame. As the gentleman has thus settled the definition of aristocracy, I trust that no man will think it a term of reproach, for who among us would not be wise? who would not be virtuous? who would not be above want? The truth is, in these republican governments we know no such ideal distinctions. We are all equally aristocrats. Officers, emoluments, honors, the roads to preferment and to wealth, are alike open to all.

The General Government and the States.
Alexander Hamilton.

1. Mr. Chairman, it has been advanced as a principle that no government but a despotism can exist in a very extensive country. This is a melancholy consideration indeed. If it were founded on truth, we ought to dismiss the idea of a republican government, even for the State of New York. But the position has been misapprehended. Its application relates only to democracies, where the body of the people meet to transact business, and where representation is unknown. The application is wrong in respect to all representative governments, but especially in relation to a confederacy of States, in which the supreme legislature has only general powers, and the civil and domestic concerns of the people are regulated by the laws of the several States. I insist that it never can be the interest or desire of the national legislature to destroy the State governments. The blow aimed at the members must give a fatal wound to the head, and the destruction of the States must be at once a political suicide. But imagine, for a moment, that a political frenzy should seize the government; suppose they should make the attempt. Certainly, sir, it would be forever impracticable. This has been sufficiently demonstrated by reason and experience. It has been proved that the members of republics have been and ever will be stronger than the head. Let us attend to one general historical example.

2. In the ancient feudal governments of Europe there was, in the first place, a monarch; subordinate to him a body of nobles, and subject to these the vassals, or the whole body of the people. The authority of the kings was limited, and that of the barons considerably independent. The histories of the feudal wars exhibit little more than a series of successful encroachments on the prerogatives of monarchy.

3. Here, sir, is one great proof of the superiority which the members in limited governments possess over their head. As long as the

barons enjoyed the confidence and attachment of the people, they had the strength of the country on their side, and were irresistible. I may be told in some instances the barons were overcome; but how did this happen? Sir, they took advantage of the depression of the royal authority, and the establishment of their own power, to oppress and tyrannize over their vassals. As commerce enlarged and wealth and civilization increased, the people began to feel their own weight and consequence; they grew tired of their oppressions; united their strength with that of the prince, and threw off the yoke of aristocracy. These very instances prove what I contend for. They prove that in whatever direction the popular weight leans, the current of power will flow; whatever the popular attachments be, there will rest the political superiority.

Patriotic Self-Sacrifice.
Clay.

1. I rose not to say one word which would wound the feelings of the President. The senator says that, if placed in like circumstances, I would have been the last man to avoid putting a direct veto upon the bill had it met my disapprobation, and he does me the honor to attribute to me high qualities of stern and unbending intrepidity. I hope that in all that relates to personal firmness, all that concerns a just appreciation of the insignificance of human life—whatever may be attempted to threaten or alarm a soul not easily swayed by opposition, or awed or intimidated by menace—a stout heart and a steady eye that can survey, unmoved and undaunted, any mere personal perils that assail this poor, transient, perishing frame—I may, without disparagement, compare with other men.

2. But there is a sort of courage which, I frankly confess, I do not possess; a boldness to which I dare not aspire; a valor which I cannot covet. I cannot lay myself down in the way of the welfare and happiness of my country. That I cannot—I have not the courage to do. I cannot interpose the power with which I may be invested—a power conferred, not for my personal benefit, not for my aggrandizement, but for my country's good—to check her onward march to greatness and glory. I have not courage enough, I am too cowardly, for that. I would not, I dare not, in the exercise of such a trust, lie down and place my body across the path that leads my country to prosperity and happiness. This is a sort of courage widely different from that which a man may display in his private conduct and private

relations. Personal or private courage is totally distinct from that higher and nobler courage which prompts the patriot to offer himself a voluntary sacrifice to his country's good.

Ambition of a Statesman.
Clay.

1. I have been accused of ambition in presenting this measure— ambition, inordinate ambition. If I had thought of myself only I should have never brought it forward. I know well the perils to which I expose myself—the risk of alienating faithful and valued friends, with but little prospect of making new ones, if any new ones could compensate for the loss of those we have long tried and loved; and I know well the honest misconception both of friends and foes. Ambition! If I had listened to its soft and seducing whispers, if I had yielded myself to the dictates of a cold, calculating and prudential policy, I would have stood still and unmoved. I might even have silently gazed on the raging storm, enjoyed its loudest thunders, and left those who are charged with the care of the vessel of State to conduct it as they could.

2. I have been heretofore often unjustly accused of ambition. Low, groveling souls, who are utterly incapable of elevating themselves to the higher and nobler duties of pure patriotism—beings who, forever keeping their own selfish ends in view, decide all public measures by their presumed influence or their aggrandizement—judge me by the venal rule which they prescribe to themselves. I have given to the winds those false accusations, as I consign that which now impeaches my motives. I have no desire for office, not even the highest. The most exalted is but a prison, in which the incarcerated incumbent daily receives his cold, heartless visitants, marks his weary hours, and is cut off from the practical enjoyment of all the blessings of genuine freedom.

3. I am no candidate for any office in the gift of the people of these States, united or separated; I never wish, never expect, to be. Pass this bill, tranquilize the country, restore confidence and affection in the Union, and I am willing to go home to Ashland and renounce public service forever. I should there find in its groves, under its shades, on its lawns, 'mid my flocks and herds, in the bosom of my family, sincerity and truth, attachment and fidelity and gratitude, which I have not always found in the walks of public life. Yes, I have ambition; but it is the ambition of being the humble instru

ment, in the hands of Providence, to reconcile a divided people: once more to revive concord and harmony in a distracted land—the pleasing ambition of contemplating the glorious spectacle of a free, united, prosperous and fraternal people.

National Character.
Maxcy.

1. The loss of a firm national character, or the degradation of a nation's honor, is the inevitable prelude to her destruction. Behold the once proud fabric of a Roman empire—an empire carrying its arts and arms into every part of the eastern continent; the monarchs of mighty kingdoms dragged at the wheels of her triumphal chariots; her eagle waving over the ruins of desolated countries. Where is her splendor, her wealth, her power, her glory? Extinguished forever. Her moldering temples, the mournful vestiges of her former grandeur, afford a shelter to her muttering monks. Where are her statesmen, her sages, her philosophers, her orators, her generals? Go to their solitary tombs and inquire. She lost her national character, and her destruction followed. The ramparts of her national pride were broken down, and vandalism desolated her classic fields.

2. Such, the warning voice of antiquity, the example of all republics, proclaim may be our fate. But let us no longer indulge these gloomy anticipations. The commencement of our liberty presages the dawn of a brighter period to the world. That bold, enterprising spirit which conducted our heroes to peace and safety, and gave us a lofty rank amid the empires of the world, still animates the bosoms of their descendants. Look back to that moment when they unbarred the dungeons of the slave and dashed his fetters to the earth; when the sword of a Washington leaped from its scabbard to avenge the slaughter of our countrymen. Place their example before you. Let the sparks of their veteran wisdom flash across your minds, and the sacred altar of your liberty, crowned with immortal honors, rise before you. Relying on the virtue, the courage, the patriotism, and the strength of our country, we may expect our national character will become more energetic, our citizens more enlightened, and we may hail the age as not far distant when will be heard, as the proudest exclamation of man, I AM AN AMERICAN!

Responsibilities of our Republic.
Joseph Story.

1. The old world has already revealed to us, in its unsealed books, the beginning and end of all its own marvelous struggles in the cause of liberty. Greece, lovely Greece, "the land of scholars and the nurse of arms," where sister republics in fair procession chanted the praises of liberty and the gods, where and what is she? For two thousand years the oppressor has bound her to the earth. Her arts are no more. The last sad relics of her temples are but the barracks of a ruthless soldiery; the fragments of her columns and her palaces are in the dust, yet beautiful in ruin. She fell not when the mighty were upon her. Her sons were united at Thermopylæ and Marathon, and the tide of her triumph rolled back upon the Hellespont. She was conquered by her own factions. She fell by the hands of her own people. The man of Macedonia did not the work of destruction. It was already done, by her own corruptions, banishments and dissensions.

2. Rome, republican Rome, whose eagles glanced in the rising and setting sun, where and what is she? The Eternal City yet remains, proud even in her desolation, noble in her decline, venerable in the majesty of religion, and calm as in the composure of death. The malaria has but traveled in the paths worn by her destroyers. More than eighteen centuries have mourned over the loss of her empire. A mortal disease was upon her vitals before Cæsar had crossed the Rubicon. The Goths and Vandals and Huns, the swarms of the North, completed only what was already begun at home. Romans betrayed Rome. The legions were bought and sold, but the people offered the tribute-money. When we reflect on what has been and is, how is it possible not to feel a profound sense of the responsibieness of this republic to all future ages! What vast motives press upon us for lofty efforts! What brilliant prospects invite our enthusiasm! What solemn warnings at once demand our vigilance and moderate our confidence!

Duty of Literary Men to their Country.
Grimke.

1 We cannot honor our country with too deep a reverence; we cannot love her with an affection too pure and fervent; we cannot serve her with an energy of purpose or a faithfulness of zeal too stead-

fast and ardent. And what is our country? It is not the East, with her hills and her valleys, with her countless sails and the rocky ramparts of her shores; it is not the North, with her thousand villages, and her harvest-home, with her frontiers of the lake and the ocean; it is not the West, with her forest-sea and her inland isles, with her luxuriant expanses, clothed in the verdant corn, with her beautiful Ohio and her majestic Missouri; nor is it yet the South, opulent in the mimic snow of the cotton, in the rich plantations of the rustling cane and in the golden robes of the rice-field. What are these but the sister families of one greater, better, holier family—our country?

2. I come not here to speak the dialect or to give the counsels of the patriot-statesman; but I come, a patriot-scholar, to vindicate the rights and to plead for the interests of American literature. And be assured that we cannot, as patriot-scholars, think too highly of that country, or sacrifice too much for her. And let us never forget—let us rather remember—with a religious awe that the union of these States is indispensable to our national independence and civil liberties, to our prosperity, happiness and improvement.

3. If, indeed, we desire to behold a literature like that which has sculptured with such energy of expression, which has painted so faithfully and vividly, the crimes, the vices, the follies of ancient and modern Europe—if we desire that our land should furnish for the orator and the novelist, for the painter and the poet, age after age, the wild and romantic scenery of war; the glittering march of armies and the revelry of the camp; the shrieks and blasphemies and all the horrors of the battle-field; the desolation of the harvest and the burning cottage; the storm, the sack and the ruin of cities—if we desire to unchain the furious passions of jealousy and selfishness, of hatred, revenge and ambition, those lions that now sleep harmless in their den; if we desire that the lake, the river, the oceans should blush with the blood of brothers; that the winds should waft from the land to the sea, from the sea to the land, the roar and the smoke of battle; that the very mountain-tops should become altars for the sacrifice of brothers; if we desire that these and such as these—the elements, to an incredible extent, of the literature of the Old World—should be the elements of our literature; then, but then only, let us hurl from its pedestal the majestic statue of our Union, and scatter its fragments over all our land.

4. But if we covet for our country the noblest, purest, holiest literature the world has ever seen, such a literature as shall honor God and bless mankind—a literature whose smiles might play upon an angel's face, whose tears "would not stain an angel's cheek;" then

let us cling to the union of these States with a patriot's love, with a scholar's enthusiasm, with a Christian's hope. In her heavenly character, as a holocaust self-sacrificed to God; at the height of her glory, as the ornament of a free, educated, peaceful, Christian people, American literature will find that the intellectual spirit is her very tree of life, and the Union her garden of paradise.

American Laborers.

Naylor.

1. The gentleman, sir, has misconceived the spirit and tendency of Northern institutions. He is ignorant of Northern character. He has forgotten the history of his country. Preach insurrection to the Northern laborers! Who are the Northern laborers? The history of your country is their history. The renown of your country is their renown. The brightness of their doings is emblazoned on every page. Blot from your annals the words and the doings of Northern laborers and the history of your country presents but a universal blank. Sir, who was he that disarmed the thunderer; wrested from his grasp the bolts of Jove; calmed the troubled ocean; became the central sun of the philosophical system of his age, shedding his brightness and effulgence on the whole civilized world—whom the great and mighty of the earth delighted to honor, who participated in the achievement of your independence, prominently assisted in molding your free institutions, and the beneficial effects of whose wisdom will be felt to the last moment of "recorded time?" Who, sir, I ask, was he? A northern laborer, a Yankee tallow-chandler's son—a printer's runaway boy!

2. And who, let me ask the honorable gentleman, who was he that, in the days of our Revolution, led forth a Northern army—yes, an army of Northern laborers—and aided the chivalry of South Carolina in their defense against British aggression, drove the spoilers from their firesides, and redeemed her fair fields from foreign invaders? Who was he? A Northern laborer, a Rhode Island blacksmith—the gallant General Greene—who left his hammer and his forge and went forth conquering and to conquer in the battle for our independence! And will you preach insurrection to men like these?

3. Sir, our country is full of the achievements of Northern laborers. Where are Concord, and Lexington, and Princeton, and Trenton, and Saratoga, and Bunker Hill, but in the North? And what, sir, has shed an imperishable renown on the never-dying names of those hal

lowed spots, but the blood and the struggles, the high daring and patriotism and sublime courage of Northern laborers? The whole North is an everlasting monument of the freedom, virtue, intelligence and indomitable independence of Northern laborers! Go, sir, go, preach insurrection to men like these!

4. The fortitude of the men of the North, under intense suffering for liberty's sake, has been almost godlike! History has so recorded it. Who comprised that gallant army, without food, without pay, shelterless, hopeless, penniless, and almost naked, in that dreadful winter—the midnight of our Revolution—whose wanderings could be traced by their blood tracks in the snow; whom no arts could seduce, no appeal lead astray, no sufferings disaffect; but who, true to their country and its holy cause, continued to fight the good fight of liberty until it finally triumphed? Who, sir, were Roger Sherman and—? But it is idle to enumerate. To name the Northern laborers who have distinguished themselves, and illustrated the history of their country, would require days of the time of this house. Nor is it necessary. Posterity will do them justice. Their deeds have been recorded in characters of fire!

NAPOLEON BONAPARTE.
Phillips.

1. He is fallen! We may now pause before that splendid prodigy which towered among us like some ancient ruin, whose frown terrified the glance its magnificence attracted. Grand, gloomy and peculiar, he sat upon the throne, a sceptered hermit, wrapt in the solitude of his own originality. A mind bold, independent and decisive; a will despotic in its dictates; an energy that distanced expedition and a conscience pliable to every touch of interest marked the outline of this extraordinary character, the most extraordinary, perhaps, that in the annals of this world ever rose or reigned or fell.

2. Flung into life in the midst of a revolution that quickened every energy of a people who acknowledge no superior, he commenced his course, a stranger by birth, and a scholar by charity. With no friend but his sword, and no fortune but his talents, he rushed into the lists where rank and wealth and genius had arrayed themselves, and competition fled from him as from the glance of destiny. He knew no motive but interest, he acknowledged no criterion but success, he worshiped no God but ambition, and, with an Eastern devotion, he knelt at the shrine of his idolatry.

3. Subsidiary to this there was no creed that he did not profess—there was no opinion that he did not promulgate. In the hope of a dynasty he upheld the Crescent; for the sake of a divorce he bowed before the Cross; the orphan of St. Louis, he became the adopted child of the Republic, and, with a parricidal ingratitude, on the ruins both of the throne and tribune, he reared the throne of his despotism. A professed Catholic, he imprisoned the Pope; a pretended patriot, he impoverished the country; and, in the name of Brutus, he grasped without remorse and wore without shame the diadem of the Cæsars! Through this pantomime of policy fortune played the clown to his caprices. At his touch crowns crumbled, beggars reigned, systems vanished, the wildest theories took the color of his whim, and all that was venerable and all that was novel changed places with the rapidity of a drama.

4. Even apparent defeat assumed the appearance of victory; his flight from Egypt confirmed his destiny; ruin itself only elevated him to empire. But if his fortune was great his genius was transcendent. Decision flashed upon his counsels, and it was the same to decide and to perform. To inferior intellects his combinations appeared perfectly impossible, his plans perfectly impracticable; but in his hands simplicity marked their development and success vindicated their adoption. His person partook the character of his mind; if the one never yielded in the cabinet, the other never bent in the field. Nature had no obstacle that he did not surmount, space no opposition that he did not spurn, and, whether amid Alpine rocks, Arabian sands, or Polar snows, he seemed proof against peril, and empowered with ubiquity!

5. The whole continent trembled at beholding the audacity of his designs and the miracle of their execution. Skepticism bowed to the prodigies of his performance; romance assumed the air of history; nor was there aught too incredible for belief or too fanciful for expectation when the world saw a subaltern of Corsica waving his imperial flag over her most ancient capitals. All the visions of antiquity became commonplaces in his contemplation. Kings were his people, nations were his outposts, and he disposed of courts and crowns and camps and churches and cabinets as if they were titular dignitaries of the chess-board. Amid all these changes he stood immutable as adamant.

6. It mattered little whether in the field or in the drawing-room, with the mob or the levee, wearing the Jacobin bonnet or the iron crown, banishing a Braganza, or espousing a Hapsburg, dictating peace on a raft to the Czar of Russia, or contemplating defeat at the gallows of Leipsic, he was still the same military despot.

7. In this wonderful combination his affectations of literature must not be omitted. The jailer of the press, he affected the patronage of letters; the proscriber of books, he encouraged philosophy; the persecutor of authors and the murderer of printers, he yet pretended to the protection of learning. Such a medley of contradictions, and, at the same time, such an individual consistency, were never united in the same character. A royalist, a republican and an emperor, a Mohammedan, a Catholic and a patron of the synagogue, a subaltern and a sovereign, a traitor and a tyrant, a Christian and an infidel, he was, through all his vicissitudes, the same stern, impatient, inflexible original, the same mysterious, incomprehensible self—the man without a model and without a shadow.

Unjust National Acquisitions.
Thomas Corwin.

1. Mr. President, the uneasy desire to augment our territory has depraved the moral sense and blighted the otherwise keen sagacity of our people. Sad, very sad, are the lessons which time has written for us. Through and in them all I see nothing but the inflexible execution of that old law which ordains as eternal the cardinal rule, "Thou shalt not covet thy neighbor's goods, nor any thing which is his." Since I have lately heard so much about the dismemberment of Mexico I have looked back to see how, in the course of events, which some call "Providence," it has fared with other nations who engaged in this work of dismemberment.

2. I see that in the latter half of the eighteenth century three powerful nations—Russia, Austria and Prussia—united in the dismemberment of Poland. They said, too, as you say, "It is our destiny." They "wanted room." Doubtless each of these thought, with his share of Poland, his power was too strong ever to fear invasion, or even insult. One had his California, another his New Mexico, and the third his Vera Cruz.

3. Did they remain untouched and incapable of harm? Alas, no! far, very far from it. Retributive justice must fulfill its destiny too. A few years pass off, and we hear of a new man, a Corsican lieutenant, the self-named "armed soldier of Democracy," Napoleon. He ravages Austria, covers her land with blood, drives the Northern Cæsar from his capital, and sleeps in his palace. Austria may now remember how her power trampled upon Poland. Did she not pay dear, very dear, for her California?

4. But has Prussia no atonement to make? You see this same Napoleon, the blind instrument of Providence, at work there. The thunders of his cannon at Jena proclaim the work of retribution for Poland's wrongs, and the successors of the Great Frederick, the drill-sergeant of Europe, are seen flying across the sandy plains that surround their capital, right glad if they may escape captivity and death.

5 But how fares it with the autocrat of Russia? Is he secure in his share of the spoils of Poland?. No. Suddenly we see, sir, six hundred thousand armed men marching to Moscow. Does his Vera Cruz protect him now? Far from it. Blood, slaughter, desolation spread abroad over the land; and, finally, the conflagration of the old commercial metropolis of Russia closes the retribution. She must pay for her share in the dismemberment of her impotent neighbor.

6. Mr. President, a mind more prone to look for the judgments of Heaven in the doings of men than mine cannot fail, in all unjust acquisitions of territory, to see the providence of God. When Moscow burned, it seemed as if the earth was lighted up that the nations might behold the scene. As that mighty sea of fire gathered and heaved and rolled upward, and yet higher, till its flames licked the stars and fired the whole heavens, it did seem as though the God of the nations was writing, in characters of flame, on the front of his throne that doom that shall fall upon the strong nation which tramples in scorn upon the weak.

Our System of Public Instruction should Distinctively Inculcate a Love of Country.

Newton Bateman.

1. The true American patriot is ever a *worshiper*. The starry symbol of his country's sovereignty is to him radiant with a diviner glory than that which meets his mortal vision. It epitomizes the splendid results of dreary ages of experiments and failures in human government; and, as he gazes upon its starry folds undulating responsive to the whispering winds of the upper air, it sometimes seems to his rapt spirit to recede farther and farther into the soft blue skies, till the heavens open, and angel hands plant it upon the battlements of Paradise. Wherever that ensign floats, on the sea or on the land, it is to him the very Shekinah of his political love and faith, luminous with the presence of that God who conducted his fathers

across the sea and through the fires of the Revolution to the Pisgah heights of civil and religious liberty. Its stars seem real; its lines of white symbol the purity of his heroic sires; those of red their patriot blood shed in defense of the right. To defend that flag is to him something more than a duty, it is a joy, a coveted privilege; akin to that which nerves the arm and directs the blow in defense of wife or child. To insult it, is worse than infamy; to make war upon it, more than treason.

2. A perfect civil government is the sublimest earthly symbol of Deity—indeed, such a government is a transcript of the divine will: its spirit and principles identical with those with which He governs he universe. Its vigilance, care and protection, are ubiquitous: its strong hand is ever ready to raise the fallen, restrain the violent, and punish the aggressor; its patient ear is bent to catch alike the complaint of the rich and strong, or the poor and weak, while unerring justice presides at the trial and settlement of every issue between man and man.

3. Now, our government is not perfect, even in theory, and still less so in practice; but it is good and strong and glorious enough to inspire a loftier patriotism than animates the people of any other nation. What element is wanting to evoke the passionate love and admiration of an American citizen for his country? Is it ancestry? Men of purer lives, sterner principles, or braver hearts than our fathers never crossed the sea. Is it motives? Not for war or conquest, but for civil and religious liberty did our fathers approach these shores. Is it perils and obstacles? Wintry storms, and icy coasts, and sterile soils; prowling beasts, and savage man, and hunger, and nakedness, and disease, and death, were the greetings our fathers received. Is it patient endurance? Not till the revelations of the final day will the dauntless fortitude of our fathers, in the midst of appalling dangers and sufferings, be disclosed. Is it heroic achievement? Again and again has the haughty lion of St. George been brought to the dust, and the titled chivalry of England overthrown by the resistless onset of the sons of liberty, led by "Mr. Washington!" Is it moral sublimity? Behold Witherspoon in the Continental Congress; Washington at Valley Forge; Clay in the Senate of 1850. Is it that we have no historical Meccas? Where shall a patriot muse and pray, if not by the shades of Vernon or Ashland—at Marshfield or the Hermitage. Have we no great names to go flaming down the ages? When will Henry's clarion voice be hushed, or Warren cease to tell men how to die for liberty? when will Adams, and Franklin, and Jefferson fade from history? Is it constitutional wisdom, excellence of laws, or

ncentives to individual exertion? No other lands can compare with ours in these respects. Is it grandeur of scenery? God has made but one Niagara, one Mississippi, one Hudson. Is it territorial extent? Our domain stretches from ocean to ocean, and from lake to gulf.

4. By all these incentives let our school-boys be fired with an enthusiastic love for the dear land of their birth, the precious heritage of their fathers; let them leave the school-room for the arena of active life, feeling that next to God and their parents, their country claims and shall receive their best affections and most uncompromising devotion; let them realize that their conduct will bring honor or dishonor upon their country, as surely as upon their parents and friends; let them learn to identify themselves as citizens with the interests of the commonwealth, blushing at whatever disgraces her, exulting in all that contributes to her glory and renown; let them feel that this great country is *their* country, that they have a personal proprietorship in the luster of her history, the honor of her name, the magnificence of her commerce, the valor of her fleets and armies, the inviolability of her Constitution and laws, and the magnitude and beneficence of her civil, social, and religious institutions.

Appeal in Behalf of Ireland.
S. S. Prentiss.

1. Fellow-citizens: It is no ordinary cause that has brought together this vast assemblage on the present occasion. We have met, not to prepare ourselves for political contests; we have met, not to celebrate the achievements of those gallant men who have planted our victorious standards in the heart of an enemy's country; we have assembled, not to respond to shouts of triumph from the West; but to answer the cry of want and suffering which comes from the East. The Old World stretches out her arms to the New. The starving parent supplicates the young and vigorous child for bread.

2. There lies upon the other side of the wide Atlantic a beautiful island, famous in story and in song. Its area is not so great as that of the State of Louisiana, while its population is almost half that of the Union. It has given to the world more than its share of genius and of greatness. It has been prolific in statesmen, warriors, and poets. Its brave and generous sons have fought successfully all battles but their own. In wit and humor it has no equal; while its harp, like its history moves to tears by its sweet but melancholy pathos.

3. Into this fair region God has seen fit to send the most terrible of all those fearful ministers that fulfill his inscrutable decrees. The earth has failed to give her increase. The common mother has forgotten her offspring, and she no longer affords them their accustomed nourishment. Famine, gaunt and ghastly famine, has seized a nation with its strangling grasp. Unhappy Ireland, in the sad woes of the present, forgets, for a moment, the gloomy history of the past.

4. O it is terrible that, in this beautiful world which the good God has given us, and in which there is plenty for us all, men should die of starvation! When a man dies of disease he alone endures the pain. Around his pillow are gathered sympathizing friends, who, if they cannot keep back the deadly messenger, cover his face and conceal the horrors of his visage as he delivers his stern mandate. In battle, in the fullness of his pride and strength, little recks the soldier whether the hissing bullet sings his sudden requiem, or the cords of life are severed by the sharp steel.

5. But he who dies of hunger wrestles alone, day by day, with his grim and unrelenting enemy. He has no friends to cheer him in the terrible conflict; for if he had friends, how could he die of hunger? He has not the hot blood of the soldier to maintain him; for his foe, vampire-like, has exhausted his veins. Famine comes not up, like a brave enemy, storming, by a sudden onset, the fortress that resists. Famine besieges. He draws his lines round the doomed garrison. He cuts off all supplies. He never summons to surrender, for he gives no quarter.

6. Alas, for poor human nature! how can it sustain this fearful warfare? Day by day the blood recedes, the flesh deserts, the muscles relax, and the sinews grow powerless. At last the mind, which at first had bravely nerved itself against the contest, gives way under the mysterious influences which govern its union with the body. Then the victim begins to doubt the existence of an overruling Providence. He hates his fellow-men, and glares upon them with the longing of a cannibal; and, it may be, dies blaspheming.

7. This is one of those cases in which we may without impiety assume, as it were, the function of Providence. Who knows but that one of the very objects of this calamity is to test the benevolence and worthiness of us upon whom unlimited abundance is showered? In the name, then, of common humanity, I invoke your aid in behalf of starving Ireland. He who is able, and will not aid such a cause, is not a man, and has no right to wear the form. He should be sent back to Nature's mint, and re-issued as a counterfeit on humanity of Nature's baser metal.

Glorious New England.

S. S. Prentiss.

1 Glorious New England, thou art still true to thy ancient fame, and worthy of thy ancestral honors. We, thy children, have assembled in this far distant land to celebrate thy birthday. A thousand fond associations throng upon us, roused by the spirit of the hour. On thy pleasant valleys rest, like sweet dews of morning, the gentle recollections of our early life; around thy hills and mountains cling, like gathering mists, the mighty memories of the Revolution; and far away in the horizon of thy past gleam, like thy own bright northern lights, the awful virtues of our pilgrim sires! But while we devote this day to the remembrance of our native land, we forget not that in which our happy lot is cast. We exult in the reflection that, though we count by thousands the miles which separate us from our birth-place, still our country is the same. We are no exiles meeting upon the banks of a foreign river to swell its waters with our home-sick tears. Here floats the same banner which rustled above our boyish heads, except that its mighty folds are wider and its glittering stars increased in number.

2. The sons of New England are found in every State of the broad republic. In the East, the South and the unbounded West their blood mingles freely with every kindred current. We have but changed our chamber in the paternal mansion; in all its rooms we are at home, and all who inhabit it are our brothers. To us the Union has but one domestic hearth; its household gods are all the same. Upon us, then, peculiarly devolves the duty of feeding the fires upon that kindly hearth, of guarding with pious care those sacred household gods.

3. We cannot do with less than the whole Union. To us it admits of no division. In the veins of our children flows Northern and Southern blood. How shall it be separated? Who shall put asunder the best affections of the heart, the noblest instincts of our nature? We love the land of our adoption, so do we that of our birth. Let us ever be true to both, and always exert ourselves in maintaining the unity of our country, the integrity of the republic.

4. Accursed, then, be the hand put forth to loosen the golden cord of union! thrice accursed the traitorous lips which shall propose its severance!

5. But no, the Union cannot be dissolved; its fortunes are too brilliant to be marred; its destinies too powerful to be resisted. Here will be their greatest triumph, their most mighty development.

6. And when, a century hence, this Crescent City shall have filled her golden horns; when within her broad-armed port shall be gathered the products of the industry of a hundred millions of freemen; when galleries of art and halls of learning shall have made classic this mart of trade; then may the sons of the Pilgrims, still wandering from the bleak hills of the North, stand upon the banks of the great river and exclaim, with mingled pride and wonder, Lo! this is our country; when did the world ever behold so rich and magnificent a city, so great and glorious a republic!

Speech Before the Virginia Convention of Delegates, March, 1775.

Patrick Henry.

1. Mr. President, it is natural for man to indulge in the illusions of hope. We are apt to shut our eyes against a painful truth and listen to the song of that siren till she transforms us into beasts. Is this the part of wise men engaged in the great and arduous struggle for liberty? Are we disposed to be of the number of those who having eyes see not, and having ears hear not, the things which so nearly concern their temporal salvation? For my part, whatever anguish of spirit it may cost, I am willing to know the whole truth; to know the worst and to provide for it.

2. I have but one lamp by which my feet are guided, and that is, the lamp of experience. I know of no way of judging of the future but by the past. And, judging by the past, I wish to know what there has been in the conduct of the British ministry for the last ten years to justify those hopes with which gentlemen have been pleased to solace themselves and the house. Is it that insidious smile with which our petition has been lately received? Trust it not, sir; it will prove a snare to your feet. Suffer not yourselves to be betrayed with a kiss. Ask yourselves how this gracious reception of our petition comports with those warlike preparations which cover our waters and darken our land. Are fleets and armies necessary to a work of love and reconciliation? Have we shown ourselves so unwilling to be reconciled that force must be called in to win back our love?

3. Let us not deceive ourselves, sir. These are the implements of war and subjugation, the last arguments to which kings resort. I ask gentlemen, sir, what means this martial array, if its purposes be

not to force us to submission? Can gentlemen assign any o.
sible motive for it? Has Great Britain any enemy in this qua.
the world to call for all this accumulation of navies and armies?
Sir, she has none. They are meant for us. They can be meant to
no other. They are sent over to bind and rivet upon us those chains
which the British ministry have been so long forging.

4. And what have we to oppose them? Shall we try argument?
Sir, we have been trying that for the last ten years. Have we any thing
new to offer upon the subject? Nothing. We have held the subject
up in every light of which it is capable; but it has been all in vain.
Shall we resort to entreaty and supplication? What terms shall we
find that have not been already exhausted? Let us not, I beseech
you, sir, deceive ourselves longer. Sir, we have done every thing
that could have been done to avert the storm that is now coming on.
We have petitioned, we have remonstrated, we have supplicated, we
have prostrated ourselves before the throne, and have implored its
interposition to arrest the tyrannical hands of the ministry and Parliament.

5. Our petitions have been slighted, our remonstrances have produced additional violence and insult, our supplications have been disregarded, and we have been spurned with contempt from the foot of the throne. In vain, after these things, may we indulge the fond hope of peace and reconciliation. There is no longer any room for hope. If we wish to be free; if we mean to preserve inviolate those inestimable privileges for which we have been so long contending; if we mean not basely to abandon the noble struggle in which we have been so long engaged, and which we have pledged ourselves never to abandon until the glorious object of our contest shall be obtained, we must fight! I repeat it, sir, we must fight! An appeal to arms and to the God of hosts is all that is left us.

6. They tell us, sir, that we are weak; unable to cope with so formidable an adversary. But when shall we be stronger? Will it be the next week or the next year? Will it be when we are totally disarmed, and when a British guard shall be stationed in every house? Shall we gather strength by irresolution and inaction? Shall we acquire the means of effectual resistance by lying supinely on our backs, and hugging the delusive phantom of hope, until our enemies shall have bound us hand and foot? Sir, we are not weak if we make a proper use of those means which the God of nature hath placed in our power.

7. Three millions of people armed in the holy cause of liberty, and in such a country as that which we possess, are invincible by any

force which our enemy can send against us. Besides, sir, we shall not fight our battles alone. There is a just God who presides over the destinies of nations, and who will raise up friends to fight our battles for us. The battle, sir, is not to the strong alone: it is to the vigilant, the active, the brave. Besides, sir, we have no election. If we were base enough to desire it, it is now too late to retire from the contest There is no retreat but in submission and slavery! Our chains are forged. Their clanking may be heard on the plains of Boston! Th war is inevitable, and let it come! I repeat, sir, let it come!

8. It is vain, sir, to extenuate the matter. Gentlemen may cry Peace, peace! but there is no peace. The war is actually begun! The next gale that sweeps from the North will bring to our ears the clash of resounding arms! Our brethren are already in the field! Why stand we here idle? What is it that gentlemen wish? What would they have? Is life so dear, or peace so sweet, as to be purchased at the price of chains and slavery? Forbid it, Almighty God! I know not what course others may take, but as for me, give me liberty or give me death!

Supposed Speech of James Otis.
Mrs. L. M. Child.

1. England may as well dam up the waters of the Nile with bulrushes as fetter the step of Freedom, more proud and firm in this youthful land than where she treads the sequestered glens of Scotland, or crouches herself among the magnificent mountains of Switzerland. Arbitrary principles, like those against which we now contest, have cost one king his life, another his crown, and they may yet cost a third his most flourishing colonies.

2. We are two millions; one fifth fighting men. We are bold and vigorous, and we call no man master. To the nation from whom we are proud to derive our origin, we ever were, and we ever will be, ready to yield unforced assistance; but it must not, and it never can be, extorted.

3. Some have sneeringly asked, "Are the Americans too poor to pay a few pounds on stamped paper?" No! America, thanks to God and herself, is rich. But the right to take ten pounds implies the right to take a thousand; and what must be the wealth that avarice, aided by power, cannot exhaust? True, the specter is now small; but the shadow he casts before him is huge enough to darken all this fair land.

4. Others, in a sentimental style, talk of the immense debt of grati-

tude which we owe to England. And what is the amount of this debt? Why, truly, it is the same that the young lion owes to the dam, which has brought it forth on the solitude of the mountain, or left it amid the winds and storms of the desert.

5. We plunged into the wave with the great charter of freedom in our teeth, because the fagot and the torch were behind us. We have waked this new world from its savage lethargy; forests have been prostrated in our path; towns and cities have grown up suddenly as the flowers of the tropics; and the fires in our autumnal woods are scarcely more rapid than the increase of our wealth and population. And do we owe all this to the kind succor of the mother country? No! we owe it to the tyranny that drove us from her, to the pelting storms which invigorated our helpless infancy.

6. But perhaps others will say, "We ask no money from your gratitude: we only demand that you should pay your own expenses." And who, I pray, is to judge of their necessity? Why, the king: and, with all due reverence to his sacred majesty, he understands the real wants of his distant subjects as little as he does the language of the Choctaws! Who is to judge concerning the *frequency* of these demands? The ministry. Who is to judge whether the money is properly expended? The cabinet behind the throne. In every instance those who *take* are to judge for those who *pay*. If this system is suffered to go into operation we shall have reason to esteem it a great privilege that *rain* and *dew* do not depend upon Parliament; otherwise, *they* would soon be taxed and dried.

7. But, thanks to God! there is freedom enough left upon earth to *resist* such monstrous injustice. The flame of liberty is extinguished in *Greece* and *Rome*, but the light of its glowing embers is still bright and strong on the shores of *America*. Actuated by its sacred influence, we will *resist* unto *death*. But we will not countenance anarchy and misrule. The wrongs that a desperate community have heaped upon their enemies shall be amply and speedily repaired. Still, it may be well for some proud men to remember, that a fire is lighted in these colonies which one breath of their king may *kindle* into such a fury that the blood of all England cannot extinguish it.

RIENZI'S ADDRESS TO THE ROMANS.
Miss Mitford.

1. I come not here to talk. You know too well
The story of our thraldom. We are slaves!
The bright sun rises to his course and lights
A race of slaves! He sets, and his last beams
Fall on a slave; not such as, swept along
By the full tide of power, the conqueror led
To crimson glory and undying fame,
But base, ignoble slaves; slaves to a horde
Of petty tyrants, feudal despots, lords,
Rich in some dozen paltry villages;
Strong in some hundred spearmen; only great
In that strange spell—a name.

2. Each hour, dark fraud,
Or open rapine, or protected murder,
Cry out against them. But this very day
An honest man, my neighbor—there he stands—
Was struck—struck like a dog by one who wore
The badge of Ursini; because, forsooth,
He tossed not high his ready cap in air,
Nor lifted up his voice in servile shouts
At sight of that great ruffian! Be we men,
And suffer such dishonor? men, and wash not
The stain away in blood? Such shames are common
I have known deeper wrongs; I, that speak to ye.
I had a brother once—a gracious boy,
Full of gentleness, of calmest hope,
Of sweet and quiet joy: there was the look
Of heaven upon his face, which limners give
To the beloved disciple.

3. How I loved
That gracious boy! Younger by fifteen years,
Brother at once, and son! He left my side;
A summer bloom on his fair cheek, a smile
Parting his innocent lips. In one short hour
That pretty, harmless boy was slain! I saw
The corse, the mangled corse, and then I cried
For vengeance! Rouse, ye Romans! rouse, ye slaves!
Have ye brave sons? Look in the next fierce brawl

To see them die. Have ye fair daughters? Look
To see them live, torn from your arms, distained,
Dishonored; and if ye dare call for justice,
Be answered by the lash!

4 Yet this is Rome,
That sat on her seven hills, and from her throne
Of beauty ruled the world! Yet we are Romans!
Why, in that elder day, to be a Roman
Was greater than a king! and once again—
Hear me, ye walls, that echoed to the tread
Of either Brutus! once, again, I swear
The eternal city shall be free!

CHAPTER XII.

ORATORICAL SUBLIME STYLE.

Some selections partake of the commingled elements of two styles.

The two following, and, in fact, all funeral orations, are of this class, containing the elements both of the Oratorical and Sublime Styles, and hence may be appropriately classed under the Oratorical Sublime.

Similar examples will frequently occur, but it has not been thought necessary to present them separately, as they are only combinations of styles already sufficiently discussed.

Death of John Quincy Adams.

L. E. Holmes.

1. Mr. Speaker, The mingled tones of sorrow, like the voice of many waters, have come unto us from a sister State—Massachusetts—weeping for her honored son. The State I have the honor in part to represent once endured, with yours, a common suffering, battled for a common cause, and rejoiced in a common triumph. Surely, then, it is meet that in this the day of your affliction we should mingle our griefs.

2. When a great man falls the nation mourns, when a patriarch is removed the people weep. Ours, my associates, is no common bereavement. The chain which linked our hearts with the gifted spirits of former times has been suddenly snapped. The lips from which flowed those living and glorious truths that our fathers uttered are closed in death.

3. Yes, my friends, death has been among us. He has not entered the humble cottage of some unknown, ignoble peasant; he has knocked audibly at the palace of a nation. His footstep has been heard in the halls of State! He has cloven down his victim in the midst of the councils of a people. He has borne in triumph from

among you the gravest, wisest, most reverend head. Ah! he has taken him as a trophy who was once chief over many statesmen, adorned with virtue and learning and truth; he has borne at his chariot wheels a renowned one of the earth.

4. How often have we crowded into that aisle, and clustered around that now vacant desk, to listen to the counsels of wisdom as they fell from the lips of the venerable sage, we can all remember, for it was but of yesterday. But what a change! How wondrous! how sudden! 'Tis like a vision of the night. That form which we beheld but a few days since is now cold in death.

5. But the last Sabbath, and in this hall, he worshiped with others. Now his spirit mingles with the noble army of martyrs, and the just made perfect in the eternal adoration of the living God. With him, "this is the end of earth." He sleeps the sleep that knows no waking. He is gone—and for ever. The sun that ushers in the morn of that next holy day, while it gilds the lofty dome of the capitol, shall rest with soft and mellow light upon the consecrated spot beneath whose turf forever lies the patriot father and the patriot sage.

Death of Alexander Hamilton.

Dr. Nott.

1. A short time since and he who is the occasion of our sorrows was the ornament of his country. He stood on an eminence, and glory covered him. From that eminence he has fallen—suddenly, forever fallen. His intercourse with the living world is now ended; and those who would hereafter find him must seek him in the grave. There, cold and lifeless, is the heart which just now was the seat of friendship. There, dim and sightless is the eye whose radiant and enlivening orb beamed with intelligence; and there, closed forever, are those lips on whose persuasive accents we have so often and so lately hung with transport.

2. From the darkness which rests upon his tomb there proceeds, methinks, a light in which it is clearly seen that those gaudy objects which men pursue are only phantoms. In this light how dimly shines the splendor of victory—how humble appears the majesty of grandeur! The bubble which seemed to have so much solidity has burst, and we again see that all below the sun is vanity.

3. True, the funeral eulogy has been pronounced; the sad and solemn procession has moved; the badge of mourning has already been decreed; and presently the sculptured marble will lift up its front,

proud to perpetuate the name of Hamilton, and rehearse to the passing traveler his virtues.

4. Just tributes of respect, and to the living useful; but to him, moldering in his narrow and humble habitation, what are they? How vain! How unavailing!

5. Approach and behold, while I lift from his sepulcher its covering. Ye admirers of his greatness, ye emulous of his talents and his fame, approach and behold him now. How pale! how silent! No martial bands admire the adroitness of his movements; no fascinated throng weep and melt and tremble at his eloquence. Amazing change! A shroud! a coffin! a narrow, subterraneous cabin! This is all that now remains of Hamilton. And is this all that remains of him? During a life so transitory, what lasting monument, then, can our fondest hopes erect?

6. My brethren, we stand on the borders of an awful gulf, which is swallowing up all things human. And is there, amid this universal wreck, nothing stable, nothing abiding, nothing immortal, on which poor, frail, dying man can fasten?

7. Ask the hero, ask the statesman, whose wisdom you have been accustomed to revere, and he will tell you. He will tell you, did I say? He has already told you from his death-bed, and his illumined spirit still whispers from the heavens, with well-known eloquence, the solemn admonition: "Mortals, hastening to the tomb, and once the companions of my pilgrimage, take warning and avoid my errors; cultivate the virtues I have recommended; choose the Saviour I have chosen. Live disinterestedly—live for immortality. And would you rescue any thing from final dissolution, lay it up in God."

CHAPTER XIII.

IMPASSIONED POETIC STYLE.

The Impassioned Poetic Style is appropriate for the delivery of impassioned poetic thought and feeling, as expressed not only in impassioned poetry, but also in the impassioned portions of speeches, orations and sermons.

Hate of the Bowl.

1. Go, feel what I have felt;
   Go, bear what I have borne;
   Sink 'neath the blow a father dealt,
   And the cold world's proud scorn:
   Then suffer on from year to year,
   Thy sole relief the scalding tear.

2. Go, kneel as I have knelt;
   Implore, beseech and pray;
   Strive the besotted heart to melt,
   The downward course to stay;
   Be dashed with bitter curse aside,
   Your prayers burlesqued, your tears defied.

3. Go weep as I have wept
   O'er a loved father's fall,
   See every promised blessing swept,
   Youth's sweetness turned to gall;
   Life's fading flowers strewed all the way,
   That brought me up to woman's day.

4. Go, see what I have seen;
   Behold the strong man bow,
   With gnashing teeth, lips bathed in blood,
   And cold and livid brow.
   Go catch his withering glance, and see
   There mirrored, his soul's misery.

5. Go to thy mother's side,
   And her crushed bosom cheer;
Thine own deep anguish hide;
   Wipe from her cheek the bitter tear,
Mark her wan cheek and pallid brow,
The gray that streaks her dark hair now,
Her failing frame and trembling limb;
And trace the ruin back to him
Whose plighted faith, in early youth,
Promised eternal love and truth;
But who, forsworn, hath yielded up
That promise to the cursed cup;
And led her down, through love and light,
And all that made her prospects bright;
And chained her there, 'mid want and strife,
That lowly thing, a drunkard's wife;
And stamped on childhood's brow so mild,
That withering blight, a drunkard's child!

6. Go, hear and feel and see and know
   All that my soul hath felt and known;
Then look upon the wine-cup's glow,
   See if its beauty can atone;
Think if its flavor you will try,
When all proclaim, 'Tis drink and die!

7. Tell me I hate the bowl—
   Hate is a feeble word:
I loathe, abhor; my very soul
   With strong disgust is stirred
Whene'er I see, or hear, or tell
Of the dark beverage of hell.

The American Flag.
Joseph Rodman Drake.

1. When Freedom, from her mountain height,
   Unfurled her standard to the air,
She tore the azure robe of night,
   And set the stars of glory there!
She mingled with its gorgeous dyes
The milky baldric of the skies,

And striped its pure celestial white
With streakings of the morning light;
Then, from his mansion in the sun,
She called her eagle-bearer down,
And gave into his mighty hand
The symbol of her chosen land!

2. Majestic monarch of the cloud!
  Who rear'st aloft thy regal form,
To hear the tempest trumpings loud,
And see the lightning-lances driven,
  When strive the warriors of the storm,
And rolls the thunder-drum of heaven!
Child of the sun! to thee 'tis given
  To guard the banner of the free,
To hover in the sulphur smoke,
To ward away the battle-stroke,
And bid its blendings shine afar,
Like rainbows on the cloud of war—
  The harbingers of victory!

3. Flag of the brave! thy folds shall fly,
The sign of hope and triumph high.
When speaks the signal trumpet tone,
And the long line comes gleaming on—
Ere yet the life-blood, warm and wet,
Has dimmed the glistening bayonet—
Each soldier's eye shall brightly turn
To where thy sky-born glories burn;
And, as his springing steps advance,
Catch war and vengeance from the glance!
And when the cannon-mouthings loud
Heave in wild wreaths the battle-shroud,
And gory sabers rise and fall,
Like shoots of flame on midnight's pall;
Then shall thy meteor glances glow,
  And cowering foes shall sink beneath
Each gallant arm that strikes below
  That lovely messenger of death.

4. Flag of the seas! on ocean wave
Thy stars shall glitter o'er the brave,
When Death, careering on the gale,
Sweeps darkly round the bellied sail,

And frighted waves rush wildly back,
Before the broadside's reeling rack;
Each dying wanderer of the sea
Shall look at once to heaven and thee,
And smile to see thy splendors fly,
In triumph o'er his closing eye.

5. Flag of the free heart's hope and home,
   By angel hands to valor given!
Thy stars have lit the welkin dome,
   And all thy hues were born in heaven.
For ever float that standard sheet!
   Where breathes the foe but falls before us,
With Freedom's soil beneath our feet,
   And Freedom's banner streaming o'er us?

The Rescue of Chicago.

H. M. Look.

I saw the city's terror,
   I heard the city's cry,
As a flame leaped out of her bosom
   Up, up to the brazen sky!
And wilder rose the tumult,
   And thicker the tidings came—
Chicago, queen of the cities,
   Is a rolling sea of flame!

Yet higher rose the fury,
   And louder the surges raved,
(Thousands were saved but to suffer,
   And hundreds never were saved,)
Till out of the awful burning
   A flash of lightning went,
As across to fair Saint Louis
   The prayer for succor was sent.

God bless thee, O true Saint Louis!
   So worthy thy royal name—
Back, back on the wing of the lightning
   Thy answer of rescue came;

But, alas! it could not enter
    Through the horrible flame and heat,
For the fire had conquered the lightning,
    And sat in the thunderer's seat!

God bless thee again, Saint Louis!
    For resting never then;
Thou calledst to all the cities
    By lightning and steam and pen:
'Ho, ho, ye hundred sisters,
    Stand forth in your bravest might!
Our sister in flame is falling,
    Her children are dying to-night!"

And through the mighty Republic
    Thy summons went rolling on,
Till it rippled the seas of the tropics,
    And ruffled the Oregon;
The distant Golden City
    Called through her golden gates,
And quickly rung the answer
    From the City of the Straits;

And the cities that sit in splendor
    Along the Atlantic sea,
Replying, called to the dwellers
    Where the proud magnolias be.
From slumber the army started
    At the far-resounding call,
"Food for a hundred thousand,
    And clothing and tents for all."

I heard through the next night's darkness
    The trains go thundering by,
Till they stood where the fated city
    Shone red in the brazen sky.
The rich gave their abundance,
    The poor their willing hands;
There was wine from all the vineyards,
    There was corn from all the lands.

At daybreak over the prairies
    Re-echoed the gladsome cry—
"Ho, look unto us, ye thousands,
    Ye shall not hunger nor die!"

Their weeping was all the answer
 That the famishing throng could give
To the million voices calling:
 "Look unto us, and live!"

Destruction wasted the city,
 But the burning curse that came
Enkindled in all the people
 Sweet charity's holy flame.
Then still to our God be glory!
 I bless him, through my tears,
That I live in the grandest nation
 That hath stood in all the years.

Sheridan's Ride.

T. Buchanan Read.

1. Up from the south at break of day,
Bringing to Winchester fresh dismay,
The affrighted air with a shudder bore,
Like a herald in haste, to the chieftain's door
The terrible grumble, and rumble, and roar,
Telling the battle was on once more,
And Sheridan twenty miles away.

2. And wilder still those billows of war
Thundered along the horizon's bar;
And louder yet into Winchester rolled
The roar of that red sea uncontrolled,
Making the blood of the listener cold,
As he thought of the stake in that fiery fray,
And Sheridan twenty miles away.

3. But there is a road from Winchester town,
A good, broad highway leading down:
And there through the flush of the morning light,
A steed, as black as the steeds of night,
Was seen to pass, as with eagle flight;
As if he knew the terrible need,
He stretched away with his utmost speed;
Hills rose and fell; but his heart was gay,
With Sheridan fifteen miles away.

4. Still sprung from those swift hoofs, thundering south,
The dust, like smoke from the cannon's mouth;
Or the trail of a comet, sweeping faster and faster,
Foreboding to traitors the doom of diaster.
The heart of the steed, and the heart of the master
Were beating like prisoners assaulting their walls,
Impatient to be where the battle-field calls;
Every nerve of the charger was strained to full play,
With Sheridan only ten miles away.

5. Under his spurning feet, the road
Like an arrowy Alpine river flowed,
And the landscape sped away behind
Like an ocean flying before the wind,
And the steed, like a bark fed with furnace ire,
Swept on, with his wild eye full of fire.
But, lo! he is nearing his heart's desire;
He is snuffing the smoke of the roaring fray,
With Sheridan only five miles away.

6. The first that the General saw were the groups
Of stragglers, and then the retreating troops;
What was done? what to do? a glance told him both,
Then striking his spurs, with a terrible oath,
He dashed down the line, 'mid a storm of huzzas,
And the wave of retreat checked its course there, because
The sight of the master compelled it to pause.
With foam and with dust the black charger was gray;
By the flush of his eye, and his red nostril's play,
He seemed to the whole great army to say,
"I have brought you Sheridan all the way
From Winchester, down to save the day."

7. Hurrah! hurrah for Sheridan!
Hurrah! hurrah for horse and man!
And when their statues are placed on high
Under the dome of the Union sky,
The American soldiers' Temple of Fame,
There with the glorious General's name
Let it be said in letters both bold and bright:
"Here is the steed that saved the day
By carrying Sheridan into the fight,
From Winchester—twenty miles away!"

CHAPTER XIV.

SHOUTING STYLE.

THE Shouting Style is chiefly used in the utterance of those words and phrases which are employed in calling and commanding. But few selections will require the Shouting Style throughout.

In the extracts given, with the exception of Tell's Address to the Alps, only those words printed in italics require the Shouting Style.

FROM THE CHARGE OF THE LIGHT BRIGADE.

Tennyson.

1. Half a league, half a league,
    Half a league onward,
   All in the valley of death
    Rode the six hundred.
   "*Forward, the Light Brigade!*"
   "*Charge for the guns,*" he said.
   Into the valley of death
    Rode the six hundred.

2. "*Forward the Light Brigade!*"
   Was there a man dismayed?
   Not though the soldier knew
    Some one had blundered.
   Theirs not to make reply,
   Theirs not to reason why,
   Theirs but to do and die.
   Into the valley of death
    Rode the six hundred.

From Marmion and Douglas.
Scott.

On the earl's cheek the flush of rage
O'ercame the ashen hue of age;
Fierce he broke forth, "And darest thou, then,
To beard the lion in his den—
 The Douglas in his hall?
And hop'st thou hence unscathed to go?
No, by Saint Bride of Bothwell, no!
Up drawbridge, grooms! what, warder, ho!
 Let the portcullis fall."

From Marco Bozzaris.
Halleck.

An hour passed on, the Turk awoke.
 That bright dream was his last.
He woke to hear his sentries shriek,
"*To arms!* they come! the Greek! the Greek!"
He woke to die 'midst flame and smoke,
And shout and groan and saber-stroke,
 And death-shots falling thick and fast
As lightnings from the mountain cloud,
And heard, with voice as trumpet loud,
 Bozzaris cheer his band:
"*Strike! till the last armed foe expires;*
Strike! for your altars and your fires;
Strike! for the green graves of your sires;
 God, and your native land!"

From the Black Regiment.
Boker.

1. "*Now,*" the flag-sergeant cried.
 "*Though death and hell betide,*
 Let the whole nation see
 If we are fit to be

*Free in this land; or bound
Down like the whining hound,
Bound with red stripes of pain
In our cold chains again!"*
O what a shout there went
From the black regiment!

2. "*Charge!*" trump and drum awoke.
Onward the bondmen broke:
Bayonet and saber-stroke
Vainly opposed their rush.
Through the wild battle's crush,
With but one thought aflush,
Driving their lords like chaff.
In the guns' mouths they laugh;
Or at the slippery brands
Leaping with open hands,
Down they tear man and horse,
Down in their awful course;
Trampling with bloody heel
Over the crashing steel,
All their eyes forward bent,
Rushed the black regiment.

3. "*Freedom!*" their battle-cry,
"*Freedom! or leave to die!*"
Ah! and they meant the word,
Not as with us 'tis heard,
Not a mere party shout:
They gave their spirits out;
Trusted the end to God,
And on the gory sod
Rolled in triumphant blood.
Glad to strike one free blow,
Whether for weal or woe;
Glad to breathe one free breath,
Though on the lips of death,
Praying—alas! in vain—
That they might fall again,
So they could once more see
That burst to liberty!
This was what "freedom" lent
To the black regiment.

Tell's Address to the Alps.
J. S. Knowles.

1. Ye crags and peaks, I'm with you once again!
I hold to you the hands you first beheld,
To show they still are free. Methinks I hear
A spirit in your echoes answer me,
And bid your tenant welcome to his home
Again. O sacred forms, how proud you look!
How high you lift your heads into the sky!
How huge you are! how mighty and how free!
Ye are things that tower, that shine, whose smile
Makes glad, whose frown is terrible, whose forms,
Robed or unrobed, do all the impress wear
Of awe divine. Ye guards of liberty,
I'm with you once again! I call to you
With all my voice! I hold my hands to you,
To show they still are free. I rush to you
As though I could embrace you.

CHAPTER XV.

VEHEMENT STYLE.

The Vehement Style is appropriate for the expression of intense passion, anger, scorn, revenge, hate, etc.

CATILINE'S DEFIANCE.
Croly.

1. Conscript Fathers!
   I do not rise to waste the night in words;
   Let that plebeian talk; 'tis not my trade;
   But here I stand for right—let him show proofs—
   For Roman right; though none, it seems, dare stand
   To take their share with me. Ay, cluster there!
   Cling to your master, judges, Romans, slaves!
   His charge is false;—I dare him to his proof.
   You have my answer. Let my actions speak!

2. But this I will avow, that I have scorned,
   And still do scorn, to hide my sense of wrong!
   Who brands me on the forehead, breaks my sword,
   Or lays the bloody scourge upon my back,
   Wrongs me not half so much as he who shuts
   The gates of honor on me—turning out
   The Roman from his birthright; and, for what?
   To fling your offices to every slave!
   Vipers, that creep where man disdains to climb,
   And, having wound their loathsome track to the top
   Of this huge, moldering monument of Rome,
   Hang hissing at the nobler man below!
   Come, consecrated lictors, from your thrones·
   Fling down your scepters; take the rod and ax
   And make the murder as you make the law!

3. Banished from Rome! What's banished, but set free
   From daily contact with the things I loathe?
   "Tried and convicted traitor!" Who says this?
   Who'll prove it, at his peril, on my head?

4. Banish'd! I thank you for't. It breaks my chain!
　 I held some slack allegiance till this hour;
　 But now my sword's my own. Smile on, my lords!
　 I scorn to count what feelings, withered hopes,
　 Strong provocations, bitter, burning wrongs,
　 I have within my heart's hot cells shut up,
　 To leave you in your lazy dignities.
　 But here I stand and scoff you! here, I fling
　 Hatred and full defiance in your face!
　 Your consul's merciful—for this all thanks;
　 He dares not touch a hair of Catiline!

5. "Traitor!" I go; but I return. This—trial?
　 Here I devote your senate! I've had wrongs
　 To stir a fever in the blood of age,
　 Or make the infant's sinews strong as steel.
　 This day's the birth of sorrow! This hour's work
　 Will breed proscriptions! Look to your hearths, my lords!
　 For there, henceforth, shall sit, for household gods,
　 Shapes hot from Tartarus!—all shames and crimes!
　 Wan treachery, with his thirsty dagger drawn;
　 Suspicion, poisoning his brother's cup;
　 Naked rebellion, with the torch and ax,
　 Making his wild sport of your blazing thrones;
　 Till anarchy comes down on you like night,
　 And massacre seals Rome's eternal grave!

6. I go; but not to leap the gulf alone.
　 I go; but, when I come, 'twill be the burst
　 Of ocean in the earthquake—rolling back
　 In swift and mountainous ruin. Fare you well!
　 You build my funeral pile; but your best blood
　 Shall quench its flame! Back, slaves! I will return!

The Seminole's Defiance.

G. W. Patten.

1. Blaze, with your serried columns! I will not bend the knee;
　 The shackle ne'er again shall bind the arm which now is free!
　 I've mailed it with the thunder, when the tempest muttered low;
　 And where it falls, ye well may dread the lightning of its blow.

I've scared you in the city; I've scalped on the plain;
Go, count your chosen where they fell beneath my leaden rain!
I scorn your proffered treaty; the pale-face I defy;
Revenge is stamped upon my spear, and "blood" my battle-cry!

2. Some strike for hope of booty; some to defend their all—
I battle for the joy I have to see the white man fall.
I love, among the wounded, to hear his dying moan,
And catch, while chanting at his side, the music of his groan.
You've trailed me through the forest; you've tracked me o'er the stream;
And struggling through the everglade your bristling bayonets gleam.
But I stand as should the warrior, with his rifle and his spear;
The scalp of vengeance still is red, and warns you—"Come not here!"

3. Think ye to find my homestead?—I gave it to the fire,
My tawny household do you seek?—I am a childless sire.
But, should you crave life's nourishment, enough I have, and good;
I live on hate—'tis all my bread; yet light is not my food.
I loathe you with my bosom! I scorn you with mine eye!
And I'll taunt you with my latest breath, and fight you till I die!
I ne'er will ask for quarter, and I ne'er will be your slave;
But I'll swim the sea of slaughter till I sink beneath the wave!

Spartacus to the Gladiators of Capua.

E. Kellogg.

1. Ye call me chief; and ye do well to call him chief who, for twelve long years, has met upon the arena every shape of man or beast the broad empire of Rome could furnish, and who never yet lowered his arm. If there be one among you who can say, that ever, in public fight or private brawl, my actions did belie my tongue, let him stand forth and say it. If there be three in all your company dare face me on the bloody sands, let them come on. And yet I was not always thus—a hired butcher, a savage chief of still more savage men!

2. My ancestors came from old Sparta, and settled among the vine-clad rocks and citron-groves of Cyrasella. My early life ran quiet as the brooks by which I sported; and when, at noon, I gathered the sheep beneath the shade, and played upon the shepherd's flute, there

was a friend, the son of a neighbor, to join me in the pastime. We led our flocks to the same pasture, and partook together our rustic meal.

3. One evening, after the sheep were folded, and we were all seated beneath the myrtle which shaded our cottage, my grandsire, an old man, was telling of Marathon and Leuctra; and how, in ancient times, a little band of Spartans, in a defile of the mountains, had withstood a whole army. I did not then know what war was; but my cheeks burned, I knew not why, and I clasped the knees of that venerable man, until my mother, parting the hair from off my forehead, kissed my throbbing temples and bade me go to rest, and think no more of those old tales and savage wars. That very night the Romans landed on our coast. I saw the breast that had nourished me trampled by the hoof of the war-horse; the bleeding body of my father flung amid the blazing rafters of our dwelling!

4. To-day I killed a man in the arena; and, when I broke his helmet-clasps, behold! he was my friend. He knew me, smiled faintly, gasped, and died—the same sweet smile upon his lips that I had marked when, in adventurous boyhood, we scaled the lofty cliff to pluck the first ripe grapes, and bear them home in childish triumph! I told the prætor that the dead man had been my friend, generous and brave; and I begged that I might bear away the body and burn it on a funeral pile, and mourn over its ashes. Ay, upon my knees, amid the dust and blood of the arena, I begged that poor boon, while all the assembled maids and matrons, and the holy virgins they call Vestals, and the rabble, shouted in derision, deeming it rare sport, forsooth, to see Rome's fiercest gladiator turn pale and tremble at sight of that piece of bleeding clay! And the prætor drew back as I were pollution, and sternly said, "Let the carrion rot; there are no noble men but Romans!" And so, fellow-gladiators, must you, and so must I, die like dogs.

5. O, Rome! Rome! thou hast been a tender nurse to me. Ay, thou hast given to that poor, gentle, timid shepherd-lad, who never knew a harsher tone than a flute note, muscles of iron and a heart of flint; taught him to drive the sword through plaited mail and links of rugged brass, and warm it in the marrow of his foe; to gaze into the glaring eye-balls of the fierce Numidian lion, even as a boy upon a laughing girl! And he shall pay thee back, until the yellow Tiber is red as frothing wine, and in its deepest ooze life-blood lies curdled!

6. Ye stand here now like giants, as ye are! The strength of brass is in your toughened sinews; but to-morrow some Roman Adonis, breathing sweet perfume from his curly locks, shall with his lily

fingers pat your red brawn, and bet his sesterces upon your blood Hark! hear ye yon lion roaring in his den? 'Tis three days since he tasted flesh; but to-morrow he shall break his fast upon yours, and a dainty meal for him ye will be!

7. If ye are beasts, then stand here like fat oxen, waiting for the butcher's knife! If ye are men—follow me! Strike down yon guard, gain the mountain passes, and there do bloody work, as did your sires at old Thermopylæ! Is Sparta dead? Is the old Grecian spirit frozen in your veins, that you do crouch and cower like a belabored hound beneath his master's lash? O comrades! warriors! Thracians! if we must fight, let us fight for ourselves! If we must slaughter, let us slaughter our oppressors! If we must die, let it be under the clear sky, by the bright waters, in noble, honorable battle!

CHAPTER XVI.

DRAMATIC STYLE.

The Dramatic is simply a combination of the previous styles. The difficulty, in the delivery of selections in the Dramatic Style, is in giving the sudden transition from one style to another, which so frequently occurs.

The following analysis will sufficiently illustrate the combination of styles and the rapid transitions:

FROM ON BOARD THE CUMBERLAND, MARCH 7, 1862.
George H. Boker.

1. "Stand to your guns, men!" Morris cried;
   Small need to pass the word;
   Our men at quarters ranged themselves
   Before the drum was heard.

2. And then began the sailors' jests:
   "What thing is that, I say?"
   "A 'long-shore meeting-house, adrift,
   Is standing down the bay!"

3. A frown came over Morris' face;
   The strange, dark craft he knew:
   "That is the iron Merrimac,
   Manned by a rebel crew."

In the above extract, "Stand to your guns, men!" should be given in the Shouting Style; "Morris cried," changes to the Didactic Style; "Small need to pass the word," etc., should be given in the Grave Style; "And then began the sailor's jests," requires the Lively Style;

SCIENCE OF ELOCUTION.

while "What thing is that, I say?" etc., can only be appropriately given in the Gay or Joyous Style.

"A frown came over Morris' face," etc., requires the Grave Style, while "That is the iron Merrimac," etc., will require the Oratorical Style.

Thus, it will be seen, there is a constant change of style with almost every line.

An analysis of any dramatic selection will disclose a similar combination of styles. No one should attempt to read or speak a selection of the Dramatic Style without first carefully analyzing it, not merely to comprehend clearly the thought, but to discover the various styles of utterance it will require. It cannot be too earnestly impressed upon the mind of the pupil that the comprehension of the sentiment does not imply the appropriate vocal delivery.

Abou Ben-Adhem.

Leigh Hunt.

1. Abou Ben-Adhem (may his tribe increase!)
Awoke one night from a deep dream of peace,
And saw, within the moonlight in his room,
Making it rich, and like a lily in bloom,
An angel, writing in a book of gold.
Exceeding peace had made Ben-Adhem bold;
And to the presence in the room he said,
"What writest thou?" The vision raised its head,
And, with a look made all of sweet accord,
Answered, "The names of those who love the Lord."
"And is mine one?" said Abou. "Nay, not so,"
Replied the angel. Abou spake more low,
But cheerily still, and said, "I pray thee, then,
Write me as one that loves his fellow-men."

2. The angel wrote, and vanished. The next night
It came again, with a great wakening light,
And showed the names whom love of God had blessed,
And lo, Ben-Adhem's name led all the rest.

DRAMATIC STYLE.

Leap for Life.
Geo. P. Morris.

1. Old Ironsides at anchor lay
    In the harbor of Mahon;
   A dead calm rested on the bay,
    And the winds to sleep had gone;
   When little Jack, the captain's son,
    With gallant hardihood,
   Climbed shroud and spar, and then upon
    The main truck rose and stood.

2. A shudder ran through every vein,
    All eyes were turned on high;
   There stood the boy, with dizzy brain,
    Between the sea and sky.
   No hold had he above, below;
    Alone he stood in air;
   At that far height none dared to go;
    No aid could reach him there.

3. We gazed, but not a man could speak;
    With horror all aghast;
   In groups, with pallid brow and cheek,
    We watched the quivering mast.
   The atmosphere grew thick and hot,
    And of a lurid hue,
   As, riveted unto the spot,
    Stood officers and crew.

4. The father came on deck—he gasped,
    "O God! thy will be done!"
   Then suddenly a rifle grasped,
    And aimed it at his son.
   "Jump! far out, boy, into the wave,
    Jump, or I fire!" he said;
   "This chance alone your life can save,
    Jump! jump!" The boy obeyed.

5. He sunk, he rose, he lived, he moved;
    He for the ship struck out;
   On board we hailed the lad beloved
    With many a manly shout.

His father drew, with silent joy,
  Those wet arms round his neck,
And folded to his heart the boy,
  Then fainted on the deck.

Lord Ullin's Daughter.
Campbell.

1. A chieftain to the Highlands bound.
  Cries, "Boatman, do not tarry!
And I'll give thee a silver pound
  To row us o'er the ferry."

2. "Now, who be ye would cross Loch Gyle,
  This dark and stormy water?"
"O I'm the chief of Ulva's isle,
  And this Lord Ullin's daughter.

3. "And fast before her father's men,
  Three days we've fled together,
For should he find us in the glen,
  My blood would stain the heather.

4. "His horsemen hard behind us ride.
  Should they our steps discover,
Then who will my bonny bride
  When t'... 'n her lover?"

5. Ou... land wight,
  "... ady:
It is n...
  But f...

6. "And, by ...
  In danger,
So, though the ...
  I'll row you o...

7. By this the storm g...
  The water-wraith ...
And, in the scowl of h...
  Grew dark as they we...

8. But still, as wilder grew the wind,
 And as the night grew drearer,
Adown the glen rode arméd men,
 Their trampling sounded nearer.

9. "O haste thee, haste!" the lady cries,
 "Though tempests round us gather,
I'll meet the raging of the skies,
 But not an angry father."

10. The boat has left the stormy land,
 A stormy sea before her,
When, O, too strong for human hand,
 The tempest gathered o'er her.

11. And while they rowed amid the roar
 Of waters fast prevailing,
Lord Ullin reached that fatal shore;
 His wrath was changed to wailing.

12. For, sore dismayed, through storm and shade,
 His child he did discover;
One lovely arm she stretched for aid,
 And one was round her lover.

13. "Come back! come back!" he cried in grief,
 Across the stormy water,
"And I'll forgive your Highland chief:
 My daughter! O, my daughter!"

14. 'Twas vain: the loud waves lashed the shore,
 Return or aid preventing:
The waters wild went o'er his child,
 And he was left lamenting.

JOHN BURNS OF GETTYSBURG.

F. Bret Harte.

1. Have you heard the story that gossips tell
Of Burns of Gettysburgh? No? Ah, well!
Brief is the glory that hero earns,
Briefer the story of poor John Burns;

He was the fellow who won renown—
The only man who didn't back down
When the rebels rode through his native town;
But held his own in the fight next day,
When all his townsfolk ran away.
That was in July, sixty-three,
The very day that General Lee,
The flower of Southern chivalry,
Baffled and beaten, backward reeled
From a stubborn Meade and a barren field.

2. I might tell how, but the day before,
John Burns stood at his cottage-door,
Looking down the village street,
  Where, in the shade of his peaceful vine,
  He heard the low of his gathered kine,
And felt their breath with incense sweet;
Or, I might say, when the sunset burned
The old farm gable, he thought it turned
The milk that fell in a babbling flood
Into the milk-pail, red as blood;
Or, how he fancied the hum of bees
Were bullets buzzing among the trees.
But all such fanciful thoughts as these
Were strange to a practical man like Burns,
Who minded only his own concerns,
Troubled no more by fancies fine
Than one of his calm-eyed, long-tailed kine—
Quite old-fashioned, and matter-of-fact,
Slow to argue, but quick to act.
That was the reason, as some folks say,
He fought so well on that terrible day.

3. And it was terrible. On the right
Raged for hours the heavy fight,
Thundered the battery's double bass—
Difficult music for men to face;
While on the left—where now the graves
Undulate like the living waves
That all the day unceasing swept
Up to the pits the rebels kept—
Round shot plowed the upland glades,
Sown with bullets, reaped with blades;

Shattered fences here and there
Tossed their splinters in the air;
The very trees were stripped and bare;
The barns that once held yellow grain
Were heaped with harvests of the slain;
The cattle bellowed on the plain,
The turkeys screamed with might and **main.**
And brooding barn-fowl left their rest
With strange shells bursting in each nest.

4. Just where the tide of battle turns,
Erect and lonely stood old John Burns.

5. How do you think the man was dressed?
He wore an ancient, long buff vest,
Yellow as saffron, but his best;
And buttoned over his manly breast
Was a bright blue coat with a rolling collar,
And large gilt buttons—size of a dollar—
With tails that country-folk called "swaller."
He wore a broad-brimmed, bell-crowned hat,
White as the locks on which it sat.
Never had such a sight been seen
For forty years on the village-green,
Since old John Burns was a country beau,
And went to the "quilting" long ago.

6. Close at his elbows all that day
Veterans of the Peninsula,
Sunburnt and bearded, charged away,
And striplings, downy of lip and chin,
Clerks that the Home Guard mustered in,
Glanced as they passed at the hat he wore,
Then at the rifle his right hand bore;
And hailed him from out their youthful lore,
With scraps of a slangy *repertoire:*
"How are you, White Hat?" "Put her through!"
"Your head's level!" and, "Bully for you!"
Called him "Daddy," and begged he'd disclose
The name of the tailor who made his clothes,
And what was the value he set on those;
While Burns, unmindful of jeer and scoff,
Stood there picking the rebels off—

With his long, brown rifle and bell-crown hat,
And the swallow-tails they were laughing at.

7. 'Twas but a moment, for that respect
Which clothes all courage their voices checked;
And something the wildest could understand,
Spake in the old man's strong right hand,
And his corded throat, and the lurking frown
Of his eyebrows under his old-bell crown;
Until, as they gazed, there crept an awe
Through the ranks in whispers, and some men saw,
In the antique vestments and long white hair,
The Past of the Nation in battle there.
And some of the soldiers since declare
That the gleam of his old white hat afar,
Like the crested plume of the brave Navarre,
That day was their oriflamme of war.
Thus raged the battle. You know the rest,
How the rebels, beaten, and backward pressed,
Broke at the final charge and ran.
At which John Burns, a practical man,
Shouldered his rifle, unbent his brows,
And then went back to his bees and cows.

8. This is the story of old John Burns;
This is the moral the reader learns:
In fighting the battle the question's whether
You'll show a hat that's white, or a feather?

POOR LITTLE JIM.

1. The cottage was a thatched one, the outside old and mean,
But all within that little cot was wondrous neat and clean;
The night was dark and stormy, the wind was howling wild,
As a patient mother sat beside the death-bed of her child:
A little worn-out creature, his once bright eyes grown dim:
It was a collier's wife and child, they called him little Jim.

2. And O! to see the briny tears fast hurrying down her cheek,
As she offered up the prayer, in thought, she was afraid to speak,
Lest she might waken one she loved far better than her life;
For she had all a mother's heart, had that poor collier's wife.
With hands uplifted, see, she kneels beside the sufferer's bed,
And prays that He would spare her boy, and take herself instead

3. She gets her answer from the child: soft fall the words from him,
"Mother, the angels do so smile, and beckon little Jim.
I have no pain, dear mother, now; but O! I am so dry,
Just moisten poor Jim's lips again, and, mother, don't you cry."
With gentle, trembling haste she held the liquid to his lip;
He smiled to thank her as he took each little, tiny sip.

4. "Tell father, when he comes from work, I said good-night to him.
And, mother, now I'll go to sleep." Alas! poor little Jim!
She knew that he was dying; that the child she loved so dear
Had uttered the last words that she might ever hope to hear:
The cottage door is opened, the collier's step is heard,
The father and the mother meet, yet neither speak a word.

5. He felt that all was over, he knew his child was dead;
He took the candle in his hand and walked toward the bed;
His quivering lips gave token of the grief he'd fain conceal,
And see, his wife has joined him—the stricken couple kneel:
With hearts bowed down by sadness, they humbly ask of Him,
In heaven once more to meet again their own poor little Jim.

The Gambler's Wife.
Coates.

1. Dark is the night! how dark—no light—no fire!
Cold, on the hearth, the last faint sparks expire!
Shivering she watches by the cradle side
For him who pledged her love—last year a bride!

2. "Hark! 'tis his footstep! No—'tis past; 'tis gone:
Tick!—Tick!—How wearily the time crawls on!
Why should he leave me thus? He once was kind!
And I believed 'twould last—how mad!—how blind!

3. "Rest thee, my babe!—rest on!—'tis hunger's cry!
Sleep!—for there is no food! the fount is dry!
Famine and cold their wearying work have done,
My heart must break!—and thou!" The clock strikes one.

4. "Hush! 'tis the dice-box! Yes, he's there, he's there,
For this! for this he leaves me to despair!
           his wife! his child! for what?
           llain—and the sot!

5. "Yet I'll not curse him! No! 'tis all in vain!
   'Tis long to wait, but sure he'll come again!
   And I could starve and bless him, but for you,
   My child!—his child!—O fiend!" The clock strikes **two**.

6. "Hark! how the sign-board creaks! The blast howls **by**!
   Moan! moan! A dirge swells through the cloudy sky!
   Ha! 'tis his knock! he comes!—he comes once more!
   'Tis but the lattice flaps! Thy hope is o'er.

7. "Can he desert me thus? He knows I stay
   Night after night in loneliness to pray
   For his return—and yet he sees no tear!
   No! no! it cannot be. He will be here.

8. "Nestle more closely, dear one, to my heart!
   Thou'rt cold! thou'rt freezing! But we will not part.
   Husband!—I die!—Father!—It is not he!
   O God! protect my child!" The clock strikes three.

9. They're gone! they're gone! the glimmering spark hath **fled**!
   The wife and child are numbered with the dead!
   On the cold hearth, out-stretched in solemn rest,
   The child lies frozen on its mother's breast!
   The gambler came at last—but all was o'er—
   Dead silence reigned around—The clock struck four!

The Beautiful Snow.
James W. Watson.

1. O the snow, the beautiful snow!
   Filling the sky and earth below!
   Over the house-tops, over the street,
   Over the heads of the people you meet,
       Dancing,
           Flirting,
               Skimming along;
   Beautiful snow! it can do no wrong;
   Flying to kiss a fair lady's cheek,
   Clinging to lips in a frolicsome freak,
   Beautiful snow from the heaven above,
   Pure as an angel, but fickle as love.

DRAMATIC STYLE. 837

2. O the snow, the beautiful snow!
How the flakes gather and laugh as they go!
Whirling about in their maddening fun
They play in their glee with every one.
      Chasing,
          Laughing,
              Hurrying by,
It lights on the face and it sparkles the eye;
And even the dogs, with a bark and a bound,
Snap at the crystals that eddy around;
The town is alive and its heart in a glow,
To welcome the coming of beautiful snow!

3. How the wild crowd goes swaying along,
Hailing each other with humor and song!
How the gay sledges, like meteors flash by,
Bright for a moment, then lost to the eye—
      Ringing,
          Swinging,
              Dashing they go,
Over the crust of the beautiful snow!
Snow so pure when it falls from the sky,
To be trampled in mud by the crowd rushing by;
To be trampled and tracked by the thousands of feet
Till it blends with the filth in the horrible street.

4. Once I was pure as the snow—but I fell!
Fell, like the snow-flakes, from heaven to hell;
Fell to be trampled as filth in the street;
Fell to be scoffed, to be spit on and beat;
      Pleading,
          Cursing,
              Dreading to die,
Selling my soul to whoever would buy;
Dealing in shame for a morsel of bread,
Hating the living and fearing the dead;
Merciful God! have I fallen so low?
And yet I was once like the beautiful snow.

5. Once I was fair as the beautiful snow,
With an eye like its crystal, a heart like its glow;

Once I was loved for my innocent grace,
Flattered and sought for the charms of my face!
   Father,
    Mother,
     Sisters, all,
God and myself, I have lost by my fall;
And the veriest wretch that goes shivering by,
Will make a wide swoop lest I wander too nigh·
For all that is on or about me I know
There is nothing that's pure but the beautiful snow.

6. How strange it should be that this beautiful snow
Should fall on a sinner with nowhere to go!
How strange it should be when the night comes again,
If the snow and the ice strike my desperate brain;
   Fainting,
    Freezing,
     Dying alone
Too wicked for prayer, too weak for my moan
To be heard in the crash of the crazy town,
Gone mad in the joy of the snow coming down,
To lie and to die in my terrible woe,
With a bed and a shroud of the beautiful snow!

MAUD MULLER.

J. G. Whittier.

Maud Muller, on a summer's day,
Raked the meadow sweet with hay.

Beneath her torn hat glowed the wealth
Of simple beauty and rustic health.

Singing, she wrought, and her merry glee
The mock-bird echoed from his tree.

But, when she glanced to the far-off town,
White from its hill-slope looking down,

The sweet song died, and a vague unrest
And a nameless longing filled her breast—

A wish, that she hardly dared to own.
For something better than she had known.

The Judge rode slowly down the lane,
Smoothing his horse's chestnut mane.

He drew his bridle in the shade
Of the apple-trees, to greet the maid,

And ask a draught from the spring that flowed
Through the meadow across the road.

She stooped where the cool spring bubbled up,
And filled for him her small tin cup,

And blushed as she gave it, looking down
On her feet so bare, and her tattered gown.

"Thanks!" said the Judge, "a sweeter draught
From a fairer hand was never quaffed."

He spoke of the grass and flowers and trees,
Of the singing birds and the humming bees:

Then talked of the haying, and wondered whether
The cloud in the west would bring foul weather.

And Maud forgot her briar-torn gown,
And her graceful ankles bare and brown;

And listened, while a pleased surprise
Looked from her long-lashed hazel eyes.

At last, like one who for delay
Seeks a vain excuse, he rode away.

Maud Muller looked and sighed: "Ah, me!
That I the Judge's bride might be!

"He would dress me up in silks so fine,
And praise and toast me at his wine.

"My father should wear a broadcloth coat;
My brother should sail a painted boat.

"I'd dress my mother so grand and gay;
And the baby should have a new toy each day.

"And I'd feed the hungry and clothe the poor,
And all should bless me who left our door."

The Judge looked back as he climbed the hill,
And saw Maud Muller standing still.

"A form more fair, a face more sweet,
Ne'er hath it been my lot to meet.

"And her modest answer and graceful air
Show her wise and good as she is fair.

"Would she were mine, and I to-day,
Like her, a harvester of hay:

"No doubtful balance of rights and wrongs,
Nor weary lawyers with endless tongues,

"But low of cattle and song of birds,
And health and quiet and loving words."

But he thought of his sisters proud and cold,
And his mother vain of her rank and gold.

So, closing his heart, the Judge rode on,
And Maud was left in the field alone.

But the lawyers smiled that afternoon,
When he hummed in court an old love-tune

And the young girl mused beside the well,
Till the rain on the unraked clover fell.

He wedded a wife of richest dower,
Who lived for fashion, as he for power.

Yet oft, in his marble hearth's bright glow
He watched a picture come and go;

And sweet Maud Muller's hazel eyes
Looked out in their innocent surprise.

Oft, when the wine in his glass was red,
He longed for the wayside well instead;

And closed his eyes on his garnished rooms,
To dream of meadows and clover-blooms.

And the proud man sighed, with a secret pain;
"Ah, that I were free again!

"Free as when I rode that day,
Where the barefoot maiden raked her hay."

She wedded a man unlearned and poor,
And many children played round her door.

And oft, when the summer sun shone hot
On the new-mown hay in the meadow lot,

And she heard the little spring brook fall
Over the roadside, through the wall,

In the shade of the apple-tree again
She saw a rider draw his rein.

And, gazing down with timid grace,
She felt his pleased eyes read her face,

Sometimes her narrow kitchen walls
Stretched away into stately halls;

The weary wheel to a spinnet turned,
The tallow candle an astral burned,

And for him who sat by the chimney lug,
Dozing and grumbling o'er pipe and mug,

A manly form at her side she saw,
And joy was duty and love was law.

Then she took up her burden of life again,
Saying only, "It might have been."

Alas for maiden, alas for Judge,
For rich repiner and household drudge!

God pity them both! and pity us all,
Who vainly the dreams of youth recall.

For of all sad words of tongue or pen,
The saddest are these: "It might have been!"

Ah, well! for us all some sweet hope lies
Deeply buried from human eyes;

And in the hereafter angels may
Roll the stone from its grave away!

John Maynard, the Hero Pilot.

Gough.

John Maynard was well known in the Lake district as a God-fearing, honest, intelligent man. He was a pilot on a steamer from Detroit to Buffalo one summer afternoon. At that time those steamers seldom carried boats. Smoke was seen ascending from below, and the captain called out, "Simpson, go down and see what that smoke is." Simpson came up with his face pale as ashes, and said, "Captain, the ship is on fire!" Then, "Fire! fire! fire! fire on ship-board!" All hands were called up. Buckets of water were dashed upon the fire, but in vain. There were large quantities of rosin and tar on board, and it was useless to attempt to save the ship. Passengers rushed forward and inquired of the pilot, "How far are we from Buffalo?" "Seven miles." "How long before we reach it?" "Three quarters of an hour at our present rate of steam." "Is there any danger?" "Danger here—see the smoke bursting out! Go forward, if you would save your lives!" Passengers and crew, men, women and children crowded the forward part of the ship. John Maynard stood at the helm. The flames burst forth in a sheet of fire, clouds of smoke arose; the captain cried out through his trumpet, "John Maynard." "Ay, ay, sir." "Are you at the helm?" "Ay, ay, sir." "How does she head?" "Southeast by east, sir." "Head her southeast and run her on shore." Nearer, nearer, yet nearer she approached the shore. Again the captain cried out, "John Maynard." The response came feebly, "Ay, ay, sir." "Can you hold on five minutes longer, John?" "By God's help I can." The old man's hair was scorched from the scalp; one hand disabled, his knee upon the stanchion, and his teeth set, with his other hand upon the wheel, he stood firm as a rock. He beached the ship—every man, woman and child was saved, as John Maynard dropped and his spirit took its flight to his God.

The Black Regiment.

PORT HUDSON, MAY 27, 1863.

G. H. Boker.

1. Dark as the clouds of even,
   Ranked in the western heaven,
   Waiting the breath that lifts
   All the dread mass, and drifts
   Tempest and falling brand
   Over a ruined land;
   So still and orderly,
   Arm to arm, knee to knee,
   Waiting the great event,
   Stands the black regiment.

2. Down the long dusky line
   Teeth gleam and eyeballs shine;
   And the bright bayonet,
   Bristling and firmly set,
   Flashed with a purpose grand,
   Long ere the sharp command
   Of the fierce rolling drum
   Told them their time had come,
   Told them that work was sent
   For the black regiment.

3. "Now," the flag-sergeant cried,
   "Though death and hell betide,
   Let the whole nation see
   If we are fit to be
   Free in this land; or bound
   Down, like the whining hound—
   Bound with red stripes of pain
   In our old chains again!"
   O what a shout there went
   From the black regiment!

4. "Charge!" Trump and drum awoke,
   Onward the bondmen broke;
   Bayonet and saber-stroke
   Vainly opposed their rush.
   Through the wild battle's crush,
   With but one thought aflush,

Driving their lords like chaff,
In the guns' mouths they laugh;
Or at the slippery brands
Leaping with open hands,
Down they tear man and horse,
Down in their awful course;
Trampling with bloody heel
Over the crashing steel,
All their eyes forward bent,
Rushed the black regiment.

5. "Freedom!" their battle-cry,
"Freedom! or leave to die!"
Ah! and they meant the word,
Not as with us 'tis heard,
Not a mere party shout:
They gave their spirits out;
Trusting the end to God,
And on the gory sod
Rolled in triumphant blood.
Glad to strike one free blow,
Whether for weal or woe;
Glad to breathe one free breath,
Though on the lips of death.
Praying—alas, in vain!
That they might fall again,
So they could once more see
That burst to liberty!
This was what "freedom" lent
To the black regiment.

6. Hundreds on hundreds fell;
But they are resting well;
Scourges and shackles strong
Never shall do them wrong.
O, to the living few,
Soldiers, be just and true!
Hail them as comrades tried;
Fight with them side by side:
Never, in field or tent,
Scorn the black regiment!

ON THE SHORES OF TENNESSEE.
Ethel L. Beers.

1. ' Move my arm-chair, faithful Pompey,
    In the sunshine, bright and strong,
   For this world is fading, Pompey,
    Massa wont be with you long;
   And I fain would hear the south wind
    Bring once more the sound to me,
   Of the wavelets softly breaking
    On the shores of Tennessee.

2. "Mournful though the ripples murmur,
    As they still the story tell,
   How no vessels float the banner
    That I've loved so long and well.
   I shall listen to their music,
    Dreaming that again I see
   Stars and Stripes on sloop and shallop
    Sailing up the Tennessee.

3. "And, Pompey, while old Massa's waiting
    For Death's last dispatch to come,
   If that exiled starry banner
    Should come proudly sailing home,
   You shall greet it, slave no longer—
    Voice and hand shall both be free
   That shout and point to Union colors
    On the waves of Tennessee."

4. "Massa's berry kind to Pompey;
    But ole darkey's happy here,
   Where he's tended corn and cotton
    For dese many a long gone year.
   Over yonder Missis' sleeping—
    No one tends her grave like me.
   Mebbe she would miss the flowers
    She used to love in Tennessee.

5. "Pears like she was watching Massa—
    If Pompey should beside him stay,
   Mebbe she'd remember better
    How for him she used to pray;

Telling him that way up yonder
  White as snow his soul would be,
If he served the Lord of heaven
  While he lived in Tennessee."

6. Silently the tears were rolling
    Down the poor old dusky face,
  As he stepped behind his master,
    In his long accustomed place.
  Then a silence fell around them
    As they gazed on rock and tree
  Pictured in the placid waters
    Of the rolling Tennessee.

7. Master, dreaming of the battle
    Where he fought by Marion's side,
  When he bid the haughty Tarlton
    Stoop his lordly crest of pride.
  Man, remembering how yon sleeper
    Once he held upon his knee,
  Ere she loved the gallant soldier,
    Ralph Vervair, of Tennessee.

8. Still the south wind fondly lingers
    'Mid the veteran's silver hair;
  Still the bondman close beside him
    Stands behind the old arm-chair.
  With his dark-hued hand uplifted,
    Shading eyes, he bends to see
  Where the woodland boldly jutting
    Turns aside the Tennessee.

9. Thus he watches cloud-born shadows
    Glide from tree to mountain-crest,
  Softly creeping, ay and ever
    To the river's yielding breast.
  Ha! above the foliage yonder
    Something flutters wild and free!
  "Massa! massa! halleluiah!
    The flag's come back to Tennessee!"

10 "Pompey, hold me on your shoulder,
    Help me stand on foot once more.
  That I may salute the colors
    As they pass my cabin door.

Here's the paper signed that frees you,
    Give a freeman's shout with me—
God and Union!' be our watchword
    Evermore in Tennessee."

1. Then the trembling voice grew fainter,
    And the limbs refused to stand;
One prayer to Jesus—and the soldier
    Glided to the better land.
When the flag went down the river
    Man and master both were free,
While the ring-dove's note was mingled
    With the rippling Tennessee.

The Vagabonds.
Trowbridge.

1. We are two travelers, Roger and I.
    Roger's my dog. Come here, you scamp!
Jump for the gentlemen—mind your eye!
    Over the table—look out for the lamp!
The rogue is growing a little old;
    Five years we've tramped through wind and weather
And slept out-doors when nights were cold,
    And ate and drank—and starved—together.

2. We've learned what comfort is, I tell you!
    A bed on the floor, a bit of rosin,
A fire to thaw our thumbs, (poor fellow!
    The paw he holds up there's been frozen,)
Plenty of catgut for my fiddle,
    (This out-door business is bad for strings,)
Then a few nice buckwheats hot from the griddle,
    And Roger and I set up for kings!

3. No, thank ye, sir—I never drink;
    Roger and I are exceedingly moral—
Aren't we, Roger? See him wink!
    Well, something hot, then—we wont quarrel.
He's thirsty, too—see him nod his head!
    What a pity, sir, that dogs can't talk!
He understands every word that's said—
    And he knows good milk from water-and-chalk.

4. The truth is, sir, now I reflect,
   I've been so sadly given to grog,
   I wonder I've not lost the respect
   (Here's to you, sir!) even of my dog.
   But he sticks by, through thick and thin;
   And this old coat, with its empty pockets,
   And rags that smell of tobacco and gin,
   He'll follow while he has eyes in his sockets.

5. There isn't another creature living
   Would do it, and prove, through every disaster,
   So fond, so faithful, and so forgiving,
   To such a miserable, thankless master!
   No, sir! see him wag his tail and grin!
   By George! it makes my old eyes water!
   That is, there's something in this gin
   That chokes a fellow. But no matter!

6. We'll have some music if you're willing,
   And Roger (hem! what a plague a cough is, sir!)
   Shall march a little. Start, you villain!
   Stand straight! 'Bout face! Salute your officer!
   Put up that paw! Dress! Take your rifle!
   (Some dogs have arms, you see!) Now hold your
   Cap while the gentlemen give a trifle
   To aid a poor old patriot soldier!

7. March! Halt! Now show how the rebel shakes
   When he stands up to hear his sentence.
   Now tell us how many drams it takes
   To honor a jolly new acquaintance.
   Five yelps—that's five; he's mighty knowing!
   The night's before us, fill the glasses!
   Quick, sir! I'm ill—my brain is going!
   Some brandy—thank you—there—it passes!

8. Why not reform? That's easily said;
   But I've gone through such wretched treatment,
   Sometimes forgetting the taste of bread,
   And scarce remembering what meat meant,
   That my poor stomach's past reform;
   And there are times when, mad with thinking,
   I'd sell out heaven for something warm
   To prop a horrible inward sinking.

DRAMATIC STYLE.

9. Is there a way to forget to think?
    At your age, sir, home, fortune, friends,
A dear girl's love—but I took to drink;—
    The same old story; you know how it ends.
If you could have seen these classic features—
    You needn't laugh, sir; they were not then
Such a burning libel on God's creatures:
    I was one of your handsome men!

10. If you had seen HER, so fair and young,
    Whose head was happy on this breast!
If you could have heard the songs I sung
    When the wine went round, you wouldn't have guessed
That ever I, sir, should be straying
    From door to door, with a fiddle and dog,
Ragged and penniless, and playing
    To you to-night for a glass of grog!

11. She's married since—a parson's wife:
    'Twas better for her that we should part—
Better the soberest, prosiest life
    Than a blasted home and a broken heart.
I have seen her? Once: I was weak and spent
    On a dusty road: a carriage stopped:
But little she dreamed, as on she went,
    Who kissed the coin that her fingers dropped!

12. You've set me talking, sir; I'm sorry;
    It makes me wild to think of the change!
What do you care for a beggar's story?
    Is it amusing? you find it strange?
I had a mother so proud of me!
    'Twas well she died before— Do you know
If the happy spirits in heaven can see
    The ruin and wretchedness here below?

13. Another glass, and strong, to deaden
    This pain; then Roger and I will start.
I wonder, has he such a lumpish, leaden,
    Aching thing, in place of a heart?
He is sad sometimes, and would weep, if he could,
    No doubt, remembering things that were—
A virtuous kennel, with plenty of food,
    And himself a sober, respectable cur.

14. I'm better now; that glass was warming.—
 You rascal! limber your lazy feet!
 We must be fiddling and performing
 For supper and bed, or starve in the street.—
 Not a very gay life to lead, you think?
 But soon we shall go where lodgings are free,
 And the sleepers need neither victuals nor drink;—
 The sooner, the better for Roger and me!

On Board the Cumberland.
G. W. Boker—March 8, 1862.

1. "Stand to your guns, men!" Morris cried.
 Small need to pass the word;
 Our men at quarters ranged themselves
 Before the drum was heard.

2. And then began the sailors' jests:
 "What thing is that, I say?"
 "A long-shore meeting-house adrift
 Is standing down the bay!"

3. A frown came over Morris' face;
 The strange, dark craft he knew.
 "That is the iron Merrimac,
 Manned by a rebel crew.

4. "So shot your guns, and point them **straight**
 Before this day goes by,
 We'll try of what her metal's made."
 A cheer was our reply.

5. "Remember, boys, this flag of ours
 Has seldom left its place;
 And when it falls, the deck it strikes
 Is covered with disgrace.

6. "I ask but this: or sink or swim,
 Or live or nobly die,
 My last sight upon earth may be
 To see that ensign fly!"

7. Meanwhile the shapeless iron mass
    Came moving o'er the wave,
 As gloomy as a passing hearse,
    As silent as the grave.

8. Her ports were closed; from stem to stern
    No sign of life appeared.
 We wondered, questioned, strained our eyes,
    Joked—every thing but feared.

9. She reached our range. Our broadside rang,
    Our heavy pivots roared;
 And shot and shell, a fire of hell,
    Against her sides we poured.

10. God's mercy! from her sloping roof
    The iron tempest glanced,
 As hail bounds from a cottage thatch,
    And round her leaped and danced;

11. Or when against her dusky hull
    We struck a fair, full blow,
 The mighty, solid iron globes
    Were crumbled up like snow.

12. On, on, with fast increasing speed
    The silent monster came,
 Though all our starboard battery
    Was one long line of flame.

13. She heeded not; no gun she fired;
    Straight on our bow she bore;
 Through riving plank and crashing frame
    Her furious way she tore.

14. Alas! our beautiful, keen bow,
    That in the fiercest blast
 So gently folded back the seas,
    They hardly felt we passed!

15. Alas! alas! my Cumberland,
    That ne'er knew grief before,
 To be so gored, to feel so deep
    The tusk of that sea-boar!

16. Once more she backward drew a space,
    Once more our side she rent;
    Then, in the wantonness of hate,
    Her broadside through us sent.

17. The dead and dying round us lay,
    But our foeman lay abeam;
    Her open port-holes maddened us;
    We fired with shout and scream.

18. We felt our vessel settling fast,
    We knew our time was brief.
    "Ho! man the pumps!" But those who worked,
    And fought not, wept with grief.

19. "O keep us but an hour afloat!
    O, give us only time
    To mete unto yon rebel crew
    The measure of their crime!"

20. From captain down to powder-boy
    No hand was idle then;
    Two soldiers, but by chance aboard,
    Fought on like sailor men.

21. And when a gun's crew lost a hand,
    Some bold marine stepped out,
    And jerked his braided jacket off,
    And hauled the gun about.

22. Our forward magazine was drowned;
    And up from the sick bay
    Crawled the wounded, red with blood,
    And round us gasping lay.

23. Yes, cheering, calling us by name,
    Struggling with failing breath
    To keep their shipmates at their post
    Where glory strove with death.

24. With decks afloat, and powder gone,
    The last broadside we gave
    From the gun's heated iron lips
    Burst out beneath the wave.

25. So sponges, rammers, and handspikes—
    As men-of-war's-men should—
  We placed within their proper racks,
    And at our quarters stood.

26. "Up to the spar-deck! save yourselves!"
    Cried Selfridge. "Up, my men!
  God grant that some of us may live
    To fight yon ship again!"

27. We turned—we did not like to go;
    Yet staying seemed but vain,
  Knee-deep in water; so we left:
    Some swore, some groaned with pain.

28. We reached the deck. There Randall stood:
    "Another turn, men—so!"
  Calmly he aimed his pivot gun:
    "Now, Tenny, let her go!"

29. It did our sore hearts good to hear
    The song our pivot sang,
  As, rushing on from wave to wave,
    The whirling bomb-shell sprang.

30. Brave Randall leaped upon the gun,
    And waved his cap in sport;
  "Well done! well aimed! I saw that shell
    Go through an open port."

31. It was our last, our deadliest shot:
    The deck was overflown;
  The poor ship staggered, lurched to port,
    And gave a living groan.

32. Down, down, as headlong through the waves
    Our gallant vessel rushed,
  A thousand gurgling watery sounds
    Around my senses gushed.

33. Then I remember little more.
    One look to heaven I gave,
  Where, like an angel's wing, I saw
    Our spotless ensign wave.

34. I tried to cheer. I cannot say
   Whether I swam or sank;
   A blue mist closed around my eyes,
   And every thing was blank.

35. When I awoke, a soldier lad,
   All dripping from the sea,
   With two great tears upon his cheeks,
   Was bending over me.

36. I tried to speak. He understood
   The wish I could not speak.
   He turned me. There, thank God! the flag
   Still fluttered at the peak!

37. And there, while thread shall hang to thread,
   O let that ensign fly!
   The noblest constellation set
   Against our northern sky.

38. A sign that we who live may claim
   The peerage of the brave;
   A monument, that needs no scroll,
   For those beneath the wave.

THE BELLS.

Edgar A. Poe.

1. Hear the sledges with the bells—
   Silver bells—
What a world of merriment their melody foretells!
   How they tinkle, tinkle, tinkle,
      In the icy air of night!
   While the stars that oversprinkle
   All the heavens, seem to twinkle
      With a crystalline delight;
   Keeping time, time, time,
   In a sort of Runic rhyme,
To the tintinnabulation that so musically swells
   From the bells, bells, bells, bells,
      Bells, bells, bells—
From the jingling and the tinkling of the bells

DRAMATIC STYLE.

2. Hear the mellow wedding-bells,
　　　　Golden bells!
What a world of happiness their harmony foretells!
　　　Through the balmy air of night
　　　How they ring out their delight!
　　　　From the molten-golden notes,
　　　　　And all in tune,
　　　　What a liquid ditty floats
To the turtle-dove that listens, while she gloats
　　　　　On the moon!
　　O, from out the sounding cells,
What a gush of euphony voluminously wells!
　　　　　How it swells!
　　　　　How it dwells
　　　　On the Future! how it tells
　　　　Of the rapture that impels
　　　To the swinging and the ringing
　　　　Of the bells, bells, bells—
　　　　Of the bells, bells, bells, bells,
　　　　　Bells, bells, bells—
To the rhyming and the chiming of the bells!

3. Hear the loud alarum bells—
　　　　Brazen bells!
What a tale of terror, now, their turbulency tells!
　　　In the startled ear of night
　　　How they scream out their affright!
　　　　Too much horrified to speak,
　　　　They can only shriek, shriek,
　　　　　Out of tune,
In a clamorous appealing to the mercy of the fire,
In a mad expostulation with the deaf and frantic fire
　　　　Leaping higher, higher, higher,
　　　　With a desperate desire,
　　　　And a resolute endeavor,
　　　　Now—now to sit or never,
　　　By the side of the pale-faced moon.
　　　　O the bells, bells, bells!
　　　　What a tale their terror tells
　　　　　Of despair!
　　　　How they clang, and clash, and roar!
　　　　What a horror they outpour
　　　On the bosom of the palpitating air!

Yet the ear, it fully knows,
 By the twanging
 And the clanging,
How the danger ebbs and flows;
Yet the ear distinctly tells,
 In the jangling
 And the wrangling,
How the danger sinks and swells,
By the sinking or the swelling in the anger of the bells,
 Of the bells—
 Of the bells, bells, bells, bells,
 Bells, bells, bells—
In the clamor and the clangor of the bells!

 4. Hear the tolling of the bells—
 Iron bells!
What a world of solemn thought their monody compels!
 In the silence of the night,
 How we shiver with affright
 At the melancholy menace of their tone!
 For every sound that floats
 From the rust within their throats
 Is a groan.
 And the people—ah, the people—
 They that dwell up in the steeple,
 All alone,
 And who tolling, tolling, tolling,
 In that muffled monotone,
 Feel a glory in so rolling
 On the human heart a stone—
 They are neither man nor woman—
 They are neither brute nor human—
 They are Ghouls:
 And their king it is who tolls;
 And he rolls, rolls, rolls, rolls,
 A pæan from the bells!
 And his merry bosom swells
 With the pæan of the bells!
 And he dances and he yells;
 Keeping time, time, time,
 In a sort of Runic rhyme,
 To the pæan of the bells—
 Of the bells;

Keeping time, time, time,
　　　In a sort of Runic rhyme,
　　　　To the throbbing of the bells—
　　　Of the bells, bells, bells,
　　　　To the sobbing of the bells;
　　　Keeping time, time, time,
　　　　As he knells, knells, knells,
　　　In a happy Runic rhyme,
　　　　To the rolling of the bells—
　　　Of the bells, bells, bells—
　　　　To the tolling of the bells,
　　　Of the bells, bells, bells, bells—
　　　　　Bells, bells, bells,
To the moaning and the groaning of the bells

The Rising, 1776.
T. Buchanan Read.

1. Out of the North the wild news came,
Far flashing on its wings of flame,
Swift as the boreal light which flies
At midnight through the startled skies.

2. And there was tumult in the air,
　　The fife's shrill note, the drum's loud beat,
And through the wide land every-where
　　The answering tread of hurrying feet;
While the first oath of Freedom's gun
Came on the blast from Lexington;
And Concord roused, no longer tame,
Forgot her old baptismal name,
Made bare her patriot arm of power,
And swelled the discord of the hour.

3. Within its shade of elm and oak
　　The church of Berkley Manor stood;
There Sunday found the rural folk,
　　And some esteemed of gentle blood.
In vain their feet with loitering tread
　　Passed 'mid the graves where rank is naught;
All could not read the lesson taught
In that republic of the dead.

4. How sweet the hour of Sabbath talk,
   The vale with peace and sunshine full,
  Where all the happy people walk,
   Decked in their homespun flax and wool!
  Where youths' gay hats with blossoms bloom;
   And every maid, with simple art,
   Wears on her breast, like her own heart,
  A bud whose depths are all perfume;
   While every garment's gentle stir
   Is breathing rose and lavender.

5. There, vailed in all the sweets that are
    Blown from the violet's purple bosom,
   The scent of lilacs from afar,
    Touched with the sweet shrub's spicy blossom,
   Walked Esther; and the rustic ranks
   Stood on each side like flowery banks,
   To let her pass—a blooming aisle,
   Made brighter by her summer smile;
   On her father's arm she seemed to be
   The last green bough of that haughty tree.

6. The pastor came: his snowy locks
    Hallowed his brow of thought and care;
   And calmly, as shepherds lead their flocks.
    He led into the house of prayer.
   Forgive the student Edgar there
   If his enchanted eyes would roam,
    And if his thoughts soared not beyond,
    And if his heart glowed warmly fond
   Beneath his hope's terrestrial dome.
   To him the maiden seemed to stand,
    Vailed in the glory of the morn,
    At the bar of the heavenly bourn,
   A guide to the golden holy land.
    When came the service low response,
   Hers seemed an angel's answering tongue;
   When with the singing choir she sung,
   O'er all the rest her sweet notes rung,
   As if a silver bell were swung
    'Mid bells of iron and of bronze.

7. At times, perchance—O, happy chance!
    Their lifting eyes together met,
    Like violet to violet,
Casting a dewy greeting glance.
For once be Love, young Love, forgiven,
    That here, in a bewildered trance,
    He brought the blossoms of romance,
And waved them at the gates of heaven.

8. The pastor rose; the prayer was strong;
The psalm was warrior David's song;
The text, a few short words of might—
"The Lord of hosts shall arm the right!"
He spoke of wrongs too long endured,
Of sacred rights to be secured;
Then from his patriot tongue of flame
The startling words for Freedom came.
The stirring sentences he spake
Compelled the heart to glow or quake,
And, rising on his theme's broad wing,
    And grasping in his nervous hand
    The imaginary battle-brand,
In face of death he dared to fling
Defiance to a tyrant king.

9. Even as he spoke, his frame, renewed
    In eloquence of attitude,
Rose, as it seemed, a shoulder higher;
Then swept his kindling glance of fire
From startled pew to breathless choir;
When suddenly his mantle wide
His hands impatient flung aside,
And, lo, he met their wondering eyes
Complete in all a warrior's guise.
    A moment there was awful pause—
When Berkley cried, "Cease, traitor! cease!
God's temple is the house of peace!"
    The other shouted, "Nay, not so,
    When God is with our righteous cause;
His holiest places then are ours,
His temples are our forts and towers
    That frown upon the tyrant foe;

In this, the dawn of Freedom's day,
There is a time to fight and pray!"

10. And now before the open door—
   The warrior priest had ordered so—
   The enlisting trumpet's sudden roar
   Rang through the chapel, o'er and o'er,
     Its long reverberating blow,
   So loud and clear, it seemed the ear
   Of dusty death must wake and hear.
   And there the startling drum and fife
   Fired the living with fiercer life;
   While overhead, with wild increase,
   Forgetting its ancient toll of peace,
     The great bell swung as ne'er before.
   It seemed as it would never cease;
   And every word its ardor flung
   From off its jubilant iron tongue
     Was, "War! war! war!"

11. "Who dares"—this was the patriot's cry,
   As striding from the desk he came—
   "Come out with me, in Freedom's name,
   For her to live, for her to die?"
   A hundred hands flung up reply,
   A hundred voices answered, "I!"

The Polish Boy.
Mrs. Ann S. Stephens.

1. Whence came those shrieks, so wild and shrill,
     That like an arrow cleave the air,
   Causing the blood to creep and thrill
     With such sharp cadence of despair?
   Once more they come! as if a heart
     Were cleft in twain by one quick blow,
   And every string had voice apart
     To utter its peculiar woe!

2. Whence came they? From yon temple, where
     An altar raised for private prayer,
   Now forms the warrior's marble bed,
     Who Warsaw's gallant armies led.

The dim funereal tapers threw
　A holy luster o'er his brow,
And burnish with their rays of light
　The mass of curls that gather bright
Above the haughty brow and eye
　Of a young boy that's kneeling by.

3. What hand is that whose icy press
　　Clings to the dead with death's own grasp,
　But meets no answering caress—
　　No thrilling fingers seek its clasp?
　It is the hand of her whose cry
　　Rang wildly late upon the air,
　When the dead warrior met her eye,
　　Outstretched upon the altar there.

4. Now with white lips and broken moan
　She sinks beside the altar stone;
　But hark! the heavy tramp of feet
　Is heard along the gloomy street.
　Nearer and nearer yet they come,
　With clanking arms and noiseless drum.
　They leave the pavement. Flowers that spread
　Their beauties by the path they tread,
　Are crushed and broken. Crimson hands
　Rend brutally their blooming bands.
　Now whispered curses, low and deep,
　Around the holy temple creep.
　The gate is burst. A ruffian band
　Rush in and savagely demand,
　With brutal voice and oath profane,
　The startled boy for exile's chain.

5. The mother sprang with gesture wild,
　And to her bosom snatched the child;
　Then with pale cheek and flashing eye,
　Shouted with fearful energy—
　"Back, ruffians, back! nor dare to tread
　Too near the body of my dead!
　Nor touch the living boy—I stand
　Between him and your lawless band!
　No traitor he. But listen! I
　Have cursed your master's tyranny.

I cheered my lord to join the band
Of those who swore to free our land,
Or fighting die; and when he pressed
Me for the last time to his breast,
I knew that soon his form would be
Low as it is, or Poland free.
He went and grappled with the foe,
Laid many a haughty Russian low;
But he is dead—the good—the brave—
And I, his wife, am worse—a slave!
Take me, and bind these arms, these hands,
With Russia's heaviest iron bands,
And drag me to Siberia's wild
To perish, if 'twill save my child!"

6. "Peace, woman, peace!" the leader cried,
Tearing the pale boy from her side;
And in his ruffian grasp he bore
His victim to the temple door.

7. "One moment?" shrieked the mother, "one
Can land or gold redeem my son?
If so, I bend my Polish knee,
And, Russia, ask a boon of thee.
Take palaces, take lands, take all,
But leave him free from Russian thrall.
Take these," and her white arms and hands
She stripped of rings and diamond bands,
And tore from braids of long black hair
The gems that gleamed like star-light there;
Unclasped the brilliant coronal
And carcanet of orient pearl;
Her cross of blazing rubies last
Down to the Russian's feet she cast.

8. He stooped to seize the glittering store;
Unspringing from the marble floor,
The mother with a cry of joy,
Snatched to her leaping heart the boy!
But no—the Russian's iron grasp
Again undid the mother's clasp.
Forward she fell, with one long cry
Of more than mother's agony.

9. But the brave child is roused at length,
  And breaking from the Russian's hold,
 He stands, a giant in the strength
  Of his young spirit, fierce and bold.

10. Proudly he towers; his flashing eye,
  So blue and fiercely bright,
 Seems lighted from the eternal sky,
  So brilliant is its light.
 His curling lips and crimson cheeks
 Foretell the thought before he speaks.
 With a full voice of proud command
 He turns upon the wondering band.

11. "Ye hold me not! no, no, nor can;
 This hour has made the boy a man.
 The world shall witness that one soul
 Fears not to prove itself a Pole.

12. "I knelt beside my slaughtered sire,
 Nor felt one throb of vengeful ire;
 I wept upon his marble brow—
 Yes, wept—I was a child; but now
 My noble mother on her knee,
 Has done the work of years for me.
 Although in this small tenement
 My soul is cramped—unbowed, unbent,
 I've still within me ample power
 To free myself this very hour.
 This dagger in my heart! and then,
  Where is your boasted power, base men?"
 He drew aside his broidered vest,
 And there, like slumbering serpent's crest,
 The jeweled haft of a poniard bright,
 Glittered a moment on the sight.
 "Ha! start ye back? Fool! coward! knave!
 Think ye my noble father's glave
 Could drink the life blood of a slave?
 The pearls that on the handle flame
 Would blush to rubies in their shame.
 The blade would quiver in thy breast,
 Ashamed of such ignoble rest!
 No; thus I rend thy tyrant's chain,
 And fling him back a boy's disdain!"

13. A moment, and the funeral light
    Flashed on the jeweled weapon bright;
    Another, and his young heart's blood
    Leaped to the floor a crimson flood.
    Quick to his mother's side he sprang,
    And on the air his clear voice rang—
    "Up, mother, up! I'm free! I'm free!
    The choice was death or slavery;
    Up! mother, up! look on my face,
    I only wait for thy embrace.
    One last, last word—a blessing, one,
    To prove thou knowest what I have done;
    No look! no word! Canst thou not feel
    My warm blood o'er thy heart congeal?
    Speak, mother, speak—lift up thy head.
    What, silent still? Then art thou dead!
    Great God, I thank thee! Mother, I
    Rejoice with thee, and thus to die."
    Slowly he falls. The clustering hair
    Rolls back and leaves that forehead bare.
    One long, deep breath, and his pale head
    Lay on his mother's bosom, dead.

COUNT CANDESPINA'S STANDARD.

"The King of Aragon now entered Castile, by way of Soria and Osma, with a powerful army; and, having been met by the queen's forces, both parties encamped near Sepulveda, and prepared to give battle.

"This engagement, called, from the field where it took place, *de la Espina*, is one of the most famous of that age. The dastardly Count of Lara fled at the first shock, and joined the queen at Burgos, where she was anxiously awaiting the issue; but the brave Count of Candespina (Gomez Gonzalez) stood his ground to the last, and died on the field of battle. His standard-bearer, a gentleman of the house of Olea, after having his horse killed under him, and both hands cut off by saber-strokes, fell beside his master, still clasping the standard in his arms, and repeating his war-cry of 'Olea!'"—*Annals of the Queens of Spain.*

1. Scarce were the splintered lances dropped,
    Scarce were the swords drawn out,
    Ere recreant Lara, sick with fear,
    Had wheeled his steed about;

2. His courser reared, and plunged, and neighed,
    Loathing the fight to yield;
  But the coward spurred him to the bone,
    And drove him from the field.

3. Gonzalez in his stirrups rose:
    "Turn, turn, thou traitor knight!
  Thou bold tongue in a lady's bower,
    Thou dastard in a fight!"

4. But vainly valiant Gomez cried
    Across the waning fray:
  Pale Lara and his craven band
    To Burgos scoured away.

5. "Now, by the God above me, sirs,
    Better we all were dead,
  Than a single knight among ye all
    Should ride where Lara led!

6. "Yet ye who fear to follow me,
    As yon traitor turn and fly;
  For I lead ye not to win a field:
    I lead ye forth to die.

7. "Olea, plant my standard here—
    Here on this little mound;
  Here raise the war-cry of thy house,
    Make this our rallying ground.

8. "Forget not, as thou hop'st for grace,
    The last care I shall have
  Will be to hear thy battle-cry,
    And see that standard wave."

9. Down on the ranks of Aragon
    The bold Gonzalez drove,
  And Olea raised his battle-cry,
    And waved the flag above..

10. Slowly Gonzalez' little band
    Gave ground before the foe,
  But not an inch of the field was won
    Without a deadly blow;

11. And not an inch o.' the field was won
    That did not draw a tear
 From the widowed wives of Aragon,
    That fatal news to hear.

12. Backward and backward Gomez fought,
    And high o'er the clashing steel,
 Plainer and plainer rose the cry,
    "Olea for Castile!"

13. Backward fought Gomez, step by step,
    Till the cry was close at hand,
 Till his dauntless standard shadowed him;
    And there he made his stand.

14. Mace, sword, and ax rang on his mail,
    Yet he moved not where he stood,
 Though each gaping joint of armor ran
    A stream of purple blood.

15. As, pierced with countless wounds, he fell,
    The standard caught his eye,
 And he smiled, like an infant hushed asleep,
    To hear the battle-cry.

16. Now one by one the wearied knights
    Have fallen, or basely flown;
 And on the mound where his post was fixed
    Olea stood alone.

17. "Yield up thy banner, gallant knight!
    Thy lord lies on the plain;
 Thy duty has been nobly done;
    I would not see thee slain."

18. "Spare pity, King of Aragon;
    I would not hear thee lie:
 My lord is looking down from heaven
    To see his standard fly."

19. "Yield, madman, yield! thy horse is down,
    Thou hast nor lance nor shield;
 Fly!—I will grant thee time." "This flag
    Can neither fly nor yield!"

20. They girt the standard round about,
　　　A wall of flashing steel;
　　But still they heard the battle-cry,
　　　"Olea for Castile!"

21. And there, against all Aragon,
　　　Full-armed with lance and brand,
　　Olea fought until the sword
　　　Snapped in his sturdy hand.

22. Among the foe, with that high scorn
　　　Which laughs at earthly fears,
　　He hurled the broken hilt, and drew
　　　His dagger on the spears.

23. They hewed the hauberk from his breast,
　　　The helmet from his head;
　　They hewed the hands from off his limbs
　　　From every vein he bled.

24. Clasping the standard to his heart,
　　　He raised one dying peal,
　　That rang as if a trumpet blew—
　　　"Olea for Castile!"

THE BARON'S LAST BANQUET.
A. G. Greene.

1. O'er a low couch the setting sun
　　　Had thrown its latest ray,
　　Where, in his last strong agony,
　　　A dying warrior lay—
　　The stern old Baron Rudiger,
　　　Whose frame had ne'er been bent
　　By wasting pain, till time and toil
　　　Its iron strength had spent.

2. "They come around me here, and say
　　　My days of life are o'er—
　　That I shall mount my noble steed
　　　And lead my band no more;

They come, and to my beard they dare
  To tell me now, that I,
Their own liege lord and master born—
  That I—ha! ha!—must die!

3 "And what is death? I've dared him
    Before the Paynim's spear—
  Think ye he's entered at my gate,
    Has come to seek me here?
  I've met him, faced him, scorned him,
    When the fight was raging hot—
  I'll try his might—I'll brave his power—
    Defy, and fear him not!

4. "Ho! sound the tocsin from the tower,
    And fire the culverin!
  Bid each retainer arm with speed,
    Call every vassal in!
  Up with my banner on the wall!
    The banquet board prepare!
  Throw wide the portal of my hall,
    And bring my armor there!"

5. A hundred hands were busy then;
    The banquet forth was spread,
  And rang the heavy oaken floor
    With many a martial tread;
  While from the rich, dark tracery,
    Along the vaulted wall,
  Lights gleamed on harness, plume, and spear,
    O'er the proud Gothic hall.

6. Fast hurrying through the outer gate,
    The mailed retainers poured
  On through the portal's frowning arch,
    And thronged around the board;
  While at its head, within his dark,
    Carved oaken chair of state,
  Armed cap-a-pie, stern Rudiger,
    With girded falchion sate.

7. "Fill every beaker up, my men!
    Pour forth the cheering wine!
  There's life and strength in every drop,
    Thanksgiving to the vine!

Are ye all there, my vassals true?—
  Mine eyes are waxing dim:
Fill round, my tried and fearless ones,
  Each goblet to the brim!

8 "Ye're there, but yet I see you not!
  Draw forth each trusty sword,
And let me hear your faithful steel
  Clash once around my board!
I hear it faintly—louder yet!
  What clogs my heavy breath?
Up, all! and shout for Rudiger,
  'Defiance unto death!'"

9. Bowl rang to bowl, steel clanged to steel,
  And rose a deafening cry,
That made the torches flare around,
  And shook the flags on high:
"Ho! cravens! do ye fear him?
  Slaves! traitors! have ye flown?
Ho! cowards, have ye left me
  To meet him here alone?

10. "But I defy him! let him come!"
  Down rang the massy cup,
While from its sheath the ready blade
  Came flashing half-way up;
And with the black and heavy plumes
  Scarce trembling on his head,
There, in his dark, carved, oaken chair,
  Old Rudiger sat—dead!

BERNARDO DEL CARPIO.

Mrs. Hemans.

1. The warrior bowed his crested head, and tamed his heart of fire,
And sued the haughty king to free his long-imprisoned sire;
"I bring thee here my fortress-keys, I bring my captive train;
I pledge thee faith, my liege, my lord!—O break my father's chain!"

2. "Rise, rise! even now thy father comes, a ransomed man this day!
Mount thy good horse, and thou and I will meet him on his way."
Then lightly rose that loyal son, and bounded on his steed,
And urged, as if with lance in rest, the charger's foamy speed.

3. And lo! from far, as on they pressed, there came a glittering band,
With one that 'midst them stately rode, as a leader in the land
"Now haste, Bernardo, haste! for there, in very truth, is he,
The father whom thy faithful heart hath yearned so long to see.'

4. His dark eye flashed, his proud breast heaved, his cheek's hue came and went;
He reached that gray-haired chieftain's side, and there, dismounting, bent;
A lowly knee to earth he bent, his father's hand he took—
What was there in its touch that all his fiery spirit shook?

5. That hand was cold—a frozen thing—it dropped from his like lead!
He looked up to the face above—the face was of the dead!
A plume waved o'er the noble brow—the brow was fixed and white;
He met, at last, his father's eyes—but in them was no sight!

6. Up from the ground he sprang and gazed; but who could paint that gaze?
They hushed their very hearts, that saw its horror and amaze—
They might have chained him, as before that stony form he stood;
For the power was stricken from his arm, and from his lip the blood.

7. "Father!" at last he murmured low, and wept like childhood then:
Talk not of grief till thou hast seen the tears of warlike men!
He thought on all his glorious hopes, and all his young renown—
He flung his falchion from his side, and in the dust sat down.

8. Then covering with his steel-gloved hands his darkly mournful brow,
"No more, there is no more," he said, "to lift the sword for now;
My king is false—my hope betrayed! My father!—O the worth,
The glory and the loveliness are passed away from earth!

9. "I thought to stand where banners waved, my sire, beside thee yet!
I would that there our kindred blood on Spain's free soil had met!
Thou wouldst have known my spirit then; for thee my fields were won;
And thou hast perished in thy chains, as though thou hadst no son!"

10. Then, starting from the ground once more, he seized the monarch's rein,
Amid the pale and wildered looks of all the courtier train;
And with a fierce, o'ermastering grasp, the rearing war-horse led,
And sternly set them face to face—the king before the dead:

11. "Came I not forth, upon thy pledge, my father's hand to kiss?
Be still, and gaze thou on, false king! and tell me, what is this?
The voice, the glance, the heart I sought—give answer, where are they?
If thou wouldst clear thy perjured soul, send life through this cold clay!

12. "Into these glassy eyes put light—be still! keep down thine ire!
Bid these white lips a blessing speak—this earth is not my sire;
Give me back him for whom I strove, for whom my blood was shed!
Thou canst not?—and a king!—his dust be mountains on thy head!"

13. He loosed the steed—his slack hand fell; upon the silent face
He cast one long, deep, troubled look, then turned from that sad place;
His hope was crushed; his after fate untold in martial strain;
His banner led the spears no more amid the hills of Spain.

THE RAVEN.
Edgar A. Poe.

1. Once upon a midnight dreary, while I pondered, weak and weary,
Over many a quaint and curious volume of forgotten lore—
While I nodded, nearly napping, suddenly there came a tapping,
As of some one gently rapping, rapping at my chamber door.
"'Tis some visitor," I muttered, "tapping at my chamber door—
Only this, and nothing more."

2. Ah, distinctly I remember, it was in the bleak December,
And each separate dying ember wrought its ghost upon the floor.
Eagerly I wished the morrow: vainly I had sought to borrow
From my books surcease of sorrow—sorrow for the lost Lenore—
For the rare and radiant maiden whom the angels named Lenore—
Nameless here for evermore.

3. And the silken, sad, uncertain rustling of each purple curtain,
Thrilled me—filled me with fantastic terrors never felt before;
So that now, to still the beating of my heart, I stood repeating,
" 'Tis some visitor entreating entrance at my chamber door—
Some late visitor entreating entrance at my chamber-door;
That it is, and nothing more."

4. Presently my soul grew stronger: hesitating then no longer,
"Sir," said I, "or Madam, truly your forgiveness I implore;
But the fact is, I was napping, and so gently you came rapping,
And so faintly you came tapping, tapping at my chamber door,
That I scarce was sure I heard you "—here I opened wide the door:
Darkness there, and nothing more.

5. Deep into that darkness peering, long I stood there, wondering, fearing,
Doubting, dreaming dreams no mortal ever dared to dream before;
But the silence was unbroken, and the darkness gave no token,
And the only word there spoken was the whispered word "Lenore!"
This *I* whispered, and an echo murmured back the word "LENORE!"
Merely this, and nothing more.

6. Back into the chamber turning, all my soul within me burning,
Soon again I heard a tapping, something louder than before.
"Surely," said I, "surely that is something at my window-lattice;
Let me see then what thereat is, and this mystery explore—
Let my heart be still a moment, and this mystery explore;—
'Tis the wind, and nothing more."

7. Open then I flung the shutter, when, with many a flirt and flutter,
In there stepped a stately raven of the saintly days of yore.
Not the least obeisance made he; not an instant stopped or stayed he;
But, with mien of lord or lady, perched above my chamber door—
Perched upon a bust of Pallas, just above my chamber door—
Perched, and sat, and nothing more.

8. Then this ebony bird beguiling my sad fancy into smiling,
　　By the grave and stern decorum of the countenance it wore,
　　"Though thy crest be shorn and shaven, thou," I said, "art sure no craven;
　　Ghastly, grim, and ancient raven, wandering from the nightly shore,
　　Tell me what thy lordly name is on the Night's Plutonian shore?'
　　　　Quoth the raven, "Nevermore!"

9. Much I marveled this ungainly fowl to hear discourse so plainly,
　　Though its answer little meaning—little relevancy bore;
　　For we cannot help agreeing that no living human being
　　Ever yet was blessed with seeing bird above his chamber door—
　　Bird or beast upon the sculptured bust above his chamber door
　　　　With such name as "Nevermore!"

10. But the raven sitting lonely on the placid bust, spoke only
　　That one word, as if his soul in that one word he did outpour.
　　Nothing further then he uttered—not a feather then he fluttered—
　　Till I scarcely more than muttered, "Other friends have flown before—
　　On the morrow *he* will leave me, as my hopes have flown before.'
　　　　Then the bird said, "Nevermore!"

11. Startled at the stillness, broken by reply so aptly spoken,
　　"Doubtless," said I, "what it utters is its only stock and store,
　　Caught from some unhappy master, whom unmerciful disaster
　　Followed fast and followed faster, till his song one burden bore—
　　Till the dirges of his hope that melancholy burden bore,
　　　　Of 'Nevermore—nevermore!'"

12. But the raven still beguiling all my sad soul into smiling,
　　Straight I wheeled a cushioned seat in front of bird, and bust, and door,
　　Then, upon the velvet sinking, I betook myself to linking
　　Fancy unto fancy, thinking what this ominous bird of yore—
　　What this grim, ungainly, ghastly, gaunt, and ominous bird of yore
　　　　Meant in croaking "Nevermore!"

3. Thus I sat engaged in guessing, but no syllable expressing
　　To the fowl, whose fiery eyes now burned into my bosom's core;
　　This and more I sat divining, with my head at ease reclining
　　On the cushion's velvet lining that the lamp-light gloated o'er,
　　But whose velvet violet lining, with the lamp-light gloating o'er
　　　　She shall press—ah! nevermore!

14. Then methought the air grew denser, perfumed from an unseen censer
 Swung by seraphim, whose faint foot-falls tinkled on the tufted floor.
 "Wretch!" I cried, "thy God hath lent thee—by these angels he hath sent thee
 Respite—respite and nepenthe from thy memories of Lenore!
 Quaff, O quaff this kind nepenthe, and forget this lost Lenore!"
  Quoth the raven, "Nevermore!"

15. "Prophet!" said I, "thing of evil!—prophet still, if bird or devil!
 Whether tempter sent, or whether tempest tossed thee here ashore,
 Desolate, yet all undaunted, on this desert land enchanted—
 On this home by Horror haunted—tell me truly, I implore—
 Is there—*is* there balm in Gilead?—tell me—tell me, I implore!"
  Quoth the raven, "Nevermore!"

16. "Prophet!" said I, "thing of evil!—prophet still, if bird or devil!
 By that heaven that bends above us—by that God we both adore,
 Tell this soul with sorrow laden, if, within the distant Aidenn,
 It shall clasp a sainted maiden, whom the angels name Lenore;
 Clasp a fair and radiant maiden, whom the angels name Lenore!"
  Quoth the raven, "Nevermore!"

17. "Be that word our sign of parting, bird or fiend!" I shrieked upstarting—
 "Get thee back into the tempest and the Night's Plutonian shore!
 Leave no black plume as a token of that lie thy soul hath spoken!
 Leave my loneliness unbroken!—quit the bust above my door!
 Take thy beak from out my heart, and take thy form from off my door!"
  Quoth the raven, "Nevermore!"

18. And the raven, never flitting, still is sitting, still is sitting
 On the pallid bust of Pallas, just above my chamber door;
 And his eyes have all the seeming of a demon that is dreaming,
 And the lamp-light o'er him streaming throws his shadow on the floor;
 And my soul from out that shadow that lies floating on the floor
  Shall be lifted—NEVERMORE!

Scene from Hamlet.

Act III. Scene III.

[*Enter* QUEEN *and* POLONIUS.]

Pol. He will come straight. Look, you lay home to him:
Tell him his pranks have been too broad to bear with;
And that your grace hath screened and stood between
Much heat and him. I'll sconce me even here.
Pray you be round with him.
   Queen. I'll warrant you—
Fear me not. Withdraw, I hear him coming.
          [*Polonius conceals himself behind the arras.*]
   Hamlet. Now, mother, what's the matter?
   Queen. Hamlet, thou hast thy father much offended.
   Hamlet. Mother, you have my father much offended.
   Queen. Come, come, you answer with an idle tongue.
   Hamlet. Go, go, you question with a wicked tongue.
   Queen. Why, how now, Hamlet?
   Hamlet.   What's the matter now?
   Queen. Have you forgot me?
   Hamlet.   No, by the rood, not so:
You are the queen: your husband's brother's wife;
And—would it were not so!—you are my mother.
   Queen. Nay, then I'll set those to you that can speak.
   Hamlet. Come, come, and sit you down; you shall not budge.
You go not till I set you up a glass
Where you may see the inmost part of you.
   Queen. What wilt thou do?—thou wilt not murder me?
   Hamlet. Leave wringing of your hands: peace; sit you down
And let me wring your heart: for so I shall
If it be made of penetrable stuff;
If damned custom have not brazed it so
That it is proof and bulwark against sense.
   Queen. What have I done, that thou darest wag thy tongue
In noise so rude against me?
   Hamlet.   Such an act,
That blurs the grace and blush of modesty;
Calls virtue, hypocrite; takes off the rose
From the fair forehead of an innocent love
And sets a blister there; makes marriage vows
As false as dicer's oath! Oh, such a deed

Lay not that flattering unction to your soul,
That not your trespass, but my madness, **speaks:**
It will but skin and film the ulcerous place,
Whilst rank corruption, mining all within,
Infects unseen. Confess yourself to Heaven;
Repent what's past; avoid what is to come;
And do not spread the compost on the weeds
To make them ranker.

    Queen. O Hamlet! thou hast cleft my heart in **twain.**

    Hamlet. Oh, throw away the worser part of it
And live the purer with the other half.
Good-night: once more, good-night!
And when you are desirous to be blest,
I'll blessing beg of you.

HUMOROUS STYLE.

THE NANTUCKET SKIPPER.

J. T. Fields.

1. Many a long, long year ago,
    Nantucket skippers had a plan
Of finding out, though "lying low,"
    How near New York their schooners ran.

2. They greased the lead before it fell,
    And then by sounding through the night,
Knowing the soil that stuck so well,
    They always guessed their reckoning right.

3. A skipper gray, whose eyes were dim,
    Could tell, by tasting, just the spot,
And so below he'd "douse the glim,"
    After, of course, his "something hot."

4. Snug in his berth, at eight o'clock,
    This ancient skipper might be found;
No matter how his craft would rock,
    He slept—for skippers' naps are sound.

5. The watch on deck would now and then
    Run down and wake him with the lead;
He'd up, and taste, and tell the men
    How many miles they went ahead

6. One night, 'twas Jotham Marden's watch,
    A curious wag—the peddler's son;
And so he mused, (the wanton wretch!)
    "To-night I'll have a grain of fun.

7. "We're all a set of stupid fools
    To think the skipper knows, by tasting,
What ground he's on; Nantucket schools
    Don't teach such stuff, with all their basting!"

8. And so he took the well-greased lead
    And rubbed it o'er a box of earth
That stood on deck, (a parsnip-bed,)
    And then he sought the skipper's berth.

9. "Where are we now, sir? Please to taste."
    The skipper yawned, put out his tongue,
And oped his eyes in wondrous haste,
    And then upon the floor he sprung!

10. The skipper stormed, and tore his hair;
    Thrust on his boots, and roared to Marden,
"Nantucket's sunk, and here we are
    Right over old Marm Hackett's garden!"

A Categorical Courtship.

I sat one night beside a blue-eyed girl—
    The fire was out, and so, too, was her mother;
A feeble flame around the lamp did curl,
    Making faint shadows, blending in each other.
'Twas nearly twelve o'clock, too, in November.
She had a shawl on also, I remember.
Well, I had been to see her every night
    For thirteen days, and had a sneaking notion
To pop the question, thinking all was right,
    And once or twice had made an awkward motion
To take her hand, and stammered, coughed, and stuttered,
But somehow nothing to the point had uttered.
I thought this chance too good now to be lost;
    I hitched my chair up pretty close beside her,
Drew a long breath, and then my legs I crossed,
    Bent over, sighed, and for five minutes eyed her·

She looked as if she knew what next was coming,
And with her foot upon the floor was drumming.
I didn't know how to begin, or where—
  I couldn't speak; the words were always choking;
I scarce could move—I seemed tied in my chair—
  I hardly breathed—'twas awfully provoking;
The perspiration from each pore was oozing;
My heart and brain and limbs their power seemed losing.
At length I saw a brindled tabby cat
  Walk purring up, inviting me to pat her;
An idea came, electric-like at that—
  My doubts, like summer clouds, began to scatter;
I seized on tabby, though a scratch she gave me,
And said, "Come, Puss, ask Mary if she'll have me?"
'Twas done at once—the murder now was out;
  The thing was all explained in half a minute;
She blushed, and, turning pussy cat about,
  Said, "Pussy, tell him yes!" Her foot was in it!
The cat had thus saved me my category,
And here's the catastrophe of my story.

ORATOR PUFF.
Thomas Moore.

1. Mr. Orator Puff had two tones to his voice,
  (The one squeaking thus, and the other down so;
In each sentence he uttered he gave you your choice;
  For one half was B alt, and the rest G below.
    Oh! Oh! Orator Puff,
    One voice for an orator's surely enough.

2. But he still talked away, spite of coughs and of frowns,
So distracting all ears with his ups and his downs,
That a wag once, on hearing the orator say,
"My voice is for war," asked him, "Which of them, pray?"
    Oh! Oh! Orator Puff,
    One voice for an orator's surely enough.

3. Reeling homeward one evening, top-heavy with gin,
  And rehearsing his speech on the weight of the crown,
He tripped near a saw-pit and tumbled right in;
  "Sinking-fund" the last words as his noddle came down.
    Oh! Oh! Orator Puff,
    One voice for an orator's surely enough

4 "Ho! help!" he exclaimed, in his he and she tones;
"Help me out! help me out! I have broken my bones!"
"Help you out!" said a Paddy, who passed; "what a bother!
Why, there's two of you there; can't you help one another?"
   Oh! Oh! Orator Puff,
   One voice for an orator's surely enough.

THE SMACK IN SCHOOL.

W. P. Palmer.

A district school, not far away
'Mid Berkshire hills, on Winter's day,
Was humming with its wonted noise
Of threescore mingled girls and boys—
Some few upon their tasks intent,
But more on furtive mischief bent;
The while the master's downward look
Was fastened on a copy-book;
When suddenly, behind his back,
Rose, loud and clear, a rousing SMACK!
As 'twere a battery of bliss
Let off in one tremendous kiss!
"What's that?" the startled master cries;
"That thir," a little imp replies,
"Wath William Willith, if you pleathe—
I thaw him kith Thuthannah Peathe!"
With frown to make a statue thrill,
The master thundered, "Hither, Will!"
Like wretch o'ertaken in his track,
With stolen chattels on his back,
Will hung his head in fear and shame,
And to the awful presence came—
A great, green, bashful simpleton,
The butt of all good-natured fun.
With smile suppressed and birch upraised,
The threatener faltered—"I'm amazed
That you, my biggest pupil, should
Be guilty of an act so rude!
Before the whole set school to boot—
What evil genius put you to't?"

" Twas she herself, sir," sobbed the lad,
" I didn't mean to be so bad;
But when Susannah shook her curls,
And whispered I was 'feared of girls,
And dassn't kiss a baby's doll,
I couldn't stand it, sir, at all!
But up and kissed her on the spot,
I know—*boo hoo*—I ought to not,
But, somehow, from her looks, *boo hoo*,
I thought she kind o' wished me to ! "

Pyramus and Thisbe.
John G. Saxe.

This tragical tale, which they say is a true one,
Is old; but the manner is wholly a new one.
One Ovid, a writer of some reputation,
Has told it before in a tedious narration;
In a style, to be sure, of remarkable fullness,
But which nobody reads on account of its dullness.

Young Peter Pyramus—I call him Peter,
Not for the sake of the rhyme or the metre;
But merely to make the name completer—
For Peter lived in the olden times,
And in one of the worst of pagan climes
That flourish now in classical fame,
Long before either noble or boor
Had such a thing as a *Christian* name.
Young Peter, then, was a nice young beau
As any young lady would wish to know;
In years, I ween, he was rather green,
That is to say, he was just eighteen—
A trifle too short, a shaving too lean,
But " a nice young man " as ever was seen,
And fit to dance with a May-day queen!

Now Peter loved a beautiful girl
As ever ensnared the heart of an earl,
In the magical trap of an auburn curl—
A little Miss Thisbe, who lived next door,
(They slept, in fact, on the very same floor,

With a wall between them and nothing more—
Those double dwellings were common of yore,)
And they loved each other, the legends say,
In that very beautiful, bountiful way,
That every young maid and every young blade
Are wont to do before they grow staid,
And learn to love by the laws of trade;
But (alack-a-day, for the girl and boy!)
A little impediment checked their joy,
And gave them awhile the deepest annoy;
For some good reason, which history cloaks,
The match didn't happen to please the old folks!

So Thisbe's father and Peter's mother
Began the young couple to worry and bother,
And tried their innocent passion to smother,
By keeping the lovers from seeing each other!
But who ever heard of a marriage deterred,
Or even deferred,
By any contrivance so very absurd
As scolding the boy and caging the bird?
Now Peter, who wasn't discouraged at all
By obstacles such as the timid appal,
Contrived to discover a hole in the wall,
Which wasn't so thick but removing a brick
Made a passage—though rather provokingly small.
Through this little chink the lover could greet her,
And secrecy made their courting the sweeter,
While Peter kissed Thisbe, and Thisbe kissed Peter—
For kisses, like folks with diminutive souls,
Will manage to creep through the smallest of holes!

'Twas here that the lovers, intent upon love,
Made a nice little plot to meet at a spot
Near a mulberry tree in a neighboring grove;
For the plan was all laid by the youth and the maid,
Whose hearts, it would seem, were uncommonly bold ones,
To run off and get married in spite of the old ones.
In the shadows of evening, as still as a mouse,
The beautiful maiden slipped out of the house,
The mulberry tree impatient to find;
While Peter, the vigilant matrons to blind,
Strolled leisurely out, some minutes behind.

While waiting alone by the trysting tree,
A terrible lion as e'er you set eye on,
Came roaring along quite horrid to see,
And caused the young maiden in terror to flee,
(A lion's a creature whose regular trade is
Blood—and "a terrible thing among ladies,")
And losing her vail as she ran from the wood,
The monster bedabbled it over with blood.

Now Peter arriving, and seeing the vail
All covered o'er and reeking with gore,
Turned, all of a sudden, exceedingly pale,
And sat himself down to weep and to wail—
For, soon as he saw the garment, poor Peter
Made up his mind in very short metre
That Thisbe was dead, and the lion had eat her!
So breathing a prayer, he determined to share
The fate of his darling, "the loved and the lost,"
And fell on his dagger, and gave up the ghost!
Now Thisbe returning, and viewing her beau,
Lying dead by her vail, (which she happened to know,
She guessed in a moment the cause of his erring;
And, seizing the knife that had taken his life,
In less than a jiffy was dead as a herring.

MORAL.

Young gentlemen!—pray recollect, if you please,
Not to make assignations near mulberry trees.
Should your mistress be missing. it shows a weak head
To be stabbing yourself till you know she is dead.
Young ladies!—you shouldn't go strolling about
When your anxious mammas don't know you are out;
And remember that accidents often befall
From kissing young fellows through holes in the wall!

A VERY IMPORTANT PROCEEDING—MR. PICKWICK.
Dickens.

Mr. Pickwick's apartments in Goswell-street, although on a limited scale, were not only of a very neat and comfortable description, but peculiarly adapted for the residence of a man of his genius and observation. His sitting-room was the first floor front, his bed-room was the second floor front; and thus, whether he was sitting at his desk in the parlor, or standing before the dressing-glass in his dormitory, he had an equal opportunity of contemplating human nature in all the numerous phases it exhibits in that not more populous than popular thoroughfare. His landlady, Mrs. Bardell—the relict and sole executrix of a deceased custom-house officer—was a comely woman of bustling manners and agreeable appearance, with a natural genius for cooking, improved by study and long practice into an exquisite talent. There were no children, no servants, no fowls. The only other inmates of the house were a large man and a small boy; the first a lodger, the second a production of Mrs. Bardell's. The large man was always at home precisely at ten o'clock at night, at which hour he regularly condensed himself into the limits of a dwarfish French bedstead in the back parlor; and the infantine sports and gymnastic exercises of Master Bardell were exclusively confined to the neighboring pavements and gutters. Cleanliness and quiet reigned throughout the house, and in it Mr. Pickwick's will was law.

To any one acquainted with these points of the domestic economy of the establishment, and conversant with the admirable regulation of Mr. Pickwick's mind, his appearance and behavior on the morning previous to that which had been fixed upon for the journey to Eatanswill would have been most mysterious and unaccountable. He paced the room to and fro with hurried steps, popped his head out of the window at intervals of about three minutes each, constantly referred to his watch, and exhibited many other manifestations of impatience very unusual with him. It was evident that something of great importance was in contemplation, but what that something was not even Mrs. Bardell herself had been enabled to discover.

"Mrs. Bardell," said Mr. Pickwick at last as that amiable female approached the termination of a prolonged dusting of the apartment.

"Sir," said Mrs. Bardell.

"Your little boy is a very long time gone."

"Why, it is a good long way to the Borough, sir," remonstrated Mrs. Bardell.

"Ah," said Mr. Pickwick, "very true; so it is."

Mr. Pickwick relapsed into silence, and Mrs. Bardell resumed her dusting.

"Mrs. Bardell," said Mr. Pickwick at the expiration of a few minutes.

"Sir," said Mrs. Bardell again.

"Do you think it's a much greater expense to keep two people than to keep one?"

"La, Mr. Pickwick," said Mrs. Bardell, coloring up to the very border of her cap, as she fancied she observed a species of matrimonial twinkle in the eyes of her lodger; "La, Mr. Pickwick, what a question!"

"Well, but do you?" inquired Mr. Pickwick.

"That depends"—said Mrs. Bardell, approaching the duster very near to Mr. Pickwick's elbow, which was planted on the table; "that depends a good deal upon the person, you know, Mr. Pickwick; and whether it's a saving and careful person, sir."

"That's very true," said Mr. Pickwick; "but the person I have in my eye (here he looked very hard at Mrs. Bardell) I think possesses these qualities, and has, moreover, a considerable knowledge of the world, and a great deal of sharpness, Mrs. Bardell, which may be of material use to me."

"La, Mr. Pickwick," said Mrs. Bardell, the crimson rising to her cap-border again.

"I do," said Mr. Pickwick, growing energetic, as was his wont in speaking of a subject which interested him; "I do, indeed· and to tell you the truth, Mrs. Bardell, I have made up my mind."

"Dear me, sir!" exclaimed Mrs. Bardell.

"You'll think it not very strange now," said the amiable Mr. Pickwick, with a good-humored glance at his companion, "that I never consulted you about this matter, and never mentioned it till I sent your little boy out this morning—eh?"

Mrs. Bardell could only reply by a look. She had long worshiped Mr. Pickwick at a distance, but here she was, all at once, raised to a pinnacle to which her wildest and most extravagant hopes had never dared to aspire. Mr. Pickwick was going to propose—a deliberate plan, too—sent her little boy to the Borough to get him out of the way—how thoughtful—how considerate!

"Well," said Mr. Pickwick, "what do you think?"

"O, Mr. Pickwick," said Mrs. Bardell, trembling with agitation, "you're very kind, sir."

"It'll save you a good deal of trouble, wont it?" said Mr. Pickwick.

"O, I never thought any thing of the trouble, sir," replied Mrs. Bardell; "and of course, I should take more trouble to please you then than ever; but it is so kind of you, Mr. Pickwick, to have so much consideration for my loneliness."

"Ah, to be sure," said Mr. Pickwick; "I never thought of that

When I am in town you'll always have somebody to sit with you. To be sure, so you will."

"I m sure I ought to be a very happy woman," said Mrs. Bardell.

"And your little boy—" said Mr. Pickwick.

"Bless his heart," interposed Mrs. Bardell, with a maternal sob.

"He, too, will have a companion," resumed Mr. Pickwick, "a lively one, who'll teach him, I'll be bound, more tricks in a week than he would ever learn in a year." And Mr. Pickwick smiled placidly.

"O you dear!" said Mrs. Bardell.

Mr. Pickwick started.

"O you kind, good, playful dear," said Mrs. Bardell; and without more ado, she rose from her chair and flung her arms around Mr Pickwick's neck, with a cataract of tears and a chorus of sobs.

"Bless my soul!" cried the astonished Mr. Pickwick; "Mrs. Bardell, my good woman—dear me, what a situation—pray consider, Mrs. Bardell, don't—if anybody should come—"

"O let them come!" exclaimed Mrs. Bardell, frantically; "I'll never leave you—dear, kind, good soul;" and, with these words, Mrs. Bardell clung the tighter.

"Mercy upon me," said Mr. Pickwick, struggling violently, "I hear somebody coming up the stairs. Don't, don't, there's a good creature, don't." But entreaty and remonstrance were alike unavailing, for Mrs. Bardell had fainted in Mr. Pickwick's arms, and before he could gain time to deposit her on a chair, Master Bardell entered the room, ushering in Mr. Tupman, Mr. Winkle, and Mr. Snodgrass.

Mr. Pickwick was struck motionless and speechless. He stood, with his lovely burden in his arms, gazing vacantly on the countenances of his friends, without the slightest attempt at recognition or explanation. They, in their turn, stared at him, and Master Bardell, in his turn, stared at every body.

The astonishment of the Pickwickians was so absorbing, and the perplexity of Mr. Pickwick was so extreme, that they might have remained in exactly the same relative situation until the suspended animation of the lady was restored, had it not been for a most beautiful and touching expression of filial affection on the part of her youthful son. Clad in a tight suit of corduroy, spangled with brass buttons of a very considerable size, he at first stood at the door astounded and uncertain; but by degrees the impression that his mother must have suffered some personal damage pervaded his partially developed mind, and considering Mr. Pickwick the aggressor, he set up an appalling and semi-earthly kind of howling, and butting forward with his head, commenced assailing that immortal gentleman about the back and legs with such blows and pinches as the strength of his arm and the violence of his excitement allowed.

"Take this little villain away," said the agonized Mr. Pickwick, "he's mad."

"What is the matter?" said the three tongue-tied Pickwickians.

"I don't know," replied Mr. Pickwick, pettishly. "Take away the boy, (here Mr. Winkle carried the interesting boy, screaming and struggling, to the farther end of the apartment.) Now help me to lead this woman down stairs."

"O I am better now!" said Mrs. Bardell, faintly.

"Let me lead you down stairs," said the ever-gallant Mr. Tupman.

"Thank you, sir, thank you!" exclaimed Mrs. Bardell hysterically. And down stairs she was led accordingly, accompanied by her affectionate son.

"I cannot conceive," said Mr. Pickwick when his friend returned, "I cannot conceive what has been the matter with that woman. I had merely announced to her my intention of keeping a man-servant when she fell into the extraordinary paroxysm in which you found her. Very extraordinary thing."

"Very," said his three friends.

"Placed me in such an extremely awkward situation," continued Mr. Pickwick.

"Very," was the reply of his followers as they coughed slightly, and looked dubiously at each other.

This behavior was not lost upon Mr. Pickwick. He remarked their incredulity. They evidently suspected him.

"There is a man in the passage now," said Mr. Tupman.

"It's the man that I spoke to you about," said Mr. Pickwick; "I sent for him to the Borough this morning. Have the goodness to call him up, Snodgrass."

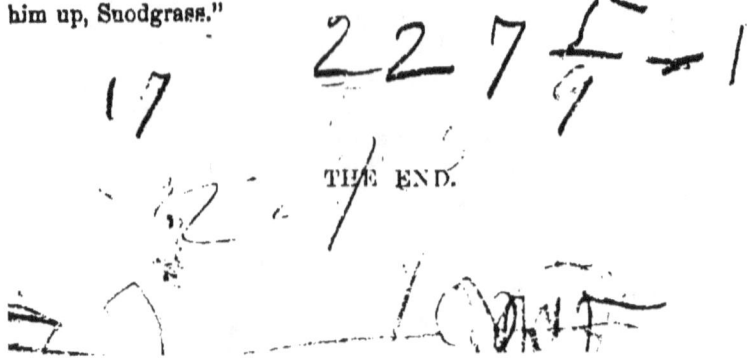

THE END.

www.ingramcontent.com/pod-product-compliance
Lightning Source LLC
Chambersburg PA
CBHW030402230426
43664CB00007BB/713